INFORMATION TECHNOLOGY, ORGANISATIONS AND PEOPLE

Will the major retail financial services companies survive into the 21st Century?

This wide-ranging volume presents in-depth research into the effect of new information technologies on organisational structure, assesses their progress towards transformation and describes the changes they are making to long-established business processes, roles, cultures and working practices. The book is based upon a series of rolling surveys carried out between 1989 and the present day, and funded by leading organisations such as IBM and KPMG. It provides a detailed picture of a sector in transition during a period of anxiety and doubt dominated by restructuring, downsizing and experimentation with re-engineering. As the 'lean and mean' emerge, they must now ask themselves if their competencies will enable them to survive into the next decade as new competitors, such as Sainsburys, Virgin, Microsoft and Ford position themselves to become major players in the sector. The book is a major contribution to the debate on the growth of knowledge work, the need for new core organisational competencies in the information age and the need for evolutionary, or radical, change.

Jeff Watkins is continuing professional development co-ordinator at the University of Bristol. His publications include *From Evolution to Revolution: The Pressure of Professional Life in the 1990s, Positioning for the Unknown: Career Development for Professionals in the 1990s* and *The Future of UK Professional Associations.*

ROUTLEDGE ADVANCES IN MANAGEMENT AND BUSINESS STUDIES

INFORMATION TECHNOLOGY, ORGANISATIONS AND PEOPLE

Transformations in the UK retail
financial services sector

Jeff Watkins

London and New York

First published 1998
by Routledge
11 New Fetter Lane, London EC4P 4EE

Simultaneously published in the USA and Canada
by Routledge
29 West 35th Street, New York, NY 10001

Typeset in Bembo by
J&L Composition Ltd, Filey, North Yorkshire
Printed and bound in Great Britain by TJ International, Padstow, Cornwall

British Library Cataloguing in Publication Data
A catalogue record for this book is available
from the British Library

Library of Congress Cataloguing in Publication Data
Watkins, Jeff, 1946–
Information technology, organisations & people:
transformations in the UK retail financial service sector/Jeff Watkins
p. cm.
Includes bibliographical references and index
ISBN 0–415–18165–8 (hardcover)
1. Financial services industry – Great Britain. 2. Information
technology. 3. Financial services industry – Employees –
Effect of automation on – Great Britain. I. Title.
HG186.A3G788 1998
332.1′0941–dc21   97–41079
CIP

ISBN 0–415–18165–8

CONTENTS

v

LIST OF FIGURES

LIST OF TABLES

ACKNOWLEDGEMENTS

I would like to thank everyone who took part in the interviews and focus group discussions for this research study. I also wish to thank the research sponsors and all those who helped to bring this project to a successful completion.

The author and publisher would like to thank the following for permission to reproduce material published elsewhere: Oxford University Press; Butter-worth Heinemann; MCB University Press.

The information upon which this report is based has been obtained from sources which we believe to be reliable, but we have not independently verified all such information and we do not guarantee that it is accurate or complete. It should not be regarded as a substitute for the exercise by the recipients of their own judgement. Under no circumstances will the publishers, authors, the university, its servants or agents accept any liability, however caused, arising from any error or inaccuracy in any opinion, advice or report arising from this work nor for any resulting damage, loss, expenses or claim.

J.W., Bristol University
1 August 1997

INTRODUCTION

During the 1990s it is predicted that the retail financial services sector will pass through a transformation similar to that which affected UK manufacturing in the early 1980s. Increased competition, more discerning customers, government intervention, particularly on the side of the customer, and the rapid introduction of new technology are all making an impact.

The focus of the research which forms the basis of this study is information technology in the organisation and its potential in a transformational role in the UK retail financial services. Research suggests that the ability to exploit the potential of IT-enabled business transformation depends on the stage of IT development reached. The critical stage is the integration stage when the development of a common IT platform enables the integration of business activities. It is also argued that new structures which facilitate the communication and flow of new ideas are needed to exploit the new business opportunities enabled by IT. In all, this involves organisations in radical change of long established business processes, roles, cultures and working practices. A successful transition and alignment of business and IT strategies requires both technological know-how and an understanding of the dynamics of change in the organisation. People, political and cultural issues, in particular those that relate to leadership, employee participation, and management control, are central to that success.

It is clear that when the study started in 1990, organisations in retail financial services faced a major transition in the way technology was being applied and in the way organisations were structured. This presented an opportunity to study a sector at a critical period in its development and to find some answers to important questions on the nature of IT-enabled transformation and the stages and key characteristics of the transformation process. It is based on the findings of a series of surveys of the sector conducted at the University of Bristol between 1990 and 1996 (for details of the surveys see the Appendix).

OUTLINE OF THE STUDY

The text is in four parts with a conclusion which draws together and sum-marises the key findings. Part I outlines the findings of the relevant research literature and specifies the research questions. Part II describes the retail financial services sector, giving an overview of key business trends and the use made of information technologies. Parts III and IV examine how the firms which took part in the surveys are changing their IT systems, restructuring and reorganising the way they work, and the progress they are making towards integration and towards realising the potential of IT for transformation.

Part 1

Background to the research (Chapter 1)

This chapter describes the changing uses of IT/IS in the organisation through the 1980s to the 1990s. It also traces key shifts in IT/IS and organisational theory and its influence on the strategies organisations adopt to keep in step with rapid change. It states the research questions and identifies the contribu-tion of the research to the wider debate on IT for transformation. It provides the context in which business transformation in the retail financial services sector is considered in this book.

Part 2

The financial services sector: an overview (Chapters 2–3)

Chapter 2 is an overview of the UK retail financial services industry, defining the sector and describing the key business challenges and its responses to them, including strategies for survival and for developing new markets.

Chapter 3 analyses the changing structure of the sector and summarises the progress made in harnessing the potential of IT to improve performance in the market-place in each of the four main areas of the financial services sector – life assurance, general insurance, banking, and building societies.

Part 3

Technology (Chapters 4–8)

This part is based on a series of surveys, carried out between 1990 and 1996 (see IT surveys in the Appendix) in the UK retail financial services sector with the aim of determining the stage of IT development in the retail financial services sector and whether or not IT is being used to achieve business transformation.

It begins, in Chapter 4, by tracing the development of stage-based models of IT growth in the organisation, showing the origin and evolution of the models selected to guide the analysis. It describes how Venkatraman's (1991) model of IT induced business transformation and Galliers and Sutherland's (1991) revised stages of growth model build upon the earlier work of Nolan *et al.* (1974, 1979) and other theorists to produce more complete explanations of the pattern of change.

Chapter 5 defines business process redesign and analyses the results of the surveys within the framework provided by Venkatraman's (1991) model of business transformation. It includes typical case studies to illustrate the stage of development reached by various companies in the sector.

Chapter 6 outlines key developments and trends in the four main areas of IT: systems architectures and systems software; information storage and retrieval; communications, networking, and the user interface; applications and services, then summarises their impact on the sector.

Chapter 7 outlines the changing approach to management of the IT function in the organisation and describes five key trends which summarise developments in the retail financial service companies surveyed. These trends, which characterise reorganisation of the IT function are analysed using Galliers and Sutherland's (1991) 'revised stages of growth model'.

Chapter 8 focuses on IT management strategy. It examines three key IT management concerns: the need for different levels of management control at different stages in the assimilation of a technology; the need to align business and IT strategies; the growing emphasis on using IT to establish and strengthen effective links with organisations in the external environment.

Part 4

IT and organisations (Chapters 9–14)

This part focuses on how the retail financial service companies surveyed are developing new organisational structures, management processes, and new roles as they seek to harness the potential of IT to enable them to meet the challenges described. It is based on the results of surveys carried out between

1990 and 1996 on changing HR policies in the sector (see HR surveys in the Appendix).

Chapter 9 considers the argument that new organisational structures are necessary if companies are to succeed in rapidly changing market conditions. The concept of the flexible organisation and the learning organisation are described and the role of IT in facilitating their development is highlighted.

Chapter 10 focuses on structural transitions and the impact of the trend towards knowledge-intensive work in the sector.

Chapters 11 to 13 discuss the effects of these trends on the working practices of clerical workers, on professionals and on middle and senior managers.

Chapter 14 focuses on the need for new ways of motivating staff as their roles change, and the development of new kinds of reward schemes.

The conclusion has two sections. Section 1: An overview of the research findings summarises the survey findings under the headings: Technology and New Organisations. Section 2: Transformation: an analysis discusses transformation under the headings: Phases of Business Transformation, The Transformation Process, and Mindset.

Part I

THE RESEARCH

1

BACKGROUND TO THE RESEARCH

This chapter describes the shift from the automating to informating uses of IT in the organisation through the 1980s to the 1990s, and the importance of integration in providing a platform for business transformation. It traces key shifts in IT/IS and organisational thinking and its influence on the strategies that organisations adopt to keep in step with rapidly changing conditions. It states the research questions and identifies the contribution of the research to the wider debate on IT for transformation. The treatment is not exhaustive but it is hoped that it is sufficient to give a taste of the key changes and to provide the context in which business transformation in the retail financial services sector is considered in the chapters that follow.

Information technology for transformation

In the early 1990s research reports in journals such as *Business Week* and the *Harvard Business Review* (Scott-Morton, 1991; Keen, 1991; Roach, 1991) focused on the disappointing results of the massive investments in IT in the services sector. Spending on technology had tripled between 1970 and 1990, yet white collar and office productivity in US businesses and organisations remained flat. Roach (1991) argued that the maintenance of current outdated IT infrastructures was adding to the burden of increasing costs in the services sector and that, for the majority of firms, the potential of IT had still to be realised. He advocated a strategic focus based on an efficient delivery system, a high quality product, and a flexible cost structure to ensure continued growth and global market presence. He stressed that the challenge was primarily managerial; that more effective ways of measuring and evaluating white collar productivity, quality, and IT were needed; and that outsourcing arrangements or strategic alliances would allow for economies of scale by sharing the costs of certain resource-hungry in-house functions.

Whilst making it clear that 'economic efficiencies' and radical change were necessary, Roach also warned that 'overzealous cost cutting' would 'hollow out the sector', affecting abilities to innovate, respond to customers, or provide quality service over the long-term.

Similar themes were developed in the *The Corporation of the 1990s: Information Technology and Organisational Transformation*, a collection of papers edited by Scott-Morton (1991). These papers described the findings of the 'MIT90s Research Programme', a five-year survey (1984–1990), supported by US industry and government agencies. It involved a multidisciplinary team with over 40 academics from the Sloan School of Management at the Massachusetts Institute of Technology in partnership with participants from sponsoring organisations. Its aim was to develop a better understanding of the managerial issues of the 1990s as they relate to anticipated advances in information technology.

Scott-Morton, like Roach, argued that, for the majority, the expected benefits of IT had yet to be reaped:

> No impact from information technology is yet visible in the macro-economic data available. A very few individual firms are demonstrably better off and there is a larger group of isolated examples of successful exploitation in particular individual functions or business units. However, on average the expected benefits are not yet visible.
>
> (Scott-Morton 1991)

Whilst the automating potential of IT had been exploited in the different functional areas, few organisations had a clear understanding of how to realise the potential of the data collected by their automated systems. Zuboff (1988) coined the term 'informating' to describe the process whereby these data can be combined or integrated to produce information that can be used to improve not only the process of production but also business coordination and control.

Advances in technology, especially the convergence of telecommunications and computing technologies, including corporate databases, present increasingly sophisticated ways of tapping the potential of integrated information. They can facilitate a level of connectivity between individuals, teams and organisations which enables a 'quantum leap' in the quantity, quality and range of stored organisational knowledge.

The combination of improved connectivity and improved organisational knowledge provides managers with increasingly flexible ways of managing and structuring their organisations. Using connectivity to leverage organisational knowledge and core competence is a key management concern in the 1990s. Knowing how to tap the potential involves a leap of the imagination. Moving from vision to practice involves the participation of all stakeholders in the organisation, directors, managers, employees, suppliers, and customers. It also requires a clear understanding of the risks. For example, whilst integration can generate information that broadens and deepens organisational knowledge and corporate memory, it can erode it too. There is already evidence in the field of inappropriate implementations leading to the loss of much of the specialist knowledge held in the separate functional areas.

New technologies support a whole range of new applications which create major challenges for managers and employees in shaping new ways of working and in balancing opportunities and risks to achieve mutual benefits and commitment (see Table 1.1).

Making the transition will be difficult without major changes in the way IT is managed, in employee competencies and in management processes. The MIT90s research stressed that IT cannot be considered in isolation, its potential for business transformation can only be understood if IT is viewed within its organisational context:

> . . . to benefit from these shifts companies must learn one key lesson from the past and present – IT can't be divorced from its organisational context.
>
> (Yates and Benjamin 1991)

It stresses that IT's role is an enabling role and that people, political and cultural issues, particularly as they relate to leadership, management control and employee participation, are central to successful change:

> IT is only an enabler . . . to actually change the jobs takes a combination of management leadership and employee participation that is, thus far, extremely rare.
>
> (Scott-Morton 1991)

Table 1.1 New applications and ways of working: supported by connectivity

• **Coordination of business tasks both within and between firms**	electronic communication links facilitate integration between procedures, functions and organisations
• **Freedom of location for individuals, teams and organisations**	electronic communication links allow teleworking for home-based individuals; teams with different skills in different locations can work collaboratively, allowing organisations to set up in countries with low labour costs
• **Support for group work and collaboration**	electronic communication links allow multiple authorship, online tracking and monitoring of projects
• **Electronic marketing, purchasing and trading**	electronic communications link multiple buyers and sellers

In describing the 'informating' potential of IT, Zuboff (1988) highlighted the deskilling/reskilling and control/empowerment conundrum it presents. How far would the information generated be used by management to exert tighter control on their workforce or to empower them and encourage their participation in designing new processes? Would the skill content of their work be reduced or increased? Would there be more 'knowledge work' where those involved not only add value to the original information but also continually monitor and adapt their own work processes? Understanding the potential risks of informating is clearly of critical importance in realising the potential benefits for all, not just the power elites.

The MIT research suggested three broad reasons to explain why the expected benefits of the new technologies were not being realised and why the transition was so difficult in the early 1990s. Their arguments, which are summarised below, are consistent with the findings of other researchers in the field, and focus on the stage of IT development reached:

- Organisations are stuck in the automation stage. Many organisations have a legacy of isolated automated systems based on outdated technologies. Most of their IT investment is being used to add to these systems, to update them and to keep them going.

- They have made no real changes in the way they work or are organised. Much of the new sophisticated hardware is used to automate more of the existing procedures to speed up outdated tasks rather than to rethink them from scratch (Caulkin, 1991). Advocates of radical BPR such as Hammer (1991) argued that as new technologies, for instance document image processing, are introduced, organisations must reshape themselves around business processes instead of the traditional functional departments. Other authors, for example Nolan, stressed that there is no point bolting new technology on to systems designed to support traditional hierarchical structures.

- Their stage of IT development is not advanced enough to exploit the potential for transformation. IT in most organisations is still at a relatively early stage of development and its impact will be much greater with the assimilation of converging new technologies. Organisations which have passed through the early stages have gained much relevant expertise in managing technology assimilation and this should ensure smoother progress in the later stages of development (see, for example, Galliers, 1990; Earl, 1989).

IT in the UK retail financial services sector

The UK retail financial services sector faced similar problems in the 1980s and early 1990s to the rest of the services sector, with massive investments in information technology resulting in diminishing returns and growing top management dissatisfaction (Scarbrough, 1992).

During this period, research showed that some leading companies were in the process of developing integrated infrastructures, but that most were in the very early stages. Fincham *et al.*'s (1994) case studies of two strategic IT projects – the Bank of Scotland's 'Cabinet Project', and Mutual Life's introduction of a new customer database system – illustrate some of the difficulties they faced in the integration process in the late 1980s.

Research in the insurance industry (Watkins in Sturdy, 1989; Watkins and Harding, 1990) and the building society sector (Watkins and Wickrama-Sekera, 1991) found evidence of two stages of IT development. Most firms in these sectors had reached a stage, summarised as Stage 1 in Table 1.2. Their focus was on short term tactical IT solutions to meet their immediate needs for new kinds of systems to support new business. A few leading-edge companies were moving on from using IT for administrative efficiency to the improvement of service quality. They were trying to introduce new customer administration systems, marketing information, point of sale and branch systems which would provide better customer service, and opportunities for strategic advantage and business transformation, but their progress towards full integration was slow.

These new systems facilitated rapid communications and decision making which enabled new ways of working. However, the hierarchical organisational structures, so typical of the financial services sector, with many layers of command and with business processes broken down into narrowly defined tasks or procedures and spread amongst several departments, were too inflexible to accommodate new working practices. Whilst the technical constraints on creating an integrated infrastructure were gradually being surmounted,

Table 1.2 IT development: the transition from Stage 1 to Stage 2

Stage 1: Automation	Stage 2: Towards Integration
• IT used for short-term tactical reasons	• IT as part of long-term strategic plan to gain competitive edge
• Reactive business IT strategy	• Integrated business IT strategy
• Administrative IT concentrating on efficiency and back office functions	• Market-led IT focusing on improved quality of service and flexibility of response
• Policy-based or account-based systems	• Integration of client administration, POS, marketing information and branch systems
• Static, administrative and paper-based management information systems	• Continuously updated quality management information systems

difficulties relating to the organisational and human factors, for example, the entrenched cultures and traditions of the status quo, were more problematic. Fincham *et al.* (1994) describe a management culture at Mutual Life in the late 1980s which was common in the sector at that time:

> With product departments run almost as independent fiefdoms . . . with historic hostilities . . . there was strong evidence of a bureau-cratic and fragmented structure.
>
> (Fincham *et al.* 1994)

By 1990, most organisations in the UK financial services sector, as in most other sectors, were intent on tracking and controlling IT expenditure and on maintaining and updating IT infrastructures and applications to keep pace with the rapid advances in technology. They were looking for productivity improvements and were particularly keen to get more value from their IT investment by tapping the strategic potential of their information systems for competitive advantage. The notion that IT used in this way could enable the kind of transformation that would ensure their survival in existing markets and their entrance into entirely new markets was especially persuasive.

However, business transformation was proving difficult to achieve and the guidance available was limited. The main conceptual frameworks and theories of management in the IT/IS field were only developed in the 1970s and 1980s and described a situation very different to that faced in the 1990s.

Frameworks to guide business transformation

Models of IT growth and IT-enabled transformation

The influential evolutionary models of IT growth in the organisation, for example, Gibson and Nolan (1974) and Nolan (1979) offered a useful starting point for understanding IT assimilation, but they had little to offer in terms of guidance on how to identify strategic information systems opportunities. Whitmore (1985) went so far as to say that their continued use as guiding frameworks through into the early 1980s had actually inhibited the strategic use of IS/IT. Their predictive capability did not extend to the new technologies and new applications, which quickly became available.

Organisations, struggling to keep pace with these changes whilst at the same time trying to forge links between isolated areas of automation based on different technologies across separate functions, found that the transition to integration was now much more complex than that described by these early evolutionary models. Their focus was on 'the development of DP/IS management' rather than 'the exploitation of DP/IS in the enterprise' (Ward, Griffiths and Whitmore, 1990).

Subsequent research and theorising through the 1980s has produced models of IT which focus more clearly on why the movement from automation to integration was so difficult; its crucial importance as a platform for transformation; and, in view of the great costs and timescales involved, the need for flexible strategic planning. For example, successive refinements of the Three Era model (DP, MIS, SIS), for example, Wiseman, 1985; Somogyi and Galliers, 1987; Ward, Griffiths and Whitmore, 1990 (see Ward *et al.* 1990); Zuboff's (1988) three-role model of IT: automating, informating, transforming; and the MIT90s models, in particular Venkatraman's (1991) five levels of IT-induced business transformation model, were especially useful. Since the transition involves a fundamental shift in emphasis from managing computers to managing information systems, they highlight the importance of a clear understanding of the nature of information and the current and future information needs of the business and the organisation in relation to the competitive environment. They also emphasise the need for a more holistic view which takes in all aspects of the organisation, its environments, the IT/IS applications and their interrelationships.

The terms used – 'shifting through stages, eras, phases, or levels' of IT use and development – suggest an ordered progression, a time-based sequence of events, which is regarded as problematic in these models as in the earlier models. However, most stress that their intention is to indicate a phased expansion of the focus of concern to include another area of IT/IS activity rather than a staged change from one activity to the next.

The MIT90s research summarised the main challenge to management in the 1990s as: the creation of flexible organisational structures which would enable companies to deal with an increasingly fast-changing, complex and competitive world. Information technology which enables the integration of business activities would play a key role as it could be used in the development of new structures which would facilitate the communication and flow of new ideas, and in the development of new business opportunities.

It stressed that the shift to this kind of organisation would be difficult because it involves changing long-established business processes, IT systems, structures, strategies, roles and cultures. Achieving a successful transition to IT-enabled business transformation would require not just the technological know-how to develop a robust IT/IS infrastructure but also an understanding of the dynamics of change as it affected all aspects of the organisation and its external environments. It highlighted the need for skilful management of the change process and investment in people, pinpointing the failure to provide these in the past as root causes for the lack of impact of IT on economic performance and productivity.

The MIT90s Research Framework (see Figure 1.1) emphasises the central role that management processes (strategic planning, budgeting, resources planning, etc.) play in the alignment of business and IT strategies in the organisation, and in maintaining organisational equilibrium. Every

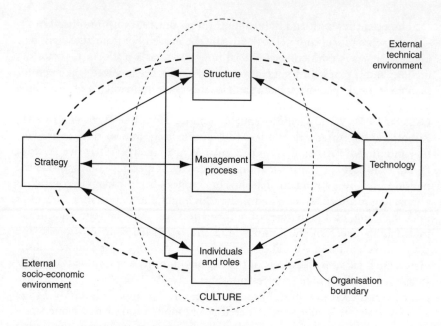

Figure 1.1 The MIT research framework.
Source: By permission of Oxford University Press.

component is influenced by external and internal environments, and changes which affect one, affect all. Changes made in one area without consideration of their likely effects on the others upset the 'dynamic equilibrium' and threaten survival and growth.

The research stressed the interdependence of organisational and technological integration. It argued that the three 'forces' in the MIT90s Research Framework (Figure 1.1) which represent 'people issues' – individuals and roles; management processes; structure – are critical in the transformation process. It highlighted 'empowerment' as the ultimate goal, and the need for investment in new skills, psychological ownership of the change process, and protection for employees, at all levels, if they are to respond wholeheartedly in the search for innovation.

Contributors to the MIT90s research tended to focus on different quadrants of the research framework (Figure 1.1) and the links between them are not always made clear in their writing.

Venkatraman's contribution explored the structural and process changes and focused on the internal forces: management processes, strategy, structure, technology. It stressed senior management involvement, the need for planning and the alignment of business, IT and organisational strategies as critical to the process of IT-enabled business transformation, which Venkatraman defines as:

The exploitation of IT capabilities for fundamental strategic choices of business scope, governance mechanisms, organisational reconfiguration and competitive action in the market place.

(Venkatraman 1991)

Venkatraman's model of IT-enabled business reconfiguration describes five levels of transformation. The first two – localised exploitation (automation) and internal integration are described as evolutionary and hierarchically linked, the success of the second building on that of the first. Subsequent levels – business process redesign, business network redesign, business scope redefinition – are described as revolutionary options which can be taken up, if relevant to the particular organisation, once the infrastructure is in place.

Venkatraman's model describes how the expansion of IT capability at each of five levels enables the transformation of business activities (see Table 1.3). As they move through Levels 1 and 2 companies build up their competencies to optimally position themselves within the existing markets. Having achieved success at these levels, the movement to Levels 3, 4 and 5 depends on their ability to develop new ways of doing business, the capacity to create fundamentally new products and services and the capacity to create new industries.

He suggests that since the risks, costs and complexity involved in these kinds of implementations are great, the incremental, evolutionary approach of the earlier stages may not provide sufficient control or momentum to achieve the kind of change required. He advocated a more carefully designed strategic

Table 1.3 Venkatraman's levels of business transformation

EVOLUTIONARY TRANSFORMATION
Level 1: Localised exploitation
Aim: to reduce costs and or improve service
Level 2: Integration
Aim: to use information as a strategic resource
REVOLUTIONARY TRANSFORMATION
Level 3: Business Process Redesign
Aim: to reengineer the business to achieve major cuts in costs and greatly improved levels of service
Level 4: Business Network Redesign
Aim: to create a virtual organisation, the company aims to occupy a central position in the network
Level 5: Business Scope Redefinition
Aim: to identify new scope for the business and the organisation

---

planning approach, stressing the importance of in-built flexibility and the dangers of rigid planning.

Whilst managers have found this model useful in developing awareness of strategic potential of IT, most still felt that the need was for a framework to help them translate these ideas into action. Development of the Strategic Alignment Model (SAM) by Venkatraman, Henderson and MacDonald (Scott-Morton, 1991) represented a step in this direction. Its iterative nature is meant to close the gap between strategy as planned and strategy as practised.

IT/IS activity based on a complex combination of DP, MIS and SIS had started to emerge in some organisations in the mid-1980s. Finding ways to plan and manage this complexity was a major concern and the alignment/ integration of IT/IS strategies became a dominant theme, stimulating renewed interest in the development of strategic planning methodologies.

Models of strategic planning

Strategic planning theorists through the 1980s produced a wide range of frameworks, many of them based on the work of Porter, Parsons and McFarlan, which focused on assessing the impact of IT and searching for IT opportunities. They have an elegant simplicity which makes them useful in raising awareness of strategic issues but leaves them open to criticism, like all frameworks and models, on the grounds that they offer limited and constricting viewpoints. The Strategic Information Systems Planning (SISP) approach, developed by IS/IT theorists, makes use of a number of these frameworks to guide the analysis for planning the application and management of IT/IS in the organisation (see Ward et al. 1990).

Although it is felt that their combined views can offer a wider and much more useful strategic perspective, these frameworks, and the SISP approach, have not been popular with managers who argue that they give no guidance on how to translate strategy into action (Brady et al. 1992). Neumann (1994) suggests that 'framework overload' may be another reason for their reluctance to use them and there are arguments (see, for example, Doyle, 1991) for a taxonomy of frameworks to help in the choice of the most appropriate and relevant views for particular conditions. Some argue for a diagnostic, computer-based meta-framework, and others for alternative approaches based on divergent thinking to supplement the traditional, convergent rational-analytical approach of the strategic planning school.

Awareness of the need for a multidimensional, multidisciplinary view on transformation and the change process had been heightened through the 1980s to the 1990s. The approaches advocated in the MIT90s Research Programme publication (Scott-Morton 1991) and the integrated strategic planning methodologies developed by, for example, Ward et al. (1990) and Cash, McFarlan, and McKenney (1992) went at least some way towards this goal.

Today, the avoidance of technologically deterministic bias, that is, the focus on the impact of IT and its benefits, is a key theme in the research field. Critics of the earlier models point out that even where human issues have been highlighted as central to the transformation process, in practice the tendency has been to consider them at the implementation stage rather than in the design stage. Research papers now call for a deeper focus on the human and political issues, underlining even more strongly their influence on the success of IT implementations. A recent paper criticising the IT/IS theorists' tendency towards a unidirectional approach, by Land (1996), an IT/IS academic himself, compares the MIT90s approach with that of the business economist Kay (1993). He argues for a composite view where human imagination and creativity are highlighted as the true-enablers of transformation.

Notwithstanding these criticisms, the research team of the MIT90s project, and other theorists of this time such as Ward *et al.*, Cash *et al.*, have all made important contributions. Their analyses are set within the kind of framework that offers a more holistic view of the organisation as a complex and dynamic set of interrelationships. They give a clear emphasis to the importance of 'empowerment' and investment in human resources to the transformation process in their writing, but at the time, this aspect was not uppermost in the minds of those seeking their advice or implementing their ideas. In their haste to get the job done, they fail to develop the synergy which can drive through the change they hope to achieve.

The tendency for complex ideas to be distorted through interpretation or simplification for practical use or used to achieve goals which differ from those assumed in the original message, as explained in more detail later, has to be considered in any criticism of the work in this field. Similar difficulties are also evident in the academic field, where authors' interpretations of each others' ideas can vary so much.

Research efforts continue to try to broaden our perspectives and to deepen our understanding of the relationship between information technology, information systems, information management, and organisational management. Use is being made of theories from both the economic and social/behavioural sciences. Their different perspectives are helping to develop more integrated and multidimensional views of IT in the organisation. Economic theories provide a focus on the cost saving/profit maximising effects of IT; social/behavioural theories – decision and control theory, sociological, post-industrial, cultural and political theories – seek to explain the effects as they are influenced by the various behaviours of the people who make up the organisation and the cultural and political environments in which they live and work (see Kumar, 1995).

Some theorists from the critical social sciences school, for example, Knights, Noble and Willmott argue that management's difficulties with the current IT-strategy discourse and SISP relate to:

excessive rationalism, a linear and hierarchical approach, the separation of planning from doing, of strategy from tactics. It has been
assumed that IT can be related to strategy by analytical means alone.
If organisations do not have an explicit strategy, one can be created
for the purpose. IT/IS is assumed to be highly malleable, subject to
managerial control and direction. Strategic applications are believed
to be discovered by means of a planning mechanism. This approach
ignores the large body of criticism and evidence against the rational
perspective which had developed both in the field of business
strategy and that of IS development and implementation.

(Knights, Noble and Willmott 1997)

Much of their research, based on detailed case studies (see, for example, the
1988/89 study of the UK banking sector, in Knights *et al.* 1997) supports the
processual view of strategy as emergent and contingent rather than rationally
planned; and confirms their views on the centrality of organisational politics
in the alignment of IT and corporate strategy. They stress that, in order to
understand how and why this is so, any analysis of the strategy process in the
organisation should incorporate a conception of power and identity. It should
consider both the internal and external political contexts.

The transformation process:
evolutionary or revolutionary?

Translating strategy into action

Research interest in explaining the gap between the actual results and the
rational intentions of strategic decision making and the notions that the
conflicting political and social agendas of different groups can delay, divert
or subvert intentions to produce unexpected outcomes, is not new. Lindblom
(1959) was one of the first to criticise the rational model of strategy formation. In a paper entitled 'The science of muddling through', he described
strategy formation as an incremental process set within a social and political
context. He argued that a limited number of strategy alternatives (not all, as in
the idealised but unattainable rational model) were compared and choices
made according to the likely success of the outcome and the ease with which
strategy could be put into action. He called this *strategy building through
successive limited comparisons.* The options most usually chosen are those that
build on the current experience of the organisation and its managers and
decisions are tested in action before being developed further.

Quinn (1980), who labelled the process *logical incrementalism,* drew a similar
perspective from interviews with managers in nine major multinational firms.
These managers viewed strategy implementation as an adaptive process which
involves continual testing to ensure that the strategy choices made are suitable

and keep the organisation in line with change. Experimentation is encouraged; there is a reluctance to specify precise objectives too soon for fear of cramping creativity; input from all levels of the organisation is encouraged; uncertainty is accepted and managers aim to be constantly 'tuned-in' to environmental change (see Johnson and Scholes, 1989). The key advantages of this evolutionary, gradual approach to change are seen to be:

- improved quality of information for decision making ensured by continual testing and feedback;
- stimulation of managerial flexibility and creativity;
- greater commitment and less resistance to change since the approach is gradual giving people time to adapt.

Since the 1970s other models of strategic thinking have emerged which recognise other motives (besides the profit motive) and the influence of social and political contexts more clearly than the rational-analytical and the incremental models. Whittington (1993) classified business strategy theories according to their assumptions about the organisation's goals (profit maximisation <-> pluralistic) and the level of strategic intent (deliberate <-> emergent). Each school of thought – classical, evolutionary, processual, systemic – has influenced and continues to influence the development of strategic management (see Figure 1.2. NB: the dates indicate the decade when the

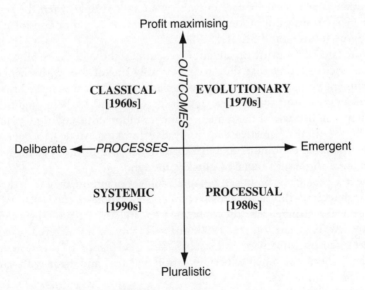

Figure 1.2 Business strategy theories.
Source: Redrawn from Whittington, 1993.

ideas of each school became influential, not the beginning and end of a period of influence).

According to Whittington, the classical theorists such as Porter and Ansoff see strategy as a rational process of long-term planning. The evolutionists such as Hannon, Freeman and Williamson, who predict a volatile future, focus on survival by optimising the fit between the organisation and the market environment. The processualists, such as Cyert and March, and Mintzberg, see strategy as an emergent process of learning and adaptation driven more by individual actions than the business environment. The systemic theorists, who argue that there are many more goals besides profit maximisation, emphasise the influence of culture and the social and political context in strategy making.

Whilst the approach to strategy formulation in most organisations through the 1980s had a rational analytical basis and was deliberate in intent, strategy tended to emerge processually and was implemented incrementally. The changes made were gradual and evolutionary.

Incremental/evolutionary and radical/revolutionary change?

Mintzberg's (1979) analysis of the different patterns of strategic response to the changing environment identifies five modes of strategy development. In the organisations he studied over many decades, he observed periods of incremental change, piecemeal change, periods of continuity with no change, a state of flux with some change but no clear direction, and rare periods of fundamental or radical changes of strategy attempted only when the organisation gets seriously out of step with its environment and must transform itself or die (see Johnson and Scholes, 1989).

In the late 1980s many organisations, including those in the retail financial services sector, found that they were seriously out of line with changes in government policies, markets, and customer demands. It was argued that the current emphasis on the classical approach, as defined by Whittington, was inappropriate because of the tendency of over rationalistic and rigid planning to stifle the kind of creative and innovative thinking needed to cope with rapidly changing conditions, and that incremental, evolutionary change could not achieve the results required quickly enough.

The need for a new approach became a subject of intense debate in the face of the perceived threat of global competition. Some argued that radical, revolutionary change was 'the right answer' and that it must be achieved quickly. At the start of the 1990s many organisations entered a period characterised by Mintzberg as a state of flux (see Figure 1.3). In this mode (Mode 2) there was much experimentation and trial and error with various new change initiatives.

A few companies began to consider a strategic shift which would involve radical change (Mode 3) throughout the organisation. Through this they

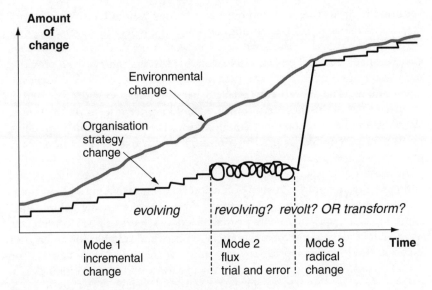

Figure 1.3 Patterns of strategy development.
Source: Adapted from Johnson 1995, based on Mintzberg, 1978.

hoped to achieve a level of transformation which would close the gap between corporate response and environmental change to ensure their future success.

However, sudden and radical change was not something many organisations had experience of unless circumstances had forced it. As we have seen, the usual strategic response in the relatively more stable conditions of earlier times has been incremental and evolutionary. Radical, revolutionary change is generally regarded as risky and only attempted when there is no other way.

Intense consultancy activity in the entrepreneurial 1980s had stimulated the rapid emergence of many new approaches to managing complexity and controlling uncertainty. Each new approach had a different prescriptive emphasis. The earlier ones, for example, mission statements, managing for excellence, quality circles, customer care, gave rise to ad hoc, isolated initiatives which were relatively low risk and could be implemented incrementally suiting the current gradual and evolutionary approach to change management. Later ones, tried out in the 1990s, for example, the learning organisation, total quality management, business process reengineering, individual career management, were designed for organisation-wide implementation and as such required integrated initiatives involving complex change across the organisation.

Packaged by consultants for easy consumption, many interpretations of these new ideas promised more than they delivered and most became little more than short-lived business fads (see Pascale, 1990: 20). This was not because the ideas were unsound but because they were often superficially or inappropriately applied in an atmosphere of panic where management gurus stressed that survival in the new global market depended on radical change and that speed was of the essence. Ideas adopted as 'the right answer' provided static solutions rather than the flexible approaches needed in a dynamic environment. The more complex ideas became distorted and corrupted as the necessities of the short term obscured any long-term focus on the future. With the emphasis still on quick solutions, the crucial fact that the ideas being implemented required long-term commitment was forgotten or never fully grasped.

Advocates of every new approach claimed to have the key to success, and although organisations achieved some kind of improvement and organisational learning with each new initiative, there were also many failures. In a paper on strategy as a dynamic process given at a recent SEMS conference, Moncrieff, Pidgeon and Smallwood (1997) provide examples of failures for each of three main approaches that have characterised the period: the planning style based on rational analysis of past success; the visioning style based on visions of future success, and the learning style based on a continuous cycle of experimentation, reflective observation and conceptualisation. They illustrate how some firms which have adopted these styles as 'the right answer' have got stuck, not only with 'plans', but also with 'visions' and 'lessons' which have become inappropriate as environments have changed.

They argue for a strategic process which resists 'the right answer' mentality; works with uncertainty rather than seeking to control it; enables an appropriate balance between analysis, visioning, and learning; and builds up the organisation's strategic capability, that is, its sensitivity, awareness and responsiveness to changing conditions (Quinn, 1989). They, like others, warn that this strategic capability is being seriously damaged by the short-term focus on restructuring, delayering and downsizing: those subjected to the ever tighter control that ensues no longer have the time or motivation to develop, maintain or apply it.

A new mindset for transformation

Overcoming the problems of rationalistic/deterministic bias

The dominant post-industrial or modernist vision of a new information society, restructured, renewed, and transformed by information technology underpins much of the rationalistic analytical approach of IT/IS management theory and strategic planning. The main protagonists of this vision (Bell, 1974; also Drucker, 1969; Toffler, 1970; Masuda, 1980) argue that the growth of the services sector in the advanced economies, as jobs in manufacturing shifted to low-wage countries, heralds the start of the transformation. Whilst acknowledging that the transition, which began in the 1960s, would be difficult, their main focus is the opportunities and benefits that would result from the application of technology. Their ideas and predictions of a shift to a knowledge economy, where knowledge and competence were valued more than hierarchy and status, stimulated intensive debate and gained widespread popular support. The social and economic benefits of an information technology revolution were extolled by governments, IT multinationals, management theorists, writers and consultants.

The warning voices of the social critics, some post-modernist in outlook, with much less optimistic views of transformation through technology were heard, but their contribution to the debate was largely ignored (see Kumar, 1995; Lyon, 1988). Since then our experience with new technologies has tempered the optimism somewhat. There is now at least some willingness to acknowledge these other perspectives and their contributions in the search for a more realistic assessment of the opportunities and threats for society and its organisations. A key concern is that an approach which stresses only benefits obscures vested interests (see Lyon, 1988). Since technology both shapes and is shaped by society, understanding its potential requires an understanding of the relationship and the mediating effects of culture, environment, structure, politics, choices made, and chance. Without this kind of understanding it will be difficult to *reshape, redirect or simply resist* unacceptable and potentially dangerous developments such as the concentration of power and the growth of an information underclass.

The current popular management of change themes centre on the need for a new *business paradigm* or a new *mindset* to shape the organisation's future, and the *resurrection of strategy*. Two of the clearest writers on business mindset in the popular management literature are Charles Handy and Richard Pascale. Handy (1989) in the *Age of Unreason* and Pascale (1990) in *Managing on the Edge*, argue that incremental or continuous change is only effective when an organisation wants to carry on doing what it already does. If it doesn't or if circumstances force it to do something different then it needs to adopt a discontinuous approach to innovation. They stress the need for a new mindset, new ways of looking at things, a way of breaking up set patterns of thought and of continually questioning deeply embedded assumptions and long-held beliefs.

Handy places the wheel of learning, with its phases of question, theory, test, reflection, at the heart of the transformation or learning process for both organisations and for individuals. The wheel is driven by 'lubricants of change' which represent an attitude of mind that allows a flexible approach to the search for innovation. They include confidence and motivation, the ability to reframe, and a positive approach to doubt and uncertainty.

Pascale talks about the engine of inquiry, fuelled by constructive contention, as the source of vitality, self-renewal and transformation; and the need for a new mindset to manage the complexity of 'fit' (internal consistency to ensure smooth functioning), 'split' (decentralisation to sustain autonomy and diversity), and 'contend' (harnessing conflict for constructive benefits) in the organisation. He argues that the seven components of the organisation – structure, strategy, systems, staff, style, shared values, skills – are held in a dynamic tension between the extremes of over-control and chaos. For each component, the different responses needed to meet new conditions tend towards either of the two extremes. For instance, planning and opportunism are the contending opposites of strategy. Too much planning leads to over-control, too much opportunism leads to chaos. The organisation needs elements of both, not held in a static equilibrium which eventually leads to stagnation, but in a dynamic tension which allows a continual repositioning as conditions change. Since all seven polarities have to be managed simulta-neously, the managerial focus is not 'static solutions' but 'orchestrating dynamic synthesis or dialectic'. Pascale sees this as the key to vitality and renewal. It involves a shift from 'either/or' thinking, to 'and/both' thinking, arriving at a synthesis, a new perspective or frame of reference from a consideration of both thesis and antithesis.

Hamel and Prahalad (1994) take up this line of thought and the notion of creative tension provided by opposites in their book *Competing for the Future*. They contend that transformation is not just about optimal positioning of the organisation within existing markets but about reinventing the industry and regenerating strategy. They argue that strategic thinking or 'strategizing' is a deeply embedded capability which uses a deep understanding of the present – trends, lifestyles, technologies, demographics, geopolitics – to project future customer needs and envisage new opportunities.

They claim that this kind of foresight should enable ' . . . a transformation process that is revolutionary in result but evolutionary in execution' and that strategy viewed as 'stretch' as well as 'fit' bridges the gap between the rational planning outlook and incrementalism. They argue for growth and diversifi-cation around core competencies, 'integrated bundles of skills and technol-ogies' with three key qualities: customer value, competitor differentiation and extendibility, which can be applied in new ways to meet customer needs.

Conclusion

When the survey started in 1990, service sector organisations, including those in the UK retail financial services sector, were at the start of a period of major business transformation. They faced a transition in the application of tech-nology, the use of information and in the way organisations were structured.

To describe this predicted transformation and its context, researchers attempted to develop more holistic models which stressed the interdepen-dence of organisational and technological integration. Models developed by the MIT90s researchers have been especially useful. One of the MIT90s models, Venkatraman's five-level model of IT enabled business transformation, is used as a starting point in this study to explore the nature of business transformation in the UK retail financial services sector.

Venkatraman's model describes transformation as an evolutionary process in the early stages as organisations build up the necessary organisational and IT competencies. Once these competencies are in place organisations can choose to move on to one or more of the three levels which support revolutionary transformation. Quinn also stresses the need for an organisation to build its strategic capability, that is, the sensitivity, awareness and responsiveness to changing conditions.

Critics of the traditional rationalistic approach to technology for transformation (see Lyons 1988 and Kumar 1995) question whether any 'real' transformation is taking place when it is clear that the underlying power structures of organisations remain largely unchanged.

Enlightened management theorists, for example, Pascale and Handy argue that real change will only be achieved if we approach it with a new mindset and new ways of looking at problems which involve continually questioning long-held beliefs and ways of doing things.

It is against this background that the research questions considered in this study are analysed. They are:

- What level of business transformation have companies in the retail financial services sector reached?

- What is the nature of the transformation process – ad hoc or integrated, incremental or radical?

The study can also contribute to the wider debate on transformation, for example, if the retail financial services sector continues with its narrow focus on IT and radical change for profit maximisation, how will this affect the strategic capability of organisations? Is there evidence that the application of new technologies is contributing to the growth of knowledge work and a shift in the balance of power?

Part II

THE FINANCIAL SERVICES SECTOR

2

UK RETAIL FINANCIAL
SERVICES AND TODAY'S
BUSINESS CHALLENGE

This chapter defines the UK retail financial services sector, highlighting the links between this sector and the other main financial services sectors, viz: corporate financial services; the City of London; and the business services sector. It outlines the pressure for change, analysing the major business challenges which face the industry, and the responses of retail financial services companies in this period of transition. It highlights the need to realise the potential of IT to enable the kind of change and transformation required for survival and future success in new markets.

The UK financial and business services sector

Taken together, the financial services and business services sectors are amongst the most successful sectors in the UK economy in terms of employment creation, output, growth and profitability. Since 1980, the number of jobs in the sector has risen from 1.6 million to 2.8 million; the real output has doubled from 11 to 20 per cent of current-price GDP, and gross profits to almost £90 billion (CSO, 1995). This expansion was due to several factors, including growing consumer wealth, deregulation and demographic changes, as well as the trend in advanced economies towards services. Financial services output, as measured by percentage of GDP, was predicted to overtake that of manufacturing some time in 1996 (McRae, 1995).

The financial services sector is made up of three interlinked and inter-dependent subsectors: retail, corporate, and City of London (see Figure 2.1). It includes banks, building societies, insurance companies, mortgage lenders, securities houses, unit and investment trusts and increasingly a large number of non-bank institutions engaged in financial activity.

The business services sector includes a wide range of professional firms such as solicitors, management consultants, accountants and computer specialists. Although both these sectors are usually considered separately, they are interlinked in two critical ways:

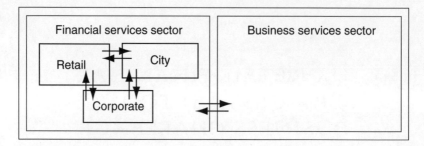

Figure 2.1 Structure of UK financial and business services sector.

- They buy services from one another, for example, the banking sector is one of the largest client groups for accountants and software services;
- They are beginning to compete for business – the movement of financial institutions into professional services is a major trend. For example, the Halifax Building Society now owns one of the largest surveying companies in the UK; and Barclays Bank has set up a large software services consultancy through outsourcing parts of its IT department.

The UK retail financial services sector

This study concentrates on the UK retail financial services sector which comprises the services provided to the personal and small business sectors by the financial institutions such as banks, mortgage lenders and insurers. This is distinguished from the services provided by these institutions to sophisticated business clients, which include large corporates, institutional investors, public services entities and governments, and from the services provided by organisations in the City of London, such as Lloyds and the Stock Exchange.

The retail financial services sector provides six main services: savings, loans, mortgages, insurance, investment, and payment facilities. In addition, a small but increasing share of their income is coming from the provision of professional advice such as tax and financial planning. These services are delivered through four main subsectors: retail banking, mortgage lending, life and pensions and general insurance (see Chapter 3). Their survival as distinct groups of service providers depends on their response to three main business challenges.

The main business challenges and pressure for change

The UK retail financial services industry now faces three main challenges: intense competition; more demanding customers; rapid technological progress (see for example, Ireland, 1994).

Intense competition

Competition has increased dramatically (see Figure 2.2).

Financial services institutions now compete aggressively across the whole range of financial services, with, for example, banks, the larger building societies, and insurers offering the whole spectrum of financial services mentioned in Figure 2.2.

These companies also face competition from a range of new entrants as diverse as Marks & Spencer, General Motors, Virgin Airways, Microsoft, British Telecom, and foreign banks. All of these organisations are capable of taking large market shares from established UK companies. Ford, for example, which owns Ford Financial Services, already provides over $100 billion of loans to its customers. The proliferation of financial products and the number of new entrants is now leading to considerable overcapacity.

The pace of competition is accelerated by the trends towards disaggregation and disintermediation. Most of the standardised core processing activities of retail financial institutions, such as mortgages, credit cards, loan instalments etc, can be outsourced to specialist companies. Disaggregation has major implications for competition because it means that any competitor with a well-known brand name and a large customer base could move into any area of financial services very quickly. As yet the process of outsourcing core processing is relatively undeveloped in the UK, whereas in the US it is quite advanced. However, it is expected to increase dramatically over the next three years.

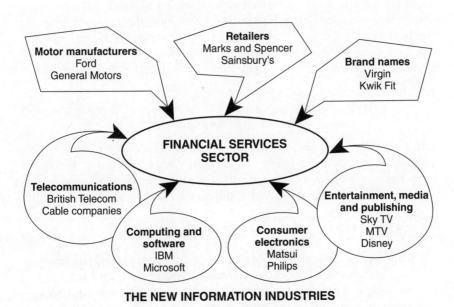

THE NEW INFORMATION INDUSTRIES

Figure 2.2 Threats from new entrants to the retail financial services sector.

The traditional role of retail financial services companies as an intermediary between depositor and borrower and between buyer and seller is also under threat. Technology such as secure networks has allowed non-financial institutions to dispense with financial intermediaries. This is more apparent in the corporate sector, for example, Ford and BP have applied to be members of SWIFT and will use it to carry payment traffic. The same trend is evident in the retail sector, for instance, Microsoft are targeting home banking as an area for future expansion. Such developments would result in a substantial reduction in the income of banks.

Markets are becoming more and more individualised, specialised and fragmented. The ability to anticipate and respond quickly to new market environments, in a highly focused way, is becoming essential for survival. Although there will be rationalisation and consolidation amongst traditional retail financial services companies, this will be accompanied by an increase in companies which focus on a particular market or customer group. For instance, the financial subsidiaries of car manufacturers such as Fiat, General Motors, Ford and Volvo have already replaced the banks as the world's principal providers of vehicle finance. Ford, in its corporate mission statement, describes automotive and financial services as its two main core businesses, and advances to its 6.7 million customers worldwide, exceed $100 billion. Its subsidiary, Ford Credit Europe is now introducing the concept of total trade cycle management, whereby the Ford car owner is provided with a whole package of services including quick and easy purchasing, flexible finance, insurance, trade in, servicing etc, intended to provide the customer with trouble-free motoring. To do this successfully, the company must be highly focused, with, for example, IT systems which are customer-based and can track their complete relationship with Ford, a well trained, financially aware dealer network, and synergy between manufacturing and finance sections.

More demanding customers

Customers' awareness of financial products has been raised by media attention on such issues as the mis-selling of pensions, poor performance of endowment-linked mortgages and the growth of negative equity. This raised awareness, together with the increased competition, is making customers more cautious, demanding and discerning, though one participant, a major bank, felt that the level of actual understanding is still limited:

> Customer awareness can be attributed in part to increased publicity from companies selling their products. There is more hard sell and more exposure to the market and the products. Customers need not necessarily understand the products but because of advertising they think they know more and feel that they have been given more of a

choice to shop around. Generally they do not settle on the best deal but on the person in whom they have the most confidence. As the customer is increasingly exercising choice, there is a need to be more customer focused.

The traditional concept of loyalty based on the old conviction that 'if you get a customer young you keep them for life' has been transformed. This is particularly apparent with mortgages. Whereas in the past it was unheard of to switch mortgages, it is now more common with borrowers moving to obtain the best deals. Customers increasingly require services and products which provide value for money in terms of cost and quality, include an element of advice, and are tailored to their individual needs. Such products are highly knowledge intensive.

Rapid technological progress

Although most areas of IT are characterised by steady progress, there are areas of discontinuity where leaps in progress are being made and where changes occur very quickly (Barron, 1994). For example, the explosion in the use of interorganisation networking via Internet and the use of video discs for compact storage of data. Technology discontinuities of this kind allow new competitors to enter the market and help to create new markets. The retail financial services sector has not really experienced any major discontinuities in its underlying technologies since the 1960s. Even the emergence of the PC has until now been superimposed upon existing, well understood technologies. Over the next five years the sector will face major technological discontinuity (see Chapter 6 for more detail).

Responses from retail financial services companies

Retail financial services companies are entering a period of consolidation and rationalisation, and are adopting a range of strategies to respond to the challenges described.

Consolidation and rationalisation

Mergers and takeovers are occurring within sub-sectors, for example, the merger of the Halifax and Leeds building societies, and Lloyds and TSB banks, and this will lead to a large reduction in the number of companies. This process will gather momentum over the next three years with mergers between major insurers, banks, and building societies. The result will be fewer larger companies in each sub-sector. This process is also occurring between sectors as seen in mergers between banks, life assurance companies, and building societies: for instance, the mergers between Lloyds Bank and the

Cheltenham and Gloucester building society; the Alliance & Leicester and Girobank; Abbey National and Scottish Mutual. This will result in fewer larger companies and they will provide a whole cross section of financial services. This is currently happening at a very rapid rate with, for example, Lloyds bank moving from being the fourteenth largest mortgage lender in 1995 to the third largest in 1996.

Strategies for survival in the short term

The first reaction of companies to these changes is to improve competitiveness and profitability through a combination of strategies:

- cost cutting;
- offering better value for money in terms of service and quality;
- extending the product range;
- extending the range of delivery channels.

Companies are now aiming to *cut costs* to best industry standards, as the expense ratios of the early 1990s testify. Since the expense ratios of companies within the same sector vary widely, some face radical cost cutting simply to equate their competitive position. For example, Equitable Life's expense ratio of 7.7 per cent as compared with that of Norwich Union at 19.5 per cent (University of Nottingham Insurance Centre, 1993); and Cheltenham & Gloucester's at 25 per cent as compared with Nationwide's at 50 per cent (Harlow Butler Ueda Ltd, 1992). Inevitably this will result in major job losses and branch closures.

They are striving to *improve quality and service* through the introduction of quality management initiatives such as customer care programmes and TQM. Several recent research surveys indicate a direct correlation between service value (quality/cost to customer), customer satisfaction, customer retention and profitability. Since it costs less to retain existing customers than to attract new ones, profitability and growth in business depend upon strategies which ensure that the same customer comes back again and again.

Companies are competing in related areas by extending their *product range*. In the financial services market, increased profitability comes most readily from selling additional products to established customers. For instance, building societies now offer current account facilities. One example, Northern Rock, attracted over 100,000 customers within eighteen months of setting up a personal banking service which offers an interest-paying current account option. With the growth in demand for life assurance and investment services, almost all of the banks and large building societies have moved into this sector, and they now account for over 10 per cent of the long-term insurance market.

Many firms are introducing new delivery channels which include intelligent ATMs, telephone sales, postal banking, and computer links from home. Some of these delivery channels, such as intelligent ATMs and home-based services, are at an early stage or have limited penetration, for example, although at least 19 banks and building societies in the UK offer telephone banking services, only 1 per cent of savings account, and 5 per cent of current account holders have accounts with postal or telephone access.

Although the introduction of telephone sales for motor insurance has been very successful, gaining 25 per cent of the market, it is likely that these new methods of delivery will replace the branch as the dominant distribution channel over the next five years. By the end of the decade, the number of people banking by telephone is expected to rise to 6 million (Ireland, 1994).

The role of information technology

IT has played an important role in reducing labour costs, improving produc-tivity and service in all four sectors. Although it will continue to be used for cost cutting, it will also be used, by those preparing for the long-term implications of rapid change in the markets, to manage information in ways which will reveal new opportunities and new markets, to enhance service to customers, and to enable and manage new kinds of information partnerships:

Managing information

To provide a better quality service, organisations require better information, both at the macro level so that they can identify key marketing trends at a company level to inform decisions, and at the point of sale so that salespeople have detailed information about their customers' needs, problems and ambi-tions. This entails improving existing customer databases, management infor-mation systems and the customer interface, for example, the use of workstations at branch level.

Enhancing customer service

Information technology can develop services which are of higher quality, can be delivered faster, more cheaply or tailored to an individual customer's exact needs. In a recent survey of high performing companies carried out by Clifford & Cavanaugh, it was found that on average more than a quarter of their sales came from products that did not exist five years ago. In the future, life cycles will become shorter and it is vital to innovate continuously. IT will play an increasingly important role in providing better customer service.

Three key aspects – *quality, time to market,* and *flexibility* – have special relevance:

- Quality – in terms of how well the ultimate product or service meets the customer's needs, and the quality of the underlying processes which deliver the service.
- *Time to Market* – New products and services have to be introduced more rapidly and existing ones managed more effectively. Technology plays a key role, for example, by improving integration of effort between departments.
- *Flexibility* – Advanced technology can be used to produce or deliver more flexible, highly complex individually tailored and targeted products or services quickly. For example, the Prudential, UK's largest pensions provider has recently introduced flexible pensions schemes with options to raise or lower payments, or halt them for a while, or switch payments from a personal pension into a top-up scheme on joining a company pension scheme. This contrasts sharply with traditional company pensions products which locked the customer in for life and took no account of the client's changing circumstances.

Managing information partnerships

The growing number of IT-enabled strategic alliances set up between organisations and their suppliers, distributors and customers, will require effective internal and external procedures to define, track, and manage joint performance. An example of this kind of alliance or partnership is that formed by fourteen UK insurers and the seven main UK brokers to develop and exploit the mutual benefits of links for commercial business. Such partnership arrangements are common in high-tech industries and will become an important part of the strategy of financial services organisations.

Whilst some firms are making progress along the lines listed above, few today have achieved any kind of IT-enabled business transformation. Many, stuck in the transition between automation and integration, are experiencing major problems. They find that integration is difficult where existing systems have developed as isolated areas of automation (Caulkin, 1991). Even where advances in technology have solved many of the technical problems, progress is hindered by both a general lack of understanding of the nature and potential of IT, and by organisational difficulties (Zuboff, 1988; Venkatraman, 1991).

Conclusion

The retail financial services sector – banking, life and general insurance and mortgage lending – was one of the most successful sectors of the UK economy in the 1980s, both in terms of employment creation and output growth. This expansion was driven by several factors including growing consumer wealth, deregulation and demographic changes, and supported by large-scale investment in IT which enabled the elimination of many routine clerical tasks and the development of more complex products. In the 1990s, the sector is entering a period of maturity, intense competition and rationalisation which will result in a large reduction in the number of companies. In this new environment, retail financial services companies must give greater emphasis to innovation, flexibility, and fast response to new market demands to survive and be successful in the long term. Achievement of business success in the future will also depend upon making full use of the capabilities of technology to enable change, innovation, and business transformation.

3

BUSINESS AND IT TRENDS IN RETAIL BANKING, MORTGAGE LENDING, LIFE AND GENERAL INSURANCE

This chapter summarises how each of the four main areas of the retail financial services sector – banking, mortgage lending, life assurance and general insurance – has changed over the last five years. It briefly describes the structure of each sector, outlines the key business trends, and the major IT challenges each faces. Most of the sectors have similar problems as described in Chapter 2, for example, the need to cut costs whilst at the same time improving quality. However, each sector has its own particular problems and these are identified too.

Employment and IT in the UK retail financial services sector

The retail financial services sector consists of four main subsectors: banking, building societies, life and pensions, and general insurance, but it also includes companies dealing with a range of associated services such as credit cards, finance and unit trusts which are not dealt with in this survey.

The largest sector, in terms of employment, is banking with over 370,000 employees (BBA, 1995), followed by the insurance sector with 270,000 employees, split roughly equally between the general and life sectors. In addition, the insurance sector employs a further 100,000 in associated industries plus 32,000 working on a self-employed basis (ABI, 1996). The building society sector employs 104,000 in total (CML, 1995).

All of these subsectors are major spenders on technology and employ large numbers of IT professionals; for example, the top ten banks in the retail banking sector invested an estimated £2.5 billion in 1995 and employed 15,000 IT professionals (Watkins, 1995). Estimates of IT spending in the insurance sector are: £1.7 billion in the life assurance sector (Insurance Marketing Review, 1995); and £600 million in the top six composites which dominate the general insurance sector. The top ten building societies spent an estimated £800 million on IT (Spikes Cavell, 1995,[1] see End Note 1).

Banking, being the largest of the four areas, is dealt with first, and since so many building societies are converting to banks, the mortgage lending sector is considered next, followed by the life assurance and general insurance sectors.

The banking sector

Retail banking in the UK is dominated by the eight major banks listed in Table 3.1 according to total liabilities/assets (BBA, 1995).

The structure of this sector has changed considerably over the past five years as banks streamline their branch networks and introduce new technology in an effort to cut their costs and remain competitive. As a result, employment in the sector, which had increased dramatically in the 1980s peaking at 460,000 in 1989, has been reduced by an estimated 90,000. Leading figures in the industry predict a further 75,000 job losses over the next few years. The major banks have also been cutting back on their expensive high street outlets and it is predicted that 20 per cent of the branch network will have been cut between 1988 and 1995 leaving an estimated 12,000 branches by 1996 (excluding Girobank). The growth of telephone banking and ATMs has also had a major impact on the number of branches. ATMs in particular increased from 11,739 in 1988 to 18,000 in 1996. Although telephone banking is still on a relatively small scale, it is predicted that it will rise rapidly in the near future.

According to the Association for Payment Clearing Services (APACS), fewer than 10 per cent of the population have no bank or building society account and fewer than 25 per cent have no bank or building society current account. As the 'unbanked' are concentrated amongst those on state benefits, and other non-working people and the unskilled working classes in social

Table 3.1 UK retail banks by assets, 1994

Bank	Total Liabilities/Assets £ millions
Barclays	159,363
National Westminster	156,893
Abbey National	90,227
Midland	79,177
Lloyds	73,200
Royal Bank of Scotland	44,896
Bank of Scotland	30,748
TSB	28,047

class D, most commentators predict that the holding of current and other accounts has reached saturation level. This area is still dominated by the big five banks, Barclays, Lloyds, NatWest, Midland, and TSB with an estimated 28 million of the 54 million account holders. The banking sector has 80 per cent of all current accounts as compared with 20 per cent held by the building societies. With regard to interest-bearing accounts, banks have 30 per cent of the market. The Building Societies Act (1986) gave building societies greater freedom to extend their products, unsecured lending, cheque accounts, and to abandon their mutual status and become public limited companies. One of the areas they have targeted is current account business. However, many building societies are either converting or considering converting to banks and in certain areas, such as current accounts, they are making considerable inroads into retail banking.

Among the main problems facing the banking sector over the next five years will be:

- Continuing over-capacity in the market with the building societies in particular extending their retail banking services;
- The continuing drive for further productivity improvement with automation and rationalisation leading to more job reductions and branch closures;
- 'The difficult task of maintaining earnings momentum in a low interest rate, low growth environment' (Derek Wanless, NatWest Bank, 1992). To achieve this, banks are now trying to push up non-interest income. This can be done in several ways: for example, through selling insurance and investment products to bank customers; through a better, more personal and more accurate service on basic banking; and through advisory services such as drawing up wills and giving advice to small business customers.

IT in retail banking: an overview

The banking sector is the largest spender on information technology and the largest employer of IT professionals. The major challenges for this sector include moving on from core data processing and automation to systems which will provide strategic advantage; and using customer databases from the core banking operations for expansion into other areas of financial services, such as investment and life assurance.

At the beginning of the 1990s, the bulk of IT expenditure was used to support the infrastructure of the retail banking operation, therefore it had either no direct competitive effect, or made a minimal contribution to increasing fee earning potential. The rapid installation of ATMs had resulted in the provision of a service which was extremely expensive to set up and maintain but contributed little to the overall profitability of the banks. Their competitive effect was simply to raise barriers to entry. As pointed out by Steiner and Teixeira (1990) the major part of systems investment supports products or services that are commodities throughout the industry.

During the last five years investment in basic data processing applications has continued, for example, much of the back office work which used to take place in each branch has been centralised into regional or national processing centres, and there has been the widespread introduction of document reader encoders into the branches. However, the investment focus has changed to the creation of customer databases, management information systems, and workstations in the branches which will give better customer service (see Chapter 6).

The building society sector – mortgage lending

Prior to the ending of the Building Societies Association (BSA) mortgage rate cartel in the 1980s, the building societies held a virtual monopoly over the supply of mortgage finance. They retained their dominant position into the mid-1980s, and in 1985 the building societies still accounted for three-quarters of the £150 billion market in mortgages outstanding, and 80 per cent of the net lending done that year. The banks had about 15 per cent of the balances outstanding and about 20 per cent of the new business. Over the past decade, the situation has changed dramatically. As a result of mergers and acquisitions, the number of building societies in the UK has been reduced dramatically from 190 to just under 80. During 1995/6 many of the largest building societies have decided to give up their mutual status and convert to banks. As a result the mortgage market is now also dominated by banks, or soon-to-be banks. Seven of the top ten mortgage lenders are now banks (see Table 3.2) and the future of the building society sector looks uncertain.

The mortgage lending sector has not experienced the same kind of employment losses as the banking sector. Since 1989 there has been a large increase in the numbers employed in this sector. However, as mergers between larger societies continue, job losses will continue at an accelerating rate.

The sector is also different from other sectors in that it has a large number of part-time employees representing over 23 per cent of the work force.

Although the number of employees has not fallen, the number of branches has been cut by almost a third from 6,954 in 1986 to under 5,000 in 1996. This trend is predicted to continue as mergers increase and also as the growing popularity of tele-sales gives the banks and building societies a new opportunity to do business through subsidiaries, such as Mortgages Direct, Nationwide Direct, Bradford and Bingley Direct, and First Direct.

IT in building societies: an overview

In many ways the building societies, having adopted sophisticated online systems linked to central computers early on, had more advanced IT systems

Table 3.2 Top 10 mortgage lenders in 1996

	Residential mortgage assets £ billions	
Halifax	73.8	Converting to bank
Abbey National	56.8	Bank
Lloyds	32.6	Bank
Nationwide	26.6	Building Society
Woolwich	21.0	Converting to bank
Alliance & Leicester	14.8	Converting to bank
NatWest	14.0	Bank
Barclays	11.9	Bank
Bradford & Bingley	10.9	Building Society
Britannia	8.0	Building Society

Source: CML 1995.

than the banks. The building societies, in common with the TSB, operated passbook accounts and customers were not allowed to overdraw. As a consequence, passbooks had to be updated from the computer each time a transaction was made. The online counter terminals involved in this data capture allowed the multi-branching of customers. This early lead has been extended with front office applications such as branch information systems.

One of the greatest strengths of the building societies is their extensive branch network. Since the 1986 Building Societies and Financial Services Act, the role of the branches has changed significantly, with a switch from distributed administrative centres to sales outlets. Branch managers are being judged by head office on their sales performance and are being set performance targets such as branch profitability, value of mortgage lending and commission income. There is a major push towards improving both the administrative efficiency and sales effectiveness of the branches. This is reflected in investment, in the late 1980s, in new branch technology to include local area networks and workstations and the phasing out of dumb terminals. The building societies were ahead of the main clearing banks with respect to customer-based as opposed to account-based mainframe systems, and had far more advanced branch technology (see Watkins, 1991).

The life assurance sector

The UK life and pensions sector is the largest in Europe with a turnover in 1994 of £43,112 million (ABI, 1995). Over the past decade this sector has experienced growth of 15 per cent per annum, making it one of the fastest growing sectors in the UK economy between 1985 and 1993. Although sales of life and pensions products fell in 1994 and 1995, the overall predictions for

Table 3.3 Top 10 life insurance companies by premium income 1993, status 1996

Company	Premium income £ million	Status 1996
Prudential	4,955	
Standard Life	4,445	Mutual
Sun Life	2,650	
Norwich Union	2,292	Mutual (changing status)
Equitable Life	2,230	Mutual
Legal & General	1,943	
Scottish Widows	1,620	Mutual
Allied Dunbar	1,462	
Clerical Medical	1,319	ex Mutual
Scottish Equitable	1,097	ex Mutual

the sector are good. An older, more affluent population will require a wide range of investment products and major growth is expected in this area as the state tries to hand over responsibility for pension provision to the individual and the private sector.

At the start of the 1990s, the life assurance sector was highly fragmented with well over 100 major companies involved, with a very strong mutual sector. In 1996, there is still a large number of mutual companies in this sector but they are increasingly being taken over. For example, the 1993 statistics provided by UNIC (1995) show that only three of the top ten companies have retained their mutual status (see Table 3.3).

The UK life assurance market remains relatively fragmented and 80 companies had a turnover in excess of £100 million in 1995. Despite predictions of a massive shake out and rationalisation in the number of companies involved in this sector this has been slow to occur. There are several reasons for this slow rationalisation, and they include:

- low brand image associated with lack of consumer recognition;
- strong growth in the sector until 1993;
- the large numbers of mutual companies in the sector make takeover more difficult.

Even though all the major banks and most of the large building societies have set up their own life companies with their own insurance, savings, and pensions products, they are looking to expand in what is seen as a major growth area. This will result in the continuing take-over of life companies by banks and ex-mortgage lenders. In response to these developments, life companies will need to make changes in three key areas:

1   They must improve the control, efficiency and effectiveness of their distribution channels. Companies such as Standard Life, Norwich

Union and Sun Life, which rely on the independent intermediary market for the bulk of their sales, are concerned about declining market share for this channel. Companies with large direct sales forces, such as Barclays and Allied Dunbar, are concerned with the expense of maintaining them. Large sales forces are expensive to run, productivity is low and there are high recruitment and training costs as a result of high turnover rates.

2   Life companies will be forced to cut their costs to compete with products offered by the banks and building societies and with other alternative investments such as unit trusts, TESSAs and investment trusts. This need will become even more urgent as government rules on disclosure take effect. Life companies will therefore have to reduce the costs associated with the sale of life and pension products dramatically.

3   The final challenge will be to move away from low-value insurance products such as whole life and endowments towards higher-value products which contain high advice and service elements. This movement started in the late 1980s and will gather momentum over the next five years (see Table 3.4).

Table 3.4 The shift from low value to higher value products

FROM *Low-value products*		TO *High-value products*
life assurance	⟶	investment
annual products	⟶	single premium products
simple products *e.g. whole life*	⟶	complex products *e.g. utilised products*
rigid products	⟶	flexible products
mass marketing	⟶	individualised marketing
low advice	⟶	high advice levels
obtaining new customers	⟶	retaining and extending services to existing customers

To survive over the next three years life companies will have to make better use of technology to meet these three demands.

IT in the life sector: an overview

The life sector is the second biggest IT spender in the sector and is a very large employer of IT professionals. Because of the need to store large amounts of information over a long period, the sector is dominated by mainframe technology with very few companies downsizing and using mid-range systems. Over 60 per cent of the companies have IBM mainframe systems. The major problem in the life sector is that the current systems were originally designed to handle low-value products of the kind summarised in the FROM column of Table 3.4. To cope with the shift to higher-value products and services, many companies are attempting to integrate their IT systems. Since the main indicator of profitability in the past has been the size and reputation of the company, life companies could continue to prosper as long as systems were adequate. However, such a situation cannot continue in the 1990s. A number of leading companies in the industry argue that survival and success now depends upon systems which can ensure speedy delivery of high-value products of the kind listed in the TO column of Table 3.4.

The general insurance sector

The general insurance sector, which had a net premium income of £34,914 million in 1994 (ABI, 1995), is the second largest general insurance market in Europe, after Germany.

The large composite insurers, which used to dominate the general insurance sector (see Table 3.5) are facing major business challenges particularly in two of their major markets, personal motor and personal property/household insurance (UNIC).

If the personal motor business follows the same trend as in the USA, about 50 per cent of the business will be written by direct insurers by the year 2000. In this area the market share of the top five composites has fallen to under 40 per cent as a result of competition, primarily from direct insurers such as Direct Line.

The property and household insurance market is dominated by the building societies and the banks which control the distribution channels. So, although the top five composites control over 50 per cent of this market, their position is vulnerable.

In order to remain profitable, the large composites are having to become *more flexible, service oriented, cost effective,* and *information intensive* as outlined below:

Table 3.5 Top 10 general insurers by net premium income 1993, status 1996

Company	Premium income £ million	Status 1996
Sun Alliance	1,788	Composite
Eagle Star	1,713	Composite
Commercial Union	1,642	Composite
Royal	1,550	Composite
General Accident	1,483	Composite
GRE	1,219	Composite
Norwich Union	969	Composite

- flexibility

  Companies are reshaping their organisation and procedures to give a better response to both policy holders and intermediaries. The aim is to adopt a more focused approach which provides a better service to a fragmenting market. Many are, for example, reorganising commercial lines and personal line accounts into separate business units at both branch and HQ.

- service orientation

  In both the commercial and personal lines markets, customers are buying mainly on price and will switch to the cheapest supplier. This affects customer retention rates. To achieve higher retention rates and to overcome price sensitivity, insurance companies are moving away from a product culture to a service culture. Examples of this movement to a service culture include:

  - the introduction of the all-embracing protection policy instead of individual products, for example, all-in-cover for professional liability, car and property insurance for a small business;
  - a major emphasis on improving the quality of service by such measures as documentation-while-you-wait, speedy reply to queries, and better claims handling, telephone advice;
  - for brokers it would include access to risk management skills and renewal incentives to retain customer loyalty.

- cost effectiveness

  To compete with niche providers and direct sales companies, the large composites, which had built up huge, inflexible infrastructures, are having to cut their costs dramatically and to set up their own direct companies.

- information intensity

  In the past the general insurance sector has suffered from poor quality information and this is particularly noticeable in underwriting. Even during the good years in the 1980s, poor underwriting results were masked by good investment performance. There were many reasons for this including poor training of underwriters, a booming market where caution was thrown to the wind (for example, mortgage indemnity policies), a cartel in the property insurance market, and lack of quality information systems on which to base decisions. In the 1990s, good underwriting is essential for survival. The information on which the underwriting is based is also becoming more sophisticated. Direct marketing companies have the advantage of starting with new systems which are client-based and have management information systems which provide data on key trends within seconds. For example, Direct Line employs a team of statisticians to identify key trends, and underwriting parameters can be adjusted on a daily basis to ensure profit levels are maintained.

In the sector there is a shift of emphasis from off-the-shelf standardised products, such as property, motor and accident insurance for the general public, to customised insurance packages for specific groups. This will result in a more loyal customer base, lower costs in acquisition and retention and less reliance on discounting. Also, higher profits are expected from tailor-made packages of services related to insurance, such as advice on security of buildings and reduction of theft.

IT in the general sector: an overview

The general insurance sector is attempting to put systems in place which meet these demands. Whilst there are clear economies of scale with regard to IT, for example, in the retail banking sector, this is not necessarily the case in the general sector. This means that identifiable niche markets can be targeted by smaller companies using new systems tailored to meet requirements exactly. It also means that a larger company may achieve greater cost effectiveness with regard to IT, if individual business units have their own systems strategies. This is the trend within the sector and could eventually lead to a highly fragmented systems approach.

The main problem faced by the sector is the need to change from systems which deliver mass produced, standardised products to highly specialised systems which provide customised insurance products for specific groups. In the property and household insurance markets, this is occurring very slowly because of the comfortable monopoly which exists between mortgage providers and insurers in this particular area. Current systems are still geared to the mass processing of property and household insurance. IT expenditure is heavily geared to the low level processing aspects, whereas competitive edge lies with quality underwriting and quality information. In many ways general insurers are hostages to banks and building societies which are extracting very large commissions. It is therefore surprising that general insurers were very late in introducing client management systems and more sophisticated underwriting which would have given them flexibility and some control over their customers. A similar situation exists with motor insurance, where systems were geared to mass marketing of standard products, whereas the market is becoming more fragmented and complex.

Conclusion

The structure of the four main subsectors has changed fairly dramatically since the late 1980s. Large sections of the building society sector are in the process of converting to banks to form an expanded banking sector in which there will be further rationalisation and concentration. What remains of the building society sector will only have a relatively small percentage of the mortgage market. The life and pensions sector will also undergo gradual rationalisation as they are taken over by banks and composite insurers. Many of the remaining mutual insurers will either convert to PLC status or be taken over.

The general insurance sector will also continue to change with mergers between some of the larger composites, and the continuing growth of direct insurance both for personal motor and household insurance.

The major IT challenges of the four main sectors are similar:

- to cut the costs of their basic financial products such as mortgages and current accounts substantially;
- to focus a far higher percentage of the IT spend on providing support to high value services such as financial advice and pensions;
- to use existing customer databases to extend the range of services – cross-selling.

Note

Estimates of IT spend in the sector vary widely according to how the sector is defined, e.g. Does banking include retail, credit cards and mortgage lending? Does life and pensions cover investment firms, PEPs and unit trusts? It also varies according to the way IT spend is calculated, for example: Does it include all IT spend not under the control of the central IT department? For instance, portable computers for sales staff may be the responsibility of the marketing department. The figures given therefore need to be treated with caution but are indicative of broad trends. The figures quoted by various authors also vary widely e.g. compare Spikes Cavell (1995) estimate of IT spend with that of Ernst & Young (1994).

Part III

TECHNOLOGY

4

ANALYSING STAGES OF
IT DEVELOPMENT

IT development in the organisation can be analysed in different ways. This chapter summarises a number of the different stage-based approaches that have evolved since the early days of computerisation. *Stages of growth* models which emerged in the 1970s were based on research in organisations which pioneered computerisation in the 1950s and 1960s. Some question whether these models, built on the experiences of the pioneers, are useful to new entrants who are implementing different technologies and are faced with different problems. More recent theories attempt to model the effects of the interaction of a range of factors, building upon the work of earlier theorists to produce refinements which offer a more complete explanation of the pattern of change. This chapter discusses briefly the origins, evolution, and limitations of some of these models. It outlines Nolan's Stages Model (1979), Galliers and Sutherland's (1991) revised stages of growth model, Friedman's Dynamic Phases Model (1989), the Three Era Model (DP-MIS-SIS), and the model selected to guide the analysis in subsequent chapters of this study: Venkatraman's (1991) model of IT induced business transformation.

Nolan's model

One of the best known and widely used models from the late 1970s and early 1980s is that developed by Nolan and Gibson in 1974, and expanded by Nolan in 1979. This model is based on the assumption that organisations pass through a series of clearly definable stages in using and managing IT. Nolan argues that stages of IT growth could be identified by analysing the amount spent on data processing as a proportion of sales revenue, that the expenditure follows an S-curve over time, and that this curve represents the learning path of the organisation with regard to the use and management of IT. Six stages are defined: initiation, contagion, control, integration, architecture, and maturity. The model, intended as a tool to identify key issues associated with further IT development, has many critics, notably Benbasat *et al.* (1984), and King and Kraemer (1984). Most criticisms, as detailed by Friedman (1989) in his evaluation of *stages of growth* models, centre on the lack of empirical evidence to support a consistent set of stages.

In spite of the views of its critics, many have found the Nolan model a useful tool for analysing stages of IT development in the organisation, and have used it as a basis for their own models. For example, Earl (1986, 1987, 1988, 1989, 1991), Bhabuta *et al.* (1988), Hirschheim *et al.* (1988), Galliers (1987), Cash, McFarlan and McKenney (1992) have all developed *stages of IT growth* models which build on the work of Nolan and Gibson. A recent paper by Friedman (1994) suggests four reasons for the continuing influence of the Nolan model:

> First it is the only explicit model of the time pattern of IS function development. Second, it is clear and easily leads to testable hypotheses. For this it has appealed to academics. Third, the model has clear prescriptive content. For this it has appealed to managers and to management consultants. Fourth, and perhaps most controversially, we would suggest that the model **does** summarise certain experiences of many organisations. The model has tested poorly because it is underspecified. Other influences on the time pattern of IS development within user organisations should be considered.
>
> (Friedman 1994)

Moving on from Nolan

Galliers and Sutherland (1991) outline key aspects of the work of Nolan, Earl, Bhabuta *et al.* and Hirschheim *et al.* in a paper which traces the development of the *stages of growth* concept and describes their own *revised stages of growth* model. They describe how Nolan's six-stage model (see Figure 4.1), an expanded version of the earlier four-stage model, focuses on four major growth processes, in addition to DP expenditure which was the focus of the earlier model. These growth processes – the scope of the applications portfolio (from DP to MIS to SIS); the focus of the DP organisation (from centralised technology management to data resource management); the focus of the DP planning and control activity (from internal to external); and the level of user awareness (from reactive to proactive to collaborative) – can all be analysed to identify the stage reached with regard to the use and management of IT. The stages are labelled: initiation, contagion, control, integration, architecture, and maturity. Whilst technology is the focus of management concern in the first three stages, a transformation point occurs after Stage 3 (Control) is complete, and the focus shifts to managing the organisation's data resources using database technology and methods.

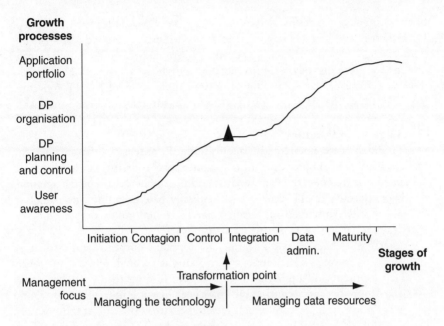

Figure 4.1 Nolan's six-stage growth model.
Source: Redrawn from Galliers and Baker (1994). By permission of Butterworth Heinemann.

Galliers and Sutherland (1991)

Galliers and Sutherland (1991) show how the subsequent work of Earl, Bhabuta *et al.* and Hirschheim *et al.* to some extent, remedy many of the inadequacies of the Nolan model. Earl (1989) focuses on the stages through which organisations pass in planning their information systems; Bhabuta's four-stage model maps the progress towards formal strategic planning of information systems; and Hirschheim puts forward a three-phase model with: a delivery phase, where the main management concern is whether the IT function can deliver the goods; a reorientation phase, where IT is exploited for competitive advantage; and a final reorganisation phase which is concerned with managing the relationships between the IS function and the rest of the organisation.

Although their work represents a substantial step forward, Galliers and Sutherland argue the need for a model which can be used not only to determine the stage an organisation has reached but also to indicate clearly what must be done to progress through the subsequent stages. The model they propose analyses the stages of IT growth within a framework of seven key elements – strategy, structure, systems, skills, staff, style, shared values – which govern the way an organisation functions. This framework of key elements is based on a model known as the 'Seven S Framework' proposed by Pascale and Athos in 1981. The combined model describes the kind of activities and organisational structures needed by an enterprise to move through six stages of IT growth: 'adhocracy'; starting the foundations; centralised dictatorship; democratic dialectic and cooperation; entrepreneurial opportunity; integrated, harmonious relationships. It indicates how an organisation might develop its use of the technology, and its organisation of the IT function. Key features of the six stages of IT growth are summarised briefly below:

Stage 1: 'adhocracy'

This first stage involves the acquisition of hardware, software and the installation of simple, operational applications. Systems are developed in an ad hoc manner; they are isolated and unconnected; their management is uncoordinated. IT skills are individually based, technology-oriented, and mostly contracted-in; business needs are only dimly perceived.

Stage 2: starting the foundations

There is a backlog of systems development projects and escalating numbers of operational applications, bought-in or developed in-house. Development and operation is centralised, leading to the establishment of a computer centre with a DP manager, growing numbers of staff, and a 'we know best' culture which sets it apart from the rest of the business. Lack of understanding of the 'whole picture', poor communications between IT and business personnel lead to confusion and fears that IT development and spending is getting out of control. End users, frustrated by long project delays, set up their own systems.

Stage 3: centralised dictatorship

In this stage, there are serious attempts to take charge of the situation by introducing top-down planning, and focusing on systems to meet real business needs. The emphasis is on structured development with careful project management. Senior management's main concern is return on investment (ROI). The DP manager either attempts to control the growth of end-user systems, or leaves them to get on with it. Either strategy is resented by the end-users, and, with the confidence gained from growing IT skills they communicate their views more forcibly.

Stage 4: democratic dialectic and cooperation

The IT department is forced to take an active part in the day-to-day business and attempts are made to bring end-users back into the fold by partial decentralisation. A 'federal approach' to IS management and development is adopted, with mini DP departments spread throughout the organisation, coordinated by an Information Services department. Systems are installed in an integrated and coordinated manner; business and IT personnel work together to ensure systems satisfy business needs. The emphasis is on cooperation and collaboration, and business skills combined with technical skills.

Stage 5: entrepreneurial opportunity

In the fifth stage, strategic systems are built on the foundations of well established core systems. The emphasis shifts to seeking opportunities for the strategic use of IT and the IT function claims strategic importance in the firm's objectives. Entrepreneurialism is encouraged. The federal approach, with strategic coalitions being made between IT and business units, as needs arise, gains dominance. Systems are more market-orientated; IT is used to add value to products and services; external data is combined with internal data to produce strategic information. IT staff have cross-disciplinary business/IT/IS skills; IT management at senior, executive level is crucial; the contribution of skilled IT end-users to systems development and training is highly valued.

Stage 6: integrated, harmonious relationships
In the final stage, IT is well integrated into the organisation and its departments; IT and business staff work harmoniously. Management's main concern, maintenance of comparative strategic advantage, involves constant reassessment of IT uses in the firm and in the market-place. Strategic alliances are in place; strategic coalitions between IT and business units are centrally coordinated; inter-organisational systems are being built; and IT-based products and services are developed. The Head of IT is now on the board and plays an active part in strategic decisions. Internally, the emphasis is on inter-dependent teamwork; externally the focus is on strategic alliances and shared information systems.

Friedman (1989, 1994)

Friedman (1989) also argues the need for a model with combined perspectives. In an evaluation of the relative merits and limitations of the different theoretical approaches, he describes how the 'stages of growth' theories which emerged in the 1970s and early 1980s tend to focus on a single agent as a driving force for change from one stage to the next. Whilst acknowledging the influence of other factors on the progress of computerisation, each one identifies a different agent of change as the primary driving force behind *all* of its stages, for example:

- the hardware generations approach of Walter (1970), Couger (1982) and others, defines stages driven by changes in computer hardware technology;
- the organisation stages approach of Churchill *et al.* (1969) proposes that the stages are driven by the progression of increasingly sophisticated types of computer applications;
- the labour process approach of Kraft (1977) describes stages driven by management's progress in imposing control over the labour process involved in programming the computer;
- the organisation stages approach of Nolan and Gibson (1979) emphasises management's short-term reactions or over-reactions to technological disruptions following the introduction of the computer, as the primary agent of change driving progress through the stages.

Friedman's main criticism is that such approaches encourage a tendency to assume that there is one best way to manage computer systems development. Since the progress of IT development in the organisation is too complex to be explained in terms of a single primary driving force, Friedman proposes a dynamic model based on an analysis of a combination of forces. To build this model, he focuses on the best elements of the 'stages' approaches, including that of Nolan and Gibson, and blends them with theories from other disciplines. The model traces the history of IT/IS management within the organisation over the past forty years and describes developments in terms of three phases, each of which is dominated by a different set of constraints. Each phase is defined by a critical factor or problem that restricts progress.

Phase 1 (from initiation to mid-1960s) is dominated by hardware constraints related to costs and limitations of capacity and reliability. Whilst advances in technology relieve these constraints, growing demand for systems and for new applications, and growing shortages of qualified labour give rise to a new set of constraints and the focus of concern shifts to software development problems.

The constraints which inhibit progress in Phase 2 (mid-1960s to early 1980s) are related to the productivity of systems developers, and difficulties in delivering reliable systems on time and within budget. Towards the end of Phase 2, users become increasingly IT literate and better able to specify the kind of systems they want. Users press for better systems and services and quality problems arising from inadequate perception of user demands and servicing of their needs start to emerge. In Phase 3 (from the early 1980s to 1990s), these user relations constraints dominate as user satisfaction becomes an increasingly important criteria of success for the IS departments.

Friedman argues that although a different constraint assumes dominance in each phase, the influence of other factors is still present: it merely fades into the background as attention is focused on relieving the problems created by the dominant constraint. As solutions are found and new opportunities are revealed, the background constraints gradually come to the fore. As the focus of concern shifts, new priorities emerge as a different constraint assumes dominance giving rise to a new phase of development. In each phase, the new priorities are reflected in the types of people recruited into computer departments, the management strategies selected for organising their work, and the relations between computer staff, users and senior management.

The interrelated forces which drive change through each of the phases in Friedman's dynamic model fall into four main groups:

- technology – rapid advances in computing, telecommunications, software development technologies;
- uses and applications – changes in the character of the demand for computer systems development, for example, the change in emphasis

from data processing to the management information systems and strategic information systems;

- markets for IT-based skills and services – monopoly markets for computer-based services and skilled-labour shortages influenced systems development in the early years; today, the trends towards outsourcing and end-user programming are having a different effect;
- organisational environment and management strategy – the environment of the organisation is shaped by management strategy and the internal reactions to management's efforts to control the systems development process has influenced the pace and character of systems development and technological change. Three key areas are the nature of management control, the new emphasis on linking business and IT strategies, and the shift in IT focus from internal to external.

What next? With regard to the future, Friedman (1989) considers three scenarios, but stresses that no single scenario can be generalised to the whole field. Different scenarios are possible in different types of organisations and in different industry sectors. The three scenarios he describes are: the possibility of a continuation of the Phase 3 strategies; the re-emergence of Phase 1 or Phase 2 type constraints; and the emergence of a new set of constraints – organisation environment constraints – which could herald a fourth phase. The organisation environment constraints of a fourth phase arise from problems connected with the interface between the internal computing systems of the organisation and agents in the external environment of the organisation. The agents include customers and clients, suppliers, competitors, partners, representatives, and public bodies. The constraints result from difficulties in:

- accurately identifying and accessing strategic information particularly about hostile and potentially hostile agents;
- establishing sufficiently cooperative relations with complementary organisations;
- reducing supplier, and particularly consumer resistance to operating through computer-mediated communications;
- agreeing and enforcing standards and protocols both for systems development and for use with cooperating organisations and customers;
- security, particularly as such systems become vulnerable to hackers and thereby industrial espionage.

Friedman's most recent paper, 1994, describes how this phases model of the history of IS systems management can be used to predict new pressures for IS executives and new directions for focusing research and education resources. It shows how the 'phases model' can supplement Nolan's stages model of computer usage within organisations and can help explain why tests of

Nolan's model have not been successful. He offers two explanations as to why new organisations in the 1970s and 1980s did not learn from the experience of the pioneers and implement appropriate controls at the outset of Stage 2 (Expansion) as Nolan recommended:

- developments in the IS field move forward rapidly so they are implementing different core technologies;
- latecomers to the IS field are generally smaller companies requiring smaller and cheaper implementations. IS consultants with experience gained in pioneer organisations are reluctant to work with them, since the profit potential is so much lower, and the knowledge is not transferred.

He points out that Nolan's articles reflect particular phases of time in the IS field: the 1974 article reflects observations of organisations experiencing Phase 2, software productivity constraints; the 1979 article reflects the coming of Phase 3, user relations constraints.

He argues that a 'new Nolanesque stages model', which takes into account the organisation environment constraints that seem to mark the transition to a fourth phase in the 1990s, would include a 'new Stage 6, (Strategic Systems)' which represents contagious growth in IS expenditure on EDI, VANs and systems for which customers and suppliers are direct end-users; and a 'new Stage 7 (Security Standards)' which focuses on inter-organisational agreements about standards, control, and security for the new inter-organisational systems.

Models based on an analysis of IT uses and applications

Analysis of the changing uses and applications of IT is a popular approach to theory development and has produced a number of models. The most common are variations on the 'Three Era' model – see, for example, the work of Wiseman, 1985; Somogy and Galliers, 1987; Ward, Griffiths, and Whitmore, 1990. Later models, such as those of Land and Lattimer 1991 (see Farbey, Land and Targett, 1995), and Venkatraman (1991) stress the transformational role of IT.

The three era model

Changes in the character of the demand for computer systems development output have influenced the progress and direction of computer systems development in the organisation. Business activities in the organisation fall into three categories – operational, control and strategic – and this has provided a useful way of analysing the effect of IT. The three era model categorises the development of IT into three overlapping eras: Data Processing (DP), Management Information Systems (MIS), and Strategic Information Systems (SIS), as outlined below. Although the model can be criticised for being over simplistic, it does provide a clear overview of trends:

Era 1: Data Processing (DP)

The first computer-based systems, focused on automating the operational activities. These involved clerical tasks which were already well formulated and understood. Systems were designed to capture, store and process data to produce operational outputs such as payslips and invoices. They also produced simple management reports for use in controlling and monitoring routine activities. The main function of IT during this era was to improve operational efficiency by automating processes. Even in the future, it is estimated that more than 50 per cent of all IT investments will be devoted to improving efficiency through data processing.

Era 2: Management Information Systems (MIS)

MIS use the computer to structure and manipulate the data in order to produce more focused information for higher level control and decision-making activities. The computer's potential for producing enhanced management information for strategic functions was soon recognised, but the transition from automating pre-existing administrative systems to producing management information systems of this kind has been slow for a number of reasons:

- The benefits from automated MIS are difficult to quantify hence the additional expenditure is difficult to justify.
- Automated MIS have been resisted by managers who see them as a threat to their role in the organisation. Their status and power ensures that their resistance is more successful than those involved in lower level tasks such as clerical work.
- Since management is not a routine task, the information requirements for MIS are difficult to specify and can change very quickly. Hence the job of analysis is much more complex.
- MIS use cross functional and external data and their effectiveness depends upon the level of integration between systems in different departments and access to external data. Integrated systems which allow the manipulation of data collected from different departments can only be developed if the data is coded and stored in a standardised format. Since systems in different departments have often been developed separately and at different times, the level of standardisation required rarely exists. Systems must be modified, upgraded or replaced in order to

establish the links that make integration possible. The level of complexity, difficulties in quantifying benefits, problems involved in changing and coordinating working practices across the different departments, and the costs associated with the increased hardware capacity required to support such systems ALL constrain the progress of integration.

The main aim of management information systems, to increase management effectiveness by satisfying their information requirements, continues to be a major problem in most organisations.

Era 3: Strategic Information Systems (SIS)

In the late 1970s and early 1980s a number of companies such as Thomson Holidays, McKesson, and American Airlines began to use IT in ways which fundamentally changed the way their business was conducted. IT had become a strategic weapon with direct influence on their competitive positioning. These new strategic information systems had the potential to restructure industry sectors, companies and markets. Commentators such as Ward *et al.* (1990) identify four main types of strategic information systems, those that:

- link the organisation via technology-based systems to its customers, consumers and or suppliers;
- produce more effective integration in the use of information in the organisations value-adding process;
- enable the organisation to develop, produce, market and deliver new or enhanced products or services based on information;
- provide executive management information to support the development and implementation of strategy.

Key differences between the SIS era and the DP and MIS eras are summarised in Table 4.1.

Table 4.1 Key differences between the DP, MIS eras and the SIS era

DP, MIS eras	SIS era
• internal focus: internal processes and issues	• external focus: customers, competitors and suppliers
• cost reduction	• added value
• efficiency emphasis	• effectiveness and differentiation
• product-led IT	• customer-led IT
• technology-driven innovation	• business-driven innovation
• clarifying requirements, agreeing total deliverables	• iterative and incremental development
• poor use of information	• information used to develop business

The MIT model of business transformation

Studies by Venkatraman (1991) at MIT suggest that organisations in the late 1980s and early 1990s are reaching a critical stage in the application of IT as they move from the automation stage to the integration stage of IT assimilation. Given that the strategic potential of IT is now well recognised, Venkatraman proposes a model of 'IT-induced business reconfiguration' to help managers reconceptualise the role of IT in business in order to exploit this potential, and to differentiate their operations from their competitors. The challenge is to identify which IT applications are most relevant to the organisation's particular strategic context, and will enable it to achieve the business goals envisaged.

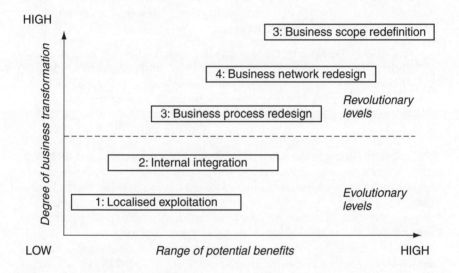

Figure 4.2 Business transformation levels.
Source: Redrawn from MIT 1991. By permission of Oxford University Press.

The model describes five levels of business transformation: localised exploitation (automation); internal integration; business process redesign; business network redesign; and business scope redefinition (see Figure 4.2). It characterises Level 2 as the integration of the tasks, processes and functions automated in Level 1, and this is made possible by the development of an internal electronic infrastructure or platform.

> While localised exploitation may provide strategic benefits in some select cases, they are invariably short-lived and can be successfully erased by competitive limitations. The real longer-term, potentially sustainable advantage accrues to an organisation because of internal

integration of business activities designed to exploit IT-enabled business opportunities differently from its competitors.

(Venkatraman 1991)

Levels 3, 4 and 5 are options which are presented once the infrastructure is in place. As an organisation moves through each level, the scale and scope of the benefits increase. At the same time, the degree of organisational change and business risk also increases dramatically.

Figure 4.2 shows the relationship between the five levels, the degree of business transformation and the range of potential benefits. Levels 1, 2 and 3 are internal and apply to business processes within the organisation, whilst Levels 4 and 5 involve changing relationships, particularly with customers and suppliers.

Venkatraman emphasises that although organisations *tend* to proceed in a stage-by-stage manner from one level to the next, some organisations make strategic leaps, rather than follow a sequential step-by-step route; other theorists take a similar line, for example:

> It is highly unlikely that any particular organisation will find itself entirely within one stage. Organisations are more likely to display characteristics associated with a number of stages; it is most likely that different parts of a single organisation will be at different stages of growth at any one time.

(Galliers and Sutherland 1994)

Venkatraman, stressing the inter-dependence of organisational and technological integration, argues that no single generic platform is suitable for all organisations even within the same industry. He proposes that the technological solution must therefore take into account the particular organisation's strategic context in order to select the most appropriate IT platform to interconnect its business activities along a chosen direction.

This involves a dynamic alignment process across four domains: business strategy, organisation infrastructure and processes, IT strategy; IT infrastructure and processes.

Framework and models for strategic alignment

Venkatraman proposes a framework for the strategic management of IT which can assist managers in achieving a successful alignment between organisational strategy and IT strategy. It is described as a staged and cyclical process with feedback loops and iterations between the various stages (for full details see Venkatraman 1991 and also McKersie in *Corporation of the 1990s*, Scott-Morton (ed.) 1991). Each cycle (they recommend a minimum of two cycles) moves through four main stages. At each stage three of the four domains (one quadrant) are considered for alignment before moving one turn to focus on the next domain in relation to two of the three considered in the previous stage. Two full cycles involve eight turns which allows sufficient feedback and iteration for convergence to occur.

Venkatraman (1991) and Earl (1996) have both developed frameworks Although they use different terminology they are very similar in many respects. As we have seen the four domains of Venkatraman's Strategic Alignment Model (SAM) are: business strategy; IT strategy; organisational infrastructure and processes; information systems infrastructure and processes. The four domains in Earl's Organisational Fit Framework (OFF) are: organisational strategy (which includes business strategy and organisational choices); IT strategy; information management strategy; information systems strategy.

Earl, in comparing OFF with SAM, states that both are concerned with relationships or linkages between IS/IT and the business; that their purpose is to guide strategic management of IT; and that both are premised on the view (limited as yet) that alignment is a *dynamic* process. The main differences, he suggests are their origin and focus: SAM, with its origins in strategic management theory, is more deductive, focusing on strategic positioning and alignment, whereas OFF, based on information management issues, is more inductive, focusing on organisational capability and synergy. He sees SAM as a conceptual framework and OFF more as a managerial check list (see Earl, 1996: 485–500).

The risks of integration

The movement to Level 2 reflects a strategic decision to exploit the benefits of integration and subsequent levels. The risks and costs associated with the move into these later stages of IT development are high.

The key inhibitors to a successful transition from automation to integration arise from both technological factors: uncertainty and the cost of integration, *and* organisational factors: the centralisation/decentralisation conflict, lack of strategic vision for integration, and organisational inertia (see Figure 4.3).

Venkatraman believes that since the technology for internal integration is readily available and affordable, the critical inhibitors are organisation-related.

Conclusion

The stage-based theories of IT development are criticised as being too simplistic, in that they propose a single path of development, and too insensitive to contextual factors, as they are derived from the experiences of mainly large companies in advanced economies. Even so, it is recognised that they do provide explicit models of the time pattern of IS function development which can lead to testable hypotheses. They predict that certain events will occur together and that others will follow a particular sequence. In addition, they appeal to managers and management consultants for having a clear, prescriptive content and for accurately summarising the experiences of most large organisations in developed countries.

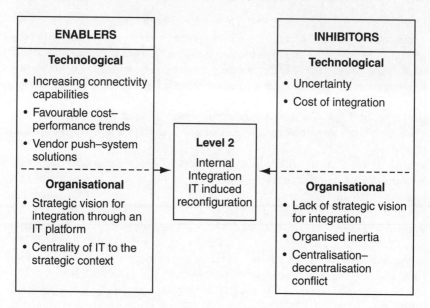

Figure 4.3 Internal integration: enablers and inhibitors.
Source: Venkatraman 1991. By permission of Oxford Universtity Press.

I have chosen Venkatraman's approach as being the most useful and relevant tool for analysing the data which forms the basis of this study of the retail financial services sector in the UK.

Venkatraman's model offers a broad brush view which emphasises the business transformation potential of current IT applications and which stresses the need to understand the inter-dependence of organisational and technological factors in managing the changes which must take place to realise this potential. It provides a very broad framework to measure the progress that organisations are making in using IT to meet the demands of rapidly changing markets. It can be combined and is consistent with IT development theories, such as that of Galliers and Sutherland (1991), and with organisational theories such as those of Mintzberg (1979), Nohria (1992), and Miles and Snow (1986).

Venkatraman stresses that as companies approach the various levels of business transformation, it is important to ensure that IT development and organisational changes are in tune. The implementation of new technologies will require parallel changes, for example, in organisational structures, systems, management strategies, and human resources policies.

The analysis also draws heavily on Galliers and Sutherland's model which takes a more holistic view of the organisation and the place of information systems management. It defines six stages of IT growth and indicates what changes are made with regard to strategy, structures, systems, skills, staff, management styles, and culture in the organisation to facilitate movement through the six stages. It is concerned with technology and its applications, the management of the IT function, and the management strategies adopted. It provides a framework which enables questions to be raised about the nature and pace of IT development at appropriate stages.

In the analysis which follows in Chapter 5, Venkatraman's model is used to provide an overview of the current stage of business transformation in the sector. Chapters 6, 7 and 8 give a more detailed analysis of transformation in three areas: technology, management of the IT function, and IT/IS management strategy.

5

TOWARDS INTEGRATION AND BUSINESS PROCESS REDESIGN

This chapter presents the results of two surveys, one conducted in 1993 covering the whole of the UK retail financial services sector, and one in 1995 covering the UK retail banking sector (Survey IT2 and Survey IT3 in the Appendix). The aim of both surveys was to determine the stage of IT development in the retail financial services sector and whether or not IT is being used to achieve business transformation as defined in Venkatraman's model (1991). The chapter begins with an overview of the model, then the results of the surveys are analysed within the framework it provides. Typical case studies are included to illustrate the stage of IT development reached by various companies in the sector and the different kind of BPR initiatives being attempted.

Venkatraman's model (1991): an overview of the stages of business transformation

Venkatraman's model identifies five levels or stages of IT-induced business transformation: local exploitation (automation); integration; business process redesign; business network redesign; and business scope redefinition, as described below:

Stage 1: localised exploitation (automation)

Over the past 20 years computers have been used to automate existing work tasks such as payroll, invoicing etc. In some areas, automation has been successful, for example, in the UK insurance sector, where productivity in terms of premium income per employee has risen dramatically. Over the same period, the complexity of the products has increased and new products, many of which would be impossible to administer manually, have been devised (for example, unit linked assurance). A large part of this increase in productivity can be attributed to the automation of existing processes. In an effort to minimise disruption, complexity and cost, most applications have been 'local' resulting in 'islands of automation'. For example, the finance, marketing and personnel departments of a company at the stage of 'localised exploitation' will each have a separate system. In banks, a single customer's accounts for savings, life assurance, mortgages, investment products, will be administered in separate unconnected systems. As a result of this kind of investment over a twenty-year period, most of the large financial services companies are faced with the following problems:

- *Cost rigidity*
  They are encumbered with a massive and rigid technology infrastructure. Such a huge systems investment makes an orderly exit from a market, if it becomes unprofitable, very difficult. They are very vulnerable to competition from new companies, smaller and more focused, which can by-pass the expensive developmental and experimental stages and pick and choose proven applications and technologies.

- *Maintenance of the status quo*
  Information technology now plays an important role in the organisation. One in eight employees in life assurance companies is an IT person. The IT specialists have a vested interest in maintaining demand for their existing skills, many of which are now obsolete, and in retaining the privileges and perks which go with the powerful company positions they now occupy.

- *Outdated IT systems*
  Much strategic planning in the financial services sector is based on strategies devised to solve past problems. IT systems planning is similarly flawed and, in view of rapidly changing markets, existing systems are now inadequate for both current and future business needs. In the life sector for example, the survey found that the bulk of the current systems were originally designed to handle low value products such as life assurance, whereas what is needed at the moment are systems which deal with high value products such as investment products.

- *Systems which are out of control*
  Many large financial services companies are now dependent on IT systems which are inherently unmanageable due to their complexity and their history of ad hoc, haphazard, piecemeal development. This tendency is confirmed in a survey of IT executives by Price Waterhouse reported in the IT Review (1993/94). Interviews in our survey revealed similar problems and typical comments from IT directors closely echoed those reported by Price Waterhouse:

'In reality we are being strangled by our old systems.'

'The basic systems infrastructure on which our company depends has become unmanageable.'

'All the larger systems on which our company depends have become over the years dangerously unstable.'

Stage 2: integration

Organisations find that further spending on automation provides fewer and fewer gains in productivity, and that *integration* is necessary if they are to make full use of the data held. Integrated systems allow data to be combined, analysed, compared and interpreted in ways which facilitate innovation. Those considering integration as the next step forward are faced with a number of major problems, for instance:

- current systems are based on manual processes, many of which are outdated;
- the costs of developing fully integrated systems are massive;
- integrated systems are large in scale and highly complex to develop;
- their development involves much disruption;
- project development timescales are lengthy;
- the large, all embracing integrated system may prove to be too unwieldy to meet the needs of markets which are becoming more and more individualised, specialised and fragmented;
- with rapidly changing markets these systems may be obsolete by the time they are installed.

It is during the transition from automation to integration, that most companies realise that integration which exploits the full potential of even the current technology is only possible if they rethink and redesign their business processes, organisational structures, and communications networks in ways which facilitate new relationships between individuals and departments.

Stage 3: business process redesign (BPR)

The many definitions of business process redesign in the literature, all emphasised fundamental organisational change and a radical redesign of the complete business system – the business processes, jobs, organisational structures, management systems – to achieve dramatic improvements in critical measures of performance.

BPR, according to Hammer (1991), in contrast to TQM and JIT which are based on continuous and incremental approaches, needs to be radical and revolutionary. He argues for company-wide implementation, and stresses that new technologies usually have to be introduced to make the new parallel processes possible, the organisation and its people need to change and a whole range of performance measures are needed to monitor the improvement (see Figure 5.1).

New simplified horizontal processes which cut across existing functional

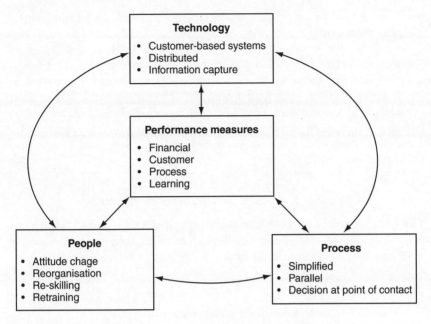

Figure 5.1 Level 3 business process redesign, an iterative process.
Source: Redrawn from Nolan Norton & Co.

departments and which enable decisions to be made at point of contact need to be identified. Introducing the new processes will result in new job descriptions which, for example, give clerical workers greater responsibility. This in turn demands new skills and new organisational structures in order to manage the work effectively.

New management systems such as budgeting, resource allocation, recruitment, are also crucial, and necessitate modification of the organisation's deep seated cultural values.

In the retail financial services sector it is virtually impossible to achieve BPR without first introducing the technology necessary to support the new parallel processes, see, for example, Case 5.2 on National Provincial. Among the main developments in technology which facilitate the introduction of BPR are client-server architecture, relational databases, imaging, and communications networks. These new technologies are enabling major organisational changes. For example, in a life company, where departments organised on policy and product lines are being reorganised along customer lines, the introduction of document image processing, together with a customer database, means that all information can be captured at one point and then passed simultaneously to different parts of the company. However, barriers to the introduction of technologies such as these can develop, for example, when the existing workforce does not want to change its work habits and when existing middle management wants to hold on to hierarchical power structures.

To manage the strategic change associated with BPR, a wide range of performance measures is required to provide an accurate and balanced assessment of progress. Traditional financial measures such as return-on-investment (ROI) need to be supplemented with other measures such as customer satisfaction surveys and the setting of targets for organisational and individual learning. In addition, improvement in the business processes needs to be monitored using techniques such as process modelling, work flow and work measurement.

Stage 4: business network redesign (BNR)

The business processes of two or more organisations are linked, leading to major cost benefits by cutting out duplicated or unnecessary processes and often resulting in collaborations between organisations which enhance joint capability.

Stage 5: business scope redefinition (BSR)

In this stage, information technology, originally intended to make the core business more effective, is used to enlarge the scope of a business, enabling entry into new profitable markets.

Results of Survey IT2, 1993

This section uses Venkatraman's model of business transformation as a framework to present the survey findings on the development of IT systems in UK retail financial services companies. Table 5.1 indicates the level of business transformation achieved by the firms participating in the survey. It shows that there had been little progress beyond Level 2 with very few companies introducing BPR as defined by Venkatraman (1991) and by Hammer (1991). Ninety per cent of the companies were still at the localised exploitation stage, as defined by Venkatraman's model, and were moving at different rates into the internal integration stage. The implementation of CCA (a

Table 5.1 Level of business transformation in the UK financial services sector 1993

		% of companies
Level 1	Localised exploitation	90
Level 2	Internal integration	8
Level 3	Business process redesign	2
Level 4	Business network redesign	0
Level 5	Business scope redefinition	0

major client-based insurance package) in the Norwich Union and Sun Alliance; the network redesign initiative at the TSB; and the Information Systems Service at NatWest are examples of major information technology projects aiming for internal integration. Eight per cent believed that they had successfully achieved internal integration. Of the hundred companies responding to the survey, only two had introduced BPR, as defined here, though the numbers will have risen since the survey was carried out in 1993. None of the companies participating in the survey claimed to be at either the BNR or BSR stage, though a number were investigating the possibilities.

In summary, the overall picture at the time was one where the majority of companies were still at Level 1 but striving for Level 2 with internal integration of IT as their aim.

Case histories from Survey IT2, 1993

Our research in 1993 found four typical examples of different kinds of BPR initiatives in the UK retail financial services sector and these are summarised below:

Case 5.1 illustrates the most common scenario, a company which was struggling to move from the localised exploitation stage to the integrated stage and is also introducing BPR in a limited way by focusing on a small functional area.

Case 5.2 describes a company undergoing radical change which concentrated initially on only one element of BPR, the people element, neglecting to change the technology simultaneously. Several UK financial services companies came into this category, for example, National Provincial Building Society.

Case 5.3 is that of a company which introduced BPR, making changes to the people, the processes and the technology simultaneously. Companies which have done this are rare, only two companies in our survey in 1993 came into this category, WPA and National Vulcan.

Case 5.4 is an example of a new start-up or parallel company.

The first case history on West Life illustrates the stage of development that most UK financial service companies had reached in 1993. They were moving from localised exploitation to integrated systems and were facing major problems; at the same time they were experimenting with localised BPR.

Case 5.1: West Life

West Life is a top ten life assurance company which sells life, investment, and pensions products, mainly through independent intermediaries. It also has a medium-sized sales force and is tied to a building
society for the sale of endowment policies. Since 1985, the importance
of IT has grown dramatically, as the statistics in Table C5.1 illustrate.

Table C5.1 Growth of IT expenditure in West Life

	1985	1994
IT expenditure	£8 million	£40 million
No. of IT staff	150	450
IT expenses (as % of group costs)	10	25

West Life had evolved as a traditional life company. It was split into
twenty different departments according to job function, e.g. marketing,
personnel, actuarial, and according to individual product types, e.g.
group life, personal pensions, unit trusts. IT systems were policy-based
so there was no way of telling whether the same person had, for
example, an endowment policy and a unit trust and it was impossible
to obtain a clear picture of the company's relationship with a client. It
provides a good example of a company in the localised exploitation
stage of IT development. To leap to the next stage of integrated IT, the
company decided, in 1989, to buy a package which, it estimated at the
time, would take three years to install, at a cost of approximately £30
million. By the time it had been installed, the costs had almost doubled
to between £50 million and £60 million. Even this could be an under-
estimate, as very few life companies cost the time of end-user involvement in the specification, design and implementation stages of
integrated systems. There were also major problems with the package,
in particular, it was too inflexible to deal with some of the new products
on the market. By the time it had been installed, the technology and the
systems had become obsolete.

When such a large strategic system is introduced, it takes years, if
ever, to transfer all business to the new system. During this time most
companies must support three layers of cost: the cost of running the
old systems, the new systems replacing them, and the interfaces

between the two. In addition to the cost of setting up new integrated systems, West Life had to contend with the following:

- a hotchpotch of old systems which in any one year may require immediate and costly replacement of some critical section in response to an acute short-term crisis;
- significant costs for patching and maintaining existing systems;
- pressure from user managers and business units for short-term tactical solutions to satisfy urgent needs. Product life cycles and launch times are much shorter. Ten years ago, a firm would spend one to two years devising and launching a product with a three-year life expectancy. Today life cycles are so short that the product must be launched within three to six months, and new systems need to be set up quickly.

By 1992 the company was saddled with a large integrated package which was obsolete and the same functional hierarchies as had existed in 1989. To overcome this problem the company tried to institute its first enterprise-wide initiative to change the way of working (processes and people) to fit in with the new system. But pressure from vested interests restricted the initiative to a subprocess – the linking of branch systems to HQ.

This is a typical example of a company facing major problems as it moves from localised exploitation to integration. A similar scenario has been re-enacted in many major banks, building societies and insurance companies.

Pearson and Skinner (1993) identify two types of BPR programme: the 'company-wide' BPR programme which is designed to change the whole organisation, achieving radical results and requiring senior management commitment; and the 'limited' BPR programme which focuses on smaller functional areas or discrete parts of the overall business to achieve incremental change benefiting the whole company and requiring divisional or functional management commitment. In almost all the companies claiming to be doing BPR, initiatives were of the second type. Though BPR may initially take a company-wide view, it rarely results in company-wide implementation because organisations are not willing to overcome difficult issues such as inter-departmental rivalry. This in turn reduces the impact and benefits of BPR.

The second case history provides an example of a company which has changed its organisational structures and people dramatically but has not improved its technology concurrently. In many major financial services companies it is impossible to introduce effective, new horizontal processes without the new technology, no matter how advanced or flexible the organisation has become.

Case 5.2: National Provincial

National Provincial, the UK's eighth largest building society in 1994, has been restructuring since the 1987 Financial Services Act. Its initial efforts split the monolithic hierarchy into a group of smaller hierarchies but it found that it was becoming detached from the requirements of the customers.

In 1990, a modified TQM approach with team-based work groups was adopted to rebuild traditional customer loyalty. This approach used the concept of team play and a game analogy with four levels – managers, coaches, captains and players – within teams. In November 1990, all current jobs were abolished, people were given roles according to competence, and teams were left to work out how best to implement them.

> At N&P, the key attribute of a team player is the ability to read what is going on and to make the right move without being told. Finding the right position for each player is critical; selecting the right team combination is critical; getting the team to plan their achievements is a challenge. The result is unique thinking implementors – not just workers.

The changes initiated – team working, empowerment, new pay structures, the breaking down of old functions etc. – resulted in increased profitability/efficiency and product quality compared with past performance. However, this is clearly not enough to enable the company to gain sustainable competitive advantage over the leaders in the field. To achieve such a position would require the introduction of streamlined processes, new organisational structures, and new technology. In the future, competition from newly created, technology-based, 'lean/mean' companies designed with BPR principles in mind, could pose a serious threat.

As with the majority of companies in the financial services sector, N&P were still burdened with an existing, relatively outdated mainframe system which had evolved in an ad hoc manner over the past decade.

When interviewed by the *Financial Times* for an article which appeared on 5 July 1993, N&P had been restructuring for three years, but in the words of the IT director:

> The main information technology expenditure has not yet started; these technology expenses will run to at least £20 million. We are concentrating on organisational changes first.

New streamlined processes had not been introduced across the board, for example, at the time the same outdated mortgage processing system was still in place:

> The average time taken to process a mortgage is 27 days. When underwriting decisions can take place at the 'coal face' and the full process is put in place, the time could theoretically be cut to 24 hours.

In many parts of the financial services sector, new processes are impossible to introduce without the new IT investment.

This mismatch is typical of what passed for BPR in the financial services sector. Pearson and Skinner's 1993 survey found that 63 per cent of the participants, who already had some form of BPR programme underway, were not prepared to change their existing database in line with BPR recommendations. Instead they would only implement technology and processes that would work with existing systems. In cases where the recommendation was to do away completely with the existing IT infrastructure the company's management were rarely willing to let it happen. This is understandable considering the man years and costs tied to the existing systems and the fact that they could disrupt the whole future of the company. Basically, almost no one wants to touch existing systems unless it is to implement non-strategic systems. The situation is highlighted in this quote from Pearson and Skinner's research report:

> It is amazing that nearly every BPR programme seems to be treating technology as a sacred cow when it is technology itself which has caused most companies to get into such a mess in the first place.
> (Pearson and Skinner 1993)

The next case history provides an example of a company which had introduced all the elements concurrently: new organisational structures, new processes and new technology.

Case 5.3: National Vulcan (Summarised from a case by Sinfield and Coghlan, 1993)

National Vulcan is a wholly owned subsidiary of the Sun Alliance Insurance Group. Its core business is the inspection of commercial and industrial equipment and machinery for safety and insurance purposes. This covers anything from the corner garage to nine of the country's nuclear power stations. In total 2.5 million items of plant are inspected annually. National Vulcan employs 1190, including 521 engineering surveyors, and has an annual net revenue of approximately £90 million. Although the company has been successful in business for almost 130 years and was the market leader with a 23 per cent market-share, by 1991 it was in terminal decline with profits falling from £9.5 million in 1989 to a loss of £6.3 million. Service standards were poor, jobs and processes had become highly specialised and fragmented, the customer was virtually ignored, and many major long-held accounts were lost.

It embarked on a BPR process and within the space of *two years* the company had turned itself around, making healthy profits and becoming the highest quality and lowest cost operator in the UK engineering insurance sector. The old ways of doing things, evolved from the Victorian era, were reconceived as three major processes: insurance administration, plant database, and reporting. The old functional departments were disbanded.

There were measurable improvements in performance as a result of the introduction of BPR, for example:

- Issuing a policy took 3 months to complete and involved 40 steps taken by at least 30 people across 10 different departments, but today after BPR, the same process takes just 24 hours, involving only 2 steps by 3 people in 1 team.
- Issuing a survey report took 8 weeks, now after BPR, the reporting process takes 24 hours, and the quality of the documents in terms of content and presentation is much higher.

New technology played a key part in the success, for example:

- Object-oriented languages and 4GLs enabled the three new systems for insurance administration, plant database and reporting to be written by a team of 30 in a nine-month period whereas normally this would have taken 3 years and a team of 60.
- Open systems enabled integration between diverse systems such as Wang, Sun, IBM PC and Ingres and between the three main systems.

This case history highlights the following key points about BPR:

- BPR is a drastic process which involves major transformation of the whole business rather than isolated parts;
- It is rarely tackled unless firms are on the verge of collapse, in which case there is often no alternative therefore it must be done quickly;
- Most business can be broken down into between three and five main interrelated processes, which in turn can be broken down into between 12 and 25 subprocesses;
- Improvements are dramatic and measurable;
- In the financial services sector the introduction of the latest new technologies, such as client-server architecture, EDI, object-oriented software, are vital for success.

There are two main kinds of companies which introduce this kind of radical BPR. The first are companies which are forced by circumstances to introduce it as a kind of last ditch effort, the second are new or parallel companies which see that if things are done differently, using BPR principles, they can take market share. In his book, *The Age of Unreason*, Charles Handy (1989) argues that, for those in charge, continuity is comfort and predictability ensures that they continue in control. Because of this, major change in most organisations seems to result in a predictable sequence of responses. These responses are summarised in Figure 5.2.

Both of the organisations identified in the survey as having implemented major BPR programmes, WPA and National Vulcan, followed a similar sequence to that shown in Figure 5.2. Both faced major problems as a result of years of complacency. New chief executives were employed with a brief to change things radically; appointments were made in key positions, for example, an IT director at board level; and external consultants were brought in to provide expertise and a new perspective. The question, 'Why do we do things this way?' was asked and major BPR investigations were conducted. In both cases new structures as well as new processes and technologies were introduced. Setting up new goals and standards placed them amongst the leaders in

FRIGHT
The possibility of bankruptcy, takeover or collapse.

NEW FACES
New people are brought in at the top.

NEW QUESTIONS
Questions, study groups, investigations into old ways and new options.

NEW STRUCTURES
The existing pattern is broken up and rearranged to give new talent scope and break up old clubs.

NEW GOALS AND STANDARDS
The new organisation sets itself new aims and standards.

Figure 5.2 Sequence of responses to change in the organisation.
Source: Based on Handy 1990.

their sectors, as judged by a range of performance measures. In both cases radical change was achieved relatively quickly over a two-year period.

Case History 5.4, which follows, is an example of a new start-up or parallel company.

Case 5.4: Direct Line

When Direct Line, an insurance company specialising in direct selling of general insurance products such as motor and house insurance, was set up, it started out with the latest technology, flexible work structures, and new streamlined processes:

- Technology
  It started out with customer databases rather than old-fashioned policy-based systems which most traditional general insurance companies still have. It was also able to develop effective management information systems to monitor such things as sales, underwriting return, and profitability on a daily basis so that the business plan could be adjusted frequently in response to changing market conditions.

- Structure
  In addition it was able to introduce flexible working patterns such as 'key time' where employees are only employed for peak periods; to operate with flattened hierarchies with only three levels; and to employ highly versatile clerical workers who are multidisciplined and able to work in project teams. In the words of the IT director of the company:

  We are an information-based organisation. Our staff share a common mission which includes a few clear objectives which everybody in the organisation understands. We work in multi-disciplined project teams and we have a flat management structure. It works – we are the most profitable company in the general insurance sector in 1993.

- Process
  Processes could be streamlined right from the start, for example, direct customer contact over the telephone, all credit transfers done automatically, and no cheques. Clerical workers were given total responsibility for the whole process of insurance purchase and for continuing customer contacts. As a result there are no functional hierarchies.

Setting up a parallel company as a new start-up company is the most common way for large traditional organisations to introduce and reap the benefits of BPR.

Almost all the major banks are moving in this direction with their telephone banking operations, and almost all the major general insurers are following a similar strategy for personal lines insurance. New parallel companies were set up with BPR principles in mind very quickly because they were not hindered by existing organisational constraints. Their success is forcing many Chief Executives to ask themselves the question: Why try to change the existing organisation with all the upheaval it will cause when it is possible to start up a new or parallel company with a minimum of disruption?

Results of survey IT3, 1995

Stages of IT development and business transformation in UK retail banking

The retail branch banking sector in the UK is dominated by eight major and a further five smaller banks, as measured by total assets and operating income.

Ten banks took part in the original IT2 survey in 1993 (see Watkins, 1994), and an additional six banks were interviewed in 1995 to determine their progress towards integration in terms of the stages described by Venkatraman's model. General trends are reported rather than details.

The results of the 1995 survey are summarised in Table 5.2 which indicates where most banks are with regard to IT development in terms of Venkatraman's classification.

In general, almost all the companies surveyed were *in a transitional phase between automation and integration*, though some had started *BPR* in some parts of their businesses, and there was also evidence of *BNR or BSR initiatives.*

The trends in these three areas are discussed in detail on page 81–2 and cases from the UK banking sector in 1995 are included to illustrate the stage of IT development reached and the progress made with BPR and BNR.

Towards integration

The survey and interviews indicated that most banks were focusing on integration. The three representative Case Histories 5.5, 5.6 and 5.7 on pages 81–2 illustrate the trends identified. All the banks, of which these three cases are typical, started the integration process in the late 1980s with the introduc-

Table 5.2 Stages of IT development in the UK retail banking sector

Venkatraman's stages of IT development (1991)	*Progress through the stages in the banking sector*
1. Localised exploitation (Automation)	Continuing automation of back office functions but now integrated rather than carried out in isolation.
2. Integration	Commenced in most companies between 1986–1989; main goals to be substantially achieved by 1996/97.
3. Business process redesign	Restricted BPR in core business plus setting up new parallel businesses based on BPR principles, e.g. telephone banking.
4. Business network redesign	Large numbers of important pilots, for example, National Westminster Bank launched its first home banking system using cable television in a small-scale trial in Cambridge in Spring 1995.
5. Business scope redefinition	Clear movement in this direction, e.g. Midland Bank now offers a will-making service; Barclays is making both its core processing and network services into profit centres which are providing an increasing part of the profits of the bank.

tion of customer databases, integration of back and front office systems, the reorganisation of IT departments and the introduction of a common IT architecture:

Case 5.5: Bank A

In 1986, Bank A decided to develop a new branch information system with four main aims: to provide a common IT infrastructure for branch outlets; to automate the back office environment; to bring online computing to the majority of staff around the country; and to introduce a customer database. The project was completed in December 1994. The estimated cost of the development was approaching £1 billion, taking everything into account, including software development, installation, capital expenditure on hardware, and associated operating costs. In 1993, it was decided to rewrite the centralised accounting system by the year 2000. Originally built in the early 1970s, this system had become outdated, highly complex and sensitive to further change. In parallel with this, it was decided to develop a new architecture which would link the branch information systems to the transaction accounting systems and also create a set of rules for the coordination of processes, databases, communications and applications.

Case 5.6: Bank B

In 1989, Bank B had three mortgage systems, three general ledger systems, two life assurance systems, and twelve separate computer centres. Each business unit, for example, retail banking, personal mortgages, life assurance had its own Human Resources, Accountancy, Marketing and IT departments. The systems were account-based as opposed to customer-based. MIS systems were incompatible and there was no company-wide customer database. A new chief executive took over in 1989 and rationalised all the systems. By 1995 this had been reduced to seven systems. There is a single data architecture to link all systems; a company-wide customer database in operation; and the telecommunications and computing operations have been merged. All support functions of the strategic business units, including IT, Finance, HR, and Marketing have been merged with common management information systems in place.

Case 5.7: Bank C

Integration started in 1989 with the appointment of a board-level IT director who reorganised the IT function by devolving responsibility for IT development to business units; making computer operations and procurement and group network services into a profit centre; creating a board-level group to set a common IT infrastructure across SBUs; commencing a company-wide IT education initiative for business users and vice versa; and integrating IT planning into business planning. A relational database captures data from the bank, credit card, financial services and other SBUs. Personal loans can now be obtained at point of sale with credit checking, loan appraisal, production of offer letters and Consumer Credit Act notices all enacted or produced by the system within minutes. The system was first introduced in 1994 and now covers the whole of UK banking.

It is clear, from the survey and the sample cases above, that UK banks are well down the road to integration which started in earnest in most companies in 1989. These are long-term projects, each costing over a billion pounds, and are expected to be completed by the year 2000. Technology, in the form of relational databases, user friendly PCs and networks, has enabled the development of customer-based systems which bank staff can use to access, at one computer terminal, information by customer name on a whole range of retail banking services such as current account, overdraft and loan facilities.

Successful integration cannot be achieved unless the appropriate IT management is in place to ensure that the technology and systems are used effectively. A common architecture, a well managed IT function and integrated IT strategic planning are all crucial for success. The findings of the survey indicate that the banks are in the process of achieving these objectives.

Towards business process redesign (BPR)

Although the main focus of the sector has been on integration, as with other sectors, retail financial services companies and senior managers have, in varying degrees, tried to implement BPR initiatives. These have ranged from large-scale business process reengineering, covering the whole company, to more restricted initiatives involving departments or specific functions. Currie and Wilcocks (1996) provide a good, illustrative case study of the kind of problems encountered by one of the top ten UK banks, the Royal

Bank of Scotland, which tried to implement a large-scale transformation programme between March 1992 and October 1995. The programme, code-named Columbus, was conceived in the early 1990s and aimed to transform the bank into 'the best retail bank in the UK by 1997'. This involved making major changes to structure, products, services, job titles and roles, training policies, technology and marketing and sales, over a relatively short period of four to five years. However, by the end of 1995 the original vision had to be scaled back ('descoped' in Currie's terminology) to include more moderate reforms. The big difference between the bank in this case study and other banks studied in the sector is its continuing commitment over a three-year period to a 'big bang' approach which, according to the case study, had major weaknesses. These, they argue, could have been highlighted and avoided if some form of risk assessment framework had been used. If such a framework had been in operation it is likely that they would have adopted a more long term, incremental approach at an earlier stage.

A more typical example is provided by Bank B (see Case 5.6) which had a similar strategic vision to the Royal Bank of Scotland. The vision, which was first described in a 1992 strategy document, predicted a major transformation of the bank with the main implementation starting in 1994 for completion by 1997. However, major difficulties in the initial stages, particularly with the introduction of a fully relational client database and the need for a complete change in HR policies and structures etc., led to an early change to a longer-term, incremental approach.

Amongst the banks interviewed for the survey, most regarded *company-wide BPR* as too risky. The few that had attempted *company-wide BPR* encountered major problems, whilst those that introduced *limited BPR,* which concentrates on manageable projects, have met with some success, for example, the Cooperative Bank (see Case 5.8).

Case 5.8: The Cooperative Bank, an example of limited BPR

The Cooperative Bank underwent Business Process Redesign of their branch network in 1993. This involved the introduction of new technology, the centralisation of branch administration and the move from functionally defined jobs to multi skilled teams. This BPR programme resulted in staff savings of 17 per cent, reduced turnaround times, and increased quality of service. The Bank now has the highest customer satisfaction rating, at 94 per cent, of any of the high street banks. (TQM, 1995)

Others are finding it is too problematic and risky to change their existing organisations at all and prefer to set up new parallel organisations designed with BPR principles in mind from the beginning, for example, see Case 5.9 below:

Case 5.9: First Direct, an example of a new parallel company

When First Direct was set up by the Midland Bank, it was able to take advantage of the latest technology since it was not encumbered by outdated systems. It began operations with a flattened hierarchy, and streamlined processes, for example, direct customer contact over the phone, and flexible working where each clerical worker is responsible for a complete banking process.

These parallel companies have major advantages over existing, old-established organisations from the technology, organisational and process points of view, and for most it is a far safer way of introducing BPR. The existing organisation is made as efficient and effective as possible but new profitable growth areas are tackled through the new company which over time may replace the parent organisation. In this way in the retail banking sector, the branch structure could eventually be allowed to wither, to be replaced by telephone banking and the virtual bank.

Towards business network redesign (BNR) and business scope redefinition (BSR)

BNR and BSR are considered together here. As banks are using telecommunications networks to diversify out of banking, other competitors are now moving in, for example, General Electric, General Motors, and Ford all expanding rapidly in this area.

Business Network Redesign involves linking the business processes of two or more organisations, leading to major cost benefits by cutting out duplicated or unnecessary processes and often resulting in collaborations between organisations which enhance joint capability. There are several BNR pilots which involve using the telecommunications networks as a delivery channel to the retail customer. The Bank of Scotland has for several years had a home and office banking system which allows a customer to pay bills, find information on new services, and transfer money electronically via a computer terminal at home (see Scarbrough, 1992). Strategic alliances are being set up between the main supermarket chains and retail banks e.g. Safeway and Abbey National.

The Cooperative Bank recently opened a chain of banking kiosks where customers can conduct all banking services and then link with a bank manager/adviser, if required, over the telecommunications network.

Business Scope Redefinition uses information technology, originally implemented to make the core business more effective, to enlarge the scope of a business, enabling entry into new profitable markets. There is a clear movement in this direction, for example, Midland Bank now offers a will-making service and Barclays is making both its core processing services and network services into profit centres which are providing an increasing part of the profits of the bank. The head of IT at Barclays, when interviewed recently, expects banks to own, run, or have equity stakes in companies which will offer consumers a 'one stop shop' for services ranging from health and education to finance. Although their core information systems are being introduced in a step-by-step manner, retail banks are creating a large number of strategic alliances to take advantage of radical new technologies, such as communications networks, and using these to rescope their businesses. For example, Barclays are linking with Cellnet to gain expertise in mobile communications; TSB are linked with Bristish Telecom to introduce telephone banking; and Midland, which is a partner in BIB, to introduce 'set-top' banking (see Case 5.10).

Case 5.10

In the spring of 1997, BSkyB, BT, Midland Bank and Matsushita Electric joined forces to launch British Interactive Broadcasting to provide a range of services to the consumer, including banking, home shopping, games, learning on line, entertainment and leisure, internet access and e-mail. This will take advantage of the latest technologies including satellite. A 'set-top' box, which acts as an interpreter of signals decoding digital satellite signals into analogue language that the TV can understand, will provide access to over 200 TV channels. A special handset will allow the viewer to tap into all these services from home, sitting in front of a TV. The 'set-top' box is initially expected to retail for £200, making it easily accessible to the majority of TV owners. However, they are not expecting this service to make a profit for at least the first five years.

The survey and interviews indicated that most banks were focusing on integration. All the banks, started the integration process in the late 1980s with the introduction of customer databases, integration of back and front office systems, the reorganisation of IT departments and the introduction of a common IT architecture.

Conclusion

Data from the two surveys make it clear that most companies are in a transition between Venkatraman's Stage 1: localised exploitation, and Stage 2: internal integration. Despite all the press coverage, very few companies are introducing BPR for a *company-wide* reorganisation encompassing all the organisation's processes. Most are introducing *limited BPR* methodologies to improve a single process. Almost all the financial service companies interviewed are faced with a similar problem to West Life with a massive and rigid technology infrastructure of outdated IT systems. As a result new technologies such as document image processing and networks can only be introduced gradually. The current situation is one where companies are attempting to introduce integrated systems and are encountering major problems.

The transfer to new systems is being carried out relatively slowly and in stages. Old systems have to be maintained until all existing business is transferred to the new system. It may take several years to build the new system and the organisation may have the expense of running two very costly systems in parallel until the transfer is satisfactorily completed. New technologies are first piloted and then integrated with older existing systems where possible. It is very difficult to impose new organisational structures on old technology, and effective organisational change cannot be completed until the new system is up and running. Some, like N&P, are tackling organisational change first.

They aim to have a functioning, highly flexible, team-based workforce in place when the new technology and processes are introduced. They argue that this will ensure quicker and easier adaptation and fewer problems during implementation.

Financial services companies which have introduced BPR, as defined by Hammer, are rare. They are usually companies in decline, confirming the view that companies only change at the point of collapse. The well publicised success of companies such as Direct Line highlights how much easier it is to implement streamlined processes in a new or parallel company which is set up from scratch with BPR principles in mind. The case examples from the banking sector highlight the long timescales needed to introduce new integrated IT systems and the dangers of introducing wholesale BPR into their core banking businesses. However, the 'step-by-step', incremental evolutionary approach to introducing technology may not be the most appropriate in a period of major technological discontinuity. The impact of this is explored in the next chapter.

6

TECHNOLOGY FOR
TRANSFORMATION

Retail financial services companies in the UK are experiencing many difficulties in achieving transformation as highlighted in the previous chapter. This chapter focuses on the technology problems they face at the stage they have reached. Reference is made to the findings of the Foresight Programme, a major government-sponsored study designed to ascertain the effect of IT on society, industry and commerce and to identify key technology trends. The likely effects of these trends on the retail financial services sector are discussed, and brief case studies are included to highlight important issues. Information is derived from the 1993 survey (IT2), which covered the whole retail financial services sector in the UK, and the 1995 survey (IT3), which covered UK retail banking.

Information technology trends

The history of computing has been characterised by an especially rapid pace of technological change, particularly with regard to the cost performance of the hardware. For example the price of computing power has steadily decreased by around a factor of ten every ten years.

Whilst technological advances in hardware have resulted in reduced costs and have made many new applications possible, the very *pace* of change and its *unevenness* offset some of these gains and hinder progress. Whilst core technologies such as CPU size and speed have grown explosively, others such as peripheral devices and software development tools have grown only slowly. Consequently the changes in cost/performance ratios of computer hardware departments has not been matched by a corresponding increase in the cost-effectiveness in the development of software.

The need to upgrade systems continually to keep pace with change has added to costs since upgraded hardware needs upgraded software and upgraded skills. Since new systems are run in parallel with old systems until fully tested and all staff retrained, running costs must include the cost of the new system, the cost of maintaining the old system, and the cost of establishing links between them and of maintaining those links for a time to allow a gradual replacement.

The technologies which encompass business data processing, telecommunications and office systems have developed independently and at different rates. Recent advances in digital communications and digital recording of sound and image have made their convergence technically possible but integration is complicated by the very different management traditions that have grown up around them.

In view of the importance of information and communications technologies to organisations, the economy, and society, governments with 'Foresight Programmes' have included the development of IT as a key area for analysis and prediction. Martin defines the 'Foresight process' as:

> The process involved in systematically attempting to look into the longer term future of science, technology, the economy, and society with the aim of identifying the areas of strategic research and the emerging generic technologies likely to yield the greatest economic and social benefits.
>
> (Martin 1995)

Foresight initiatives are now widespread throughout the developed world. For example, the Japanese Science and Technology Agency has been carrying out a series of long-term forecasts every five years since 1970 with the aim of providing a comprehensive, holistic overview of longer-term trends in technology and innovation. In 1988, the Dutch government launched its own Foresight programme, the objective of which was to provide information about emerging technologies that would have wide ranging potential applications for Dutch industry over the next five to ten years.

The UK launched its own Foresight initiative in 1993. Its overall objective was to enhance wealth creation and the quality of life in the UK. During 1994 and 1995, the UK government set up expert panels in fifteen sectors of the economy to predict key technology developments over the next ten to twenty years. The IT and Electronics (ITE) Foresight programme began in early 1993 and the final report was published in mid-1995. The expert panel was made up of 26 leading authorities from academia and industry. In consultation with other experts, the panel published a series of preliminary reports on key trends in the field. This was followed by a Delphi study involving 260 leading experts which aimed to validate important assumptions made in the initial report as well as obtaining a wide cross-section of expert opinion about the timing of key developments in IT markets and technologies. Subsequently, a series of focus group meetings/workshops were conducted where issues could be discussed in depth. The final stage involved assessing priorities and identifying key trends.

'The Demographics Roadmap' (Barron, 1994), one of a series of reports on the results, identifies 28 key technologies which could radically affect organisations over the next ten years. Some of these developments, those which will have an impact over the next two years on the financial services sector, are the focus of this chapter. The ITE Foresight programme raised two issues which are of vital importance to the retail financial services sector:

- How do companies deal with major technology discontinuities?
- How do companies introduce more advanced technologies which are often incompatible with the current status quo?

Technology discontinuities enabling strategic leaps

In a paper entitled 'System Demographics' (see p. B3 in 'The Demographics Roadmap', Barron, 1994), ITE panel member, Ian Barron argues that although most areas of IT are characterised by steady progress, there are areas of *discontinuity* where *leaps in progress* are being made and where changes occur very quickly, for example, the explosion in the use of inter-organisation networking via the Internet; the use of video discs for storage of data; the use of new technologies which enable companies to implement strategic information systems.

Technology discontinuities which enable strategic leaps of this kind help to create new markets, and forecasting, in his view, should be based on identifying these opportunities. He offers three examples of technological discontinuities which will occur in the near future, and each could have a major effect on the retail financial services sector:

- the convergence between the TV set, the PC and other office products could change delivery patterns to consumers of products such as bank accounts and insurance;
- the convergence of computing, telecommunications, and broadband communication enables the delivery of completely new products and services, for example, interactive financial advice;
- business communication through networks is nearing critical mass which will enable most businesses to switch to computer-based communications. This development could have a dramatic effect on employment patterns in the sector as duplicated effort is eliminated.

The retail financial services sector has not really experienced any major discontinuities in its underlying technologies since the 1960s. Even the emergence of the PC has until now been superimposed upon existing well understood technologies.

Various authors, for example Rajan (1984) and Watkins (1990) researching in the insurance sector and Ernst and Young Consultancy (1994) researching in the banking sector, comment on how companies in these sectors in the UK go through a step-by-step process building on existing well proven technologies with different companies taking the lead in implementing new technologies at different times.

Arthur Andersen (1988) carried out a survey to compare the impact of three different IT strategies – 'to pioneer or to lead the field; to move with the pack; or to trail' – on different aspects of performance in the insurance sector in the USA. The subsequent report, published in 1988, drew the following conclusions (summarised in Table 6.1):

- Pioneers in the use of IT will attract and retain customers and talented personnel. This will give an important competitive edge and improve productivity. However, the potentially higher profit must be weighed against the higher degree of risk.
- Moving with the pack will reap similar benefits to those enjoyed by the pioneers, but does not offer the same potential for competitive advantage. For many of the US insurers surveyed, this was acceptable, given the lower level of risk associated with this strategy. Similarly, with few exceptions, it is the preferred option for the majority of UK insurers. Most financial services companies adhere to Andrew Carnegie's maxim: 'It is better to be a follower than a pioneer. The pioneers get scalped.'
- Trailers will tend to lose competitive advantage. In addition, they could find it very difficult to catch up, particularly as the costs involved would be relatively high, effectively acting as a barrier to competition.

In the past, the best position was probably that of the 'fast follower', that is, allow the leaders to pilot the new technology and make the mistakes, and then move quickly to exploit the technology once it was proven. However, as

Table 6.1 Impact of technology strategies in the US insurance sector

| | ←——————IT strategy——————→ | | |
	Pioneer	Move with the pack	Trailer
Ability to attract policy holders	+	+	−
Ability to retain policy holders	+	+	−
Ability to raise capital	+	+	−
Ability to attract talented personnel	+	+	−
Profitability	+	+	−
General business risk avoidance	−	0	?
Office staff productivity	+	+	−
Management productivity	+	+	−
Ability to attract and retain agents	+	+	−

Key:
+ Improved position   0 Neither advantage nor disadvantage
− Worse position   ? Mixed option

Barron (1994) stresses we are currently in a stage of major technology discontinuity where it is possible to make strategic leaps. Retail financial services sector companies have to decide whether to introduce technology steadily in a step-by-step approach, as in the past (Rajan, 1986; Andersen, 1988; Watkins, 1990), or make these strategic leaps.

A step-by-step approach to IT development

In the previous chapter, the case studies from the banking sector (Cases 5.5–5.7) provide examples of banks adopting a step-by-step strategy for the introduction of new technology. This can be seen from the way they have introduced two key applications: customer databases and management information systems. Prior to 1990 most financial services companies had account-based systems, i.e. every account opened was indexed according to the account number rather than customer name in hierarchical databases which were not integrated with systems from other departments such as finance, sales and marketing.

During the late 1980s they started moving from account-based to customer-based systems; from hierarchical to relational databases; and to integrated management information systems, as described below:

- *From account-based to customer-based systems*
  As banks move to provide better customer service, the old account-based systems are replaced with more modern client administration systems. These provide integrated information which enables the bank to improve customer service and to cut out excessive duplication, for example, a customer is now sent a single letter with information on all his or her different product accounts instead of separate letters for each one. Table 6.2 summarises the advantages of customer-based or client administration systems over account-based systems.
- *From hierarchical to relational databases*
  Until recently, core administrative functions such as the general ledger, accounts receivable, personnel, etc. were all developed on hierarchically

Table 6.2 Towards customer-based systems

Account-based systems	Customer-based systems
• Cross-selling difficulty	• Better marketing and company image

• Cross-servicing difficulty
   *e.g.: combined billing,
      address change*
	• Better service with integrated
	   product lines

• Duplication of function	• Control of distribution
• Inconsistency of reporting	• Consistent management information

structured databases. In this kind of database establishing links between files containing related information can be very cumbersome and complex. Often the links have to be built into the design of the database when it is first set up. Thus the end user must know at the outset what relations need to be specified making it difficult to alter the system as business needs change. In contrast, relational databases do not require the user to anticipate relations in advance. Instead, they allow the user to ask any reasonable question requiring data from a number of files.

Query Languages have been developed to facilitate the search for information on relationships and this is more in tune with the way in which most managers and knowledge workers use information. Relational databases allow more efficient access to more of the company's data. For example, in a bank, a relational database which holds details of a customer's personal bank account, business account, insurance policy details, mortgage account etc., enables the bank to map out its complete business relationship with that customer quickly. As stated this can be done with the earlier hierarchical databases but with greater difficulty.

- *Towards management information systems*
  Management Information Systems (MIS) aim to increase management effectiveness by satisfying their information requirements. MIS structure and manipulate cross-functional and external data to produce more focused information for higher level control and decision-making activities. Their effectiveness depends upon the level of integration between systems in different departments and access to external data. Integrated systems which allow the manipulation of data collected from different departments can only be developed if the data is coded and stored in a standardised format. The level of complexity, difficulties in quantifying benefits, problems involved in changing and coordinating working practices across the different departments, and the costs associated with the increased hardware capacity required to support such systems all constrain the progress of integration and the development of MIS for strategic functions.

This process is still going on but most of the firms interviewed in the survey aimed for completion by 1997. In the late 1980s, the majority of financial services companies still had static, administrative and paper-based management information systems of the kind categorised as Phase 1 MIS in Table 6.3 below (see, for example, Watkins, 1991).

The brief case study of the Top 10 UK banks describes the step-by-step approach adopted by a medium-sized bank:

Table 6.3 Management information systems in the financial services

PHASE 1 MIS	PHASE 2 MIS
Static information	**Continuous information**
Monthly reports	Information is available continuously on
Annual statistics	key statistics which are updated regularly. Organisations can act on the latest trends in business activity quickly.
Administration	**Managerial**
Concentrates on administrative records	Timely, cost effective, relevant information which supports decision making.
Paper-based	**Computer-based**
Monthly printed reports	Continuously updated database.

Case 6.1: A Top 10 UK bank (1996)

In the late 1980s, this Top 10 UK bank decided to move from an account-based system with a hierarchical database to a customer information system (CIS) based on a relational database. The prime objective of the CIS is to maintain a central repository for all customer relationship information across all products and business units. Having a totally integrated view of a customer relationship, including products used and profitability to the bank, provides a platform to enhance customer service, quality and marketing strategy initiatives.

The CIS was first implemented in 1992 so that branch clerks could access customer information directly but on dumb terminals. However, it took a further two years to integrate the CIS with a number of accounting systems and the sales and marketing function. In 1995 the latest workstations were introduced at branch level, giving branch staff interactive access to vital customer details. Prior to this, that is until 1994, the bank's sales and marketing function had relatively poor quality information on key issues such as customer and product profitability. It was also untimely since it was produced mainly in the form of monthly printed reports. Now that the three systems are integrated, the CIS is able to provide in-depth information on the customer (Phase 2 MIS type information as described in Table 6.3) which greatly improves the overall customer-bank relationship.

There are also operational efficiencies associated with the CIS, for example, the amendment to the name and address of a customer needs only to be keyed in on the CIS and the integrated accounting systems are updated automatically. Sales and marketing have been introduced on two levels: centrally in the marketing department to support national sales (telesales/direct mail) and advertising campaigns; and locally on the branch servers using downloaded information from the CIS to support local sales drive initiatives. On contact with a customer, staff in the organisation should be able to make use of existing data from previous contacts, collating information from different sources to produce the right solution for the customer. Systems are capable of informing staff on how the rest of the process will be handled and what is required from the customer at each stage so they can monitor the progress of the transaction.

To provide the kind of services required, the bank adopted a step-by-step approach to IT development, a typical response when faced with the need to integrate a wide variety of old and new technologies and systems.

Developing the new CIS involved finding ways to integrate the following:

- accounting systems on various platforms, some on technologies dating back a decade;
- the core customer information system (based on CICS from IBM) written almost entirely in COBOL, a language first introduced in 1959, and DB2, a mainframe relational database;
- marketing and sales systems, state-of-the-art PC-systems using modern object-oriented languages such as C++;
- workstations at branches based on PCs with Windows and systems built with C++.

As this case study illustrates, companies using the step-by-step approach are taking a long time to create strategic systems as defined in Chapter 2. They face a strong competitive threat from new entrants who are now able to make strategic leaps using new technologies. They are also spending considerable sums on integrating old and new technologies. The advantages and disadvantages of this approach are summarised in Table 6.4.

Table 6.4 The step-by-step approach: advantages and disadvantages

Advantages	Disadvantages
• Incremental development is less disruptive to the business than leaping into the unknown with entirely new systems.	• Danger of firms from other sectors with large client databases setting up new companies with the latest technologies as competitors in the market e.g. Kwik Fit, Marks & Spencer, Virgin. There is a very big danger of very powerful, new competitors emerging from the new, fast-growing information industries.
• Less chance of major failure/ reduction of risk.	
• Move with the pack – a safe bet – in view of the sector's innate conservatism it is unlikely that the whole industry will make a strategic leap.	• Slow to develop Strategic Information Systems, e.g. customer databases, which are vital in this new market environment.
• New technologies, e.g. multimedia, can be introduced gradually in pilot schemes which test their potential.	• Too much effort is expended on creating links between old and new technologies.
• Ensures that technology is not in advance of the customer e.g. home banking failed to take off because the customer was not ready for it.	
• Staff able to adapt gradually with planned retraining to cope with new technologies.	

New technologies enabling strategic leaps

In the 'Demographics Roadmap' report (Barron, 1994), Foresight's ITE panel identifies four generic areas where major technology developments over the next five years could enable companies to make strategic leaps. These are:

• Systems Architecture and Systems Software
• Information Storage and Retrieval
• Communications, Networking, and the User Interface
• Applications and Services

Each of these headings are discussed in turn to show how the developments in each area relate to the retail financial services sector.

Systems architecture and systems software

Three major trends are identified which are of vital importance to the retail financial services sector: the shift from mainframes, to PCs and client-servers; from mainframe as host, to mainframe as client-server; and from proprietary systems, to open systems. The mainframe has dominated the sector over the past 25 years but, as the power of personal computers grows and with the introduction of client-server architectures, questions are being asked about the future role of the mainframe.

Client-server architecture

The ITE panel highlights the trend to client-server as one of the most important technological developments. It offers greater flexibility and places the future of the mainframe in some doubt. Client-server is a term used to describe a configuration of linked systems where 'servers' provide services, on request, to applications programs on 'clients'. The services provided by the server or servers are usually to do with access and storing of data. On a stand-alone PC, an application's five main functions – data capture; user interface; application logic; logical data handling; and physical data access – are all handled by the PC; on a client-server configuration, the application is split so that some of these functions take place on a server and others on the client. Client-server configurations where the application runs on the client and the data is managed and stored on the server are most often preferred, since they offer the user greater flexibility, minimise the volume of traffic across the network, and maximise the number of clients able to share the same data. However, the functions may be split in other ways – the choice depends on individual priorities.

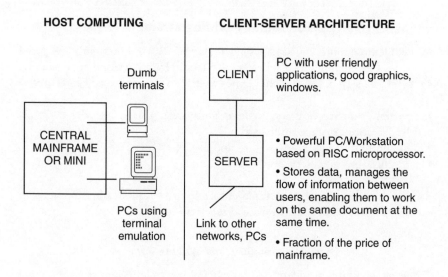

Figure 6.1 Host vs. client-server architecture.

Figure 6.1 contrasts traditional host computing with client-server architecture. Client-server computing is sometimes referred to as 'distributed network computing'.

Those who prefer to protect the life of their mainframe, do so by changing their function to that of *corporate-server*. Instead of driving applications from the centre as in traditional host computing, the corporate-server responds to requests from user systems (PCs), it manages and controls the interface between user systems and specialist servers, the links to external systems, and the distribution of software and licensing agreements. It manages the massive volumes of data required by the organisation, ensuring its integrity and security, and runs online transaction processing with dumb or intelligent terminals as front ends. It provides archiving and back-up facilities for departmental servers. It coordinates the whole information infrastructure of the company, managing software distribution and licence agreements.

The major problem at the moment with client-server systems is the development and testing of the applications in what can be very complex run-time environments. Consequently, the 1993 survey found relatively few companies using client-servers; those who did tended to be smaller companies such as the one in the case outlined below:

Case 6.2: Client-server networks in a life company

Large financial services companies such as banks, building societies, and insurance companies need to provide *on-line transaction processing (OLTP)* to large numbers of customers. Although in the past networked PCs have not been up to the task, today we see many such installations running large-scale OLTP. For example, Richmond Savings Credit Union, a Canadian-based bank has the largest PC-based OLTP network in the world, handling 100,000 transactions a day for 250,000 accounts spread over 350 PC workstations.

In the UK, client-server networks can make a major impact on knowledge intensive and highly focused financial services companies with a relatively small client database (up to 250,000 records) providing flexible and high value products with high levels of customer service. A typical example of such a company was set up in 1990, by a long-established life assurance/investment firm, as a separate concern to cater for professional people who had some kind of business relationship with the parent company as well as holding a policy with them. They dealt with over 100,000 professional people such as solicitors, doctors, accountants and surveyors.

As a start-up company unhindered by systems compatibility concerns, they were able to install an OLTP system based on client-server network architecture within six months and at a fraction of the cost of an advanced life assurance/investment system of the kind required by established firms with traditional host-computing. Such systems consisting of a million lines of code typically take 25 man years to develop, whilst the client-server-based system, consisting of 250,000 lines of code, took only 12 man years to develop.

Their sophisticated client management system now allows them to respond very quickly to changing market conditions, and growth and profitability have soared over the past two years. Since the clerical functions have been automated, over 80 per cent of the employees of the company are now professionals or knowledge workers. The network allows them to communicate effectively with one another and to develop new products and ideas online.

From proprietary systems to open systems

In the past, the retail financial services depended heavily on proprietary, mainly mainframe, computing hardware and operating systems, and were tied to a particular supplier. For example, IBM have dominance in the life assurance sector (see Watkins, 1990). However, with the development of open operating systems such as MsDos for PCs, and UNIX for mainframes, the demand for open systems which make wider links possible are gaining ground.

Open systems offer a number of advantages as outlined below:

- reduced hardware costs – the company is free to select hardware from the supplier with the best price for a standard measure of computing performance;
- reduced software costs – standardised software components can be purchased 'off the shelf' ('Lego' modules) e.g. accounting modules;
- reduced programming support – if systems are compatible less programming effort is required;
- better information management – no need to transfer information between incompatible systems;
- reduced cost of change management and end–user training;
- reduced risk – if suppliers go out of business, they can easily be replaced. The company can keep up with and install the most up-to-date technology. It is easier to migrate to new technology.

The 1993 survey found that, although nearly 40 per cent of the companies had an open system installed, only 10 per cent considered open systems as vital to their strategy. The majority of systems had been installed for particular application packages rather than as part of a radical appraisal. However, 10 per cent of the companies had made a strategic decision to use open systems for their main processing and a further 5 per cent are considering the move. Nevertheless, this constituted a slow but steady movement towards open systems in the sector.

Information storage and retrieval

The most important information to be shared across any organisation uses data describing the primary objects and events of the enterprise, such as staff, customers, products, orders, collections and so on. These kinds of data have always been stored by organisations but often on media such as paper, or other forms which made it difficult to distribute, to interpret or process further.

The introduction of magnetic discs was the first step towards storing large quantities of electronic data in a form which could be accessed easily and immediately on-line. The introduction of database management software was the corresponding step needed to make this data available to authorised individuals in a shared environment. Foresight's ITE panel predicts major developments in both areas of database management and information storage as outlined below.

Database management

More sophisticated databases are now being developed which offer numerous benefits: for example, fully distributed databases, which allow transactions to be initiated and updated across different proprietary databases and hardware, enable more effective intercompany collaboration; and object-oriented databases which allow the manipulation of complex data including multimedia information such as documents, programs and images. Applying parallel hardware architectures with parallel database servers will mean the cost and time of processing transactions will be greatly reduced.

Storage media

The price of data storage is decreasing by a factor of ten every ten years approximately, and the price of optical storage is falling even faster. The three main media are DRAM (semi-conductor); magnetic; and the newer optical storage. The ITE panel stresses that the three will coexist but since each has different advantages in terms of speed and capacity, the choice is dependent on priorities and on what tradeoffs can be made. The fast online response systems will continue to utilise magnetic rather than optical storage, because speed is a priority; with document archiving systems, the priority is capacity, and optical storage is more cost effective.

Current information technology manages the flow of a mere 5 per cent of the business information used in UK companies today. Approximately 95 per cent is still stored on paper, and it is estimated that the use of imaging technology will halve this amount. Imaging technology enables organisations to capture, store, retrieve, display, manage and manipulate information held in non-digital media such as paper, photographs and voice. Technically, imaging can also be fully integrated with text, numerical data and graphics.

The main advantage of document image processing (DIP) is the ease of manipulation of information which is facilitated by faster access, more efficient storage, ease of transportation and effective dissemination. For example, imaging enables an insurance company to retrieve correspondence from its files in seconds rather than hours. This has major implications in improving customer service. Large amounts of material can be stored in a relatively small space: for example, optical discs are capable of storing 80,000 scanned pages of data which enables companies to save considerable amounts of money as compared with traditional paper filing systems. DIP also allows more efficient transportation and sharing of information. For example, a pharmaceutical company which in the past delivered approval documentation to the Federal Drugs Authority (FDA) in 40-foot long trailers, now delivers it on a small number of optical discs. This information can be shared amongst individuals and groups involved in the approval process in the FDA.

Of the companies taking part in the 1993 survey, 15 per cent had installed DIP for part of their business. However, the real advantage of this technology arises when it is integrated into the transaction processing systems – only 5 per cent had achieved this.

Communications, networking and the user interface

Foresight's ITE panel predicts that the movement towards a client-server architecture will encourage autonomous enterprises, specialising in a particular area of work, to connect with each other over the information highway and to form federations (see Figure 6.2). The threat of client-server technology has already been discussed.

Two other developments – *multimedia* and *the Information Superhighway* – linked to client-servers have major implications for the financial services sector. Multimedia can be used to sell financial services products without direct human contact, and telecommunications networks offer ways of cutting out the branch network and delivering services to people at home or work.

Multimedia

Multimedia systems bring together a wide range of services and information based on image, video, voice, and text, making them available to the user at the desk-top. Individuals will have ready access to textual, pictorial, video and spoken information which is currently stored in information libraries of various kinds, such as film and music libraries.

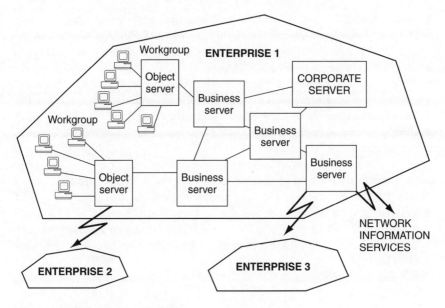

Figure 6.2 IT for Enterprise 2000.
Source: A.J. Herbert in 'Technology Foresight' OST 1994.

In the near future it will be possible to access multimedia information, through a TV as well as a PC. Televisions fitted with 'set-top boxes' which add interactive capabilities are being developed to enable the consumer to connect and interact with the system. Over time, televisions and PCs will merge and carry out identical functions.

There are many potential inhibitors to the growth of this market and to the widespread acceptance of services such as interactive TV. They include limits on the availability of the base infrastructure (including high band-width data networks); problems associated with the security of systems, and with charging mechanisms; social implications such as the rate of acceptability of the technology; and the availability of sufficient high quality information and entertainment material.

The Information Superhighway

Existing networks such as the Internet, the Super Janet network for academia, government networks and various commercial and trading networks, are being linked and developed to form the 'Information Superhighway'. It is defined as a secure, widely accessible, broadband communications infrastructure capable of carrying data, voice and video. When it is in place, individuals will be able to access a wide range of new services from a number of connecting points or systems platforms such as the telephone, personal computers and TV. Over the next five years many new platforms will be added, especially 'personal digital assistants' (PDAs) which can be worn by the individual. Spectacle displays, wristwatch PCs and advanced mobile phones are examples of PDAs.

Services such as electronic trading, multimedia publishing, home shopping, medical consultations etc. will become widely available over the Information Superhighway (see Table 6.5). However, many social, legal, security, and cultural constraints will emerge and these must be resolved before this potential can be fully realised.

Agreement on the exact nature of the communications infrastructure, which will enable the transmission of voice, video, image and data across the same communication link and therefore allow the true integration and management of these services, has yet to be reached. Foresight's ITE panel predicts that it will be complete by the year 2001, but that a comprehensive network based on the ATM protocol will not be available until the year 2005.

Table 6.5 Information Superhighway 2000

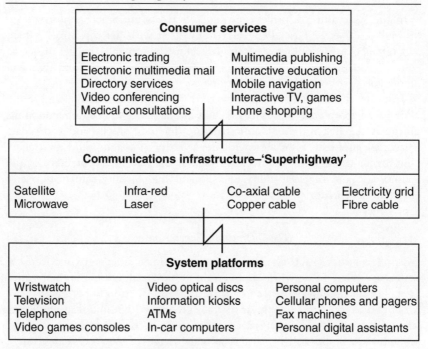

Consumer services		
Electronic trading		Multimedia publishing
Electronic multimedia mail		Interactive education
Directory services		Mobile navigation
Video conferencing		Interactive TV, games
Medical consultations		Home shopping

Communications infrastructure–'Superhighway'			
Satellite	Infra-red	Co-axial cable	Electricity grid
Microwave	Laser	Copper cable	Fibre cable

System platforms		
Wristwatch	Video optical discs	Personal computers
Television	Information kiosks	Cellular phones and pagers
Telephone	ATMs	Fax machines
Video games consoles	In-car computers	Personal digital assistants

Source: Technology Foresight, OST, 1994.

Applications and services

Foresight's ITE panel identifies several key trends with regard to software development. Two which have important implications in the retail financial services sector – *the growth of third party software suppliers*, and *modular programming* – are discussed here.

Third party software suppliers

There will be a large reduction in the amount of programming carried out by the IT department, as shown in Figure 6.3. The function of the department will change radically (this issue is discussed in more detail in Chapter 7). Much of the work of internal IT departments will be taken over by professionals from product companies such as IBM who produce code that is embedded in the product. One of the main aims of this is to simplify applications coding. There will be a large increase in software produced by external software companies such as Microsoft or Logica. This will increasingly be in the form of modules or specific applications packages.

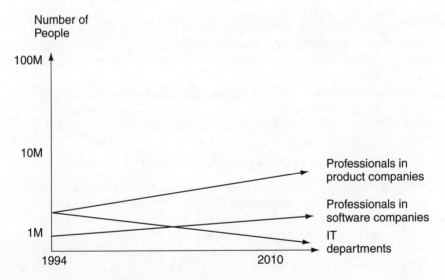

Figure 6.3 Who will produce software?
Source: Based on Software 2000 in 'Technology Foresight' OST 1994.

Applications packages

Applications packages – programs or a set of programs designed to carry out a specific and commonly required business task, such as mortgage processing, personnel records, payroll, accounts – have many advantages over bespoke software, whether written in-house, that is, in the organisation's own DP department, or by an external company:

- they are usually cheaper than bespoke software, since the cost of analysis, programming, testing and maintenance is shared by all those who purchase the package;
- implementation can take place very quickly;
- the package supplier has a pool of expertise to deal with all problems.

The main disadvantages of such packages are:

- they are designed for use by a large number of companies, and although they try to cover as wide a range of requirements as possible, it is unlikely that they will satisfy every requirement of every user;
- rather than face the cost of tailoring the package to suit every detail of their own needs, most companies will change their method of working to conform to the package. This does not always work to their advantage.

Because of these difficulties, packages offering a greater degree of flexibility are being developed. These include modular packages which allow users to select those modules which best suit their purpose, and parameterised packages, which allow users to change the program settings to tailor the package to their own requirements.

Applications packages are now commonplace in the retail financial services sector with, for example, 17 out of the Top 20 UK life companies having introduced one in the last eight years (Insurance Marketing Review, 1995).

The growth of modular programming for applications development

Foresight highlights the need to reuse standard software modules to reduce the cost of developing new applications, and the role that object-oriented techniques will play in this (see Figure 6.4).

Although it predicts that future applications will not be written in the conventional sense, but assembled from standard modules using object-oriented techniques, it stresses that it will be some time before this happens – the techniques need further development and existing developers need to be retrained.

Object technology and fifth generation languages

Wyllie and Sprigge (1990) in *Computing, Communications and Media: Trend Monitor* predict that the 'life-cycle' methodologies of software systems development and the Case tools only recently adopted to implement them will

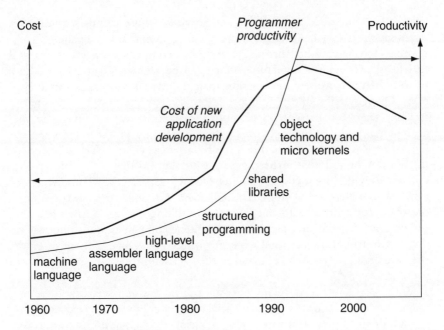

Figure 6.4 Applications development.
Source: IBM in 'Technology Foresight' OST 1994.

soon be obsolete and replaced by an 'evolutionary' approach based on object technology. Object-oriented systems analysis can be applied regardless of the underlying technology and development tools. The object-oriented approach to programming is said to be able to deal with unstructured and uncertain information better than structured system design. It can model complex problems and will be especially useful in developing executive and management information systems. Modular applications can be developed much more quickly; modules can be continually improved; new modules can easily be added as they are needed or developed; and modules can be stored in software libraries and reused in other related systems reducing programming time and costs.

Although object-oriented programming languages, for example C+++ and Smalltalk, are being used, they have had little impact on the software development process as yet. Foresight (OST, 1994) pinpoints object technology as a key technology for use in software engineering over the next five years, but stresses that the object-oriented approach to analysis is immature and further development is required. Object technology-based programming languages which combine tools for coding and 'prototyping' are under development and are, or will be, known as fifth generation languages.

In the four main areas described – Systems Architecture and Systems Software; Information Storage and Retrieval; Communications, Networking, and the User Interface; Applications and Services – there are opportunities for organisations to make strategic leaps gaining competitive advantage over existing, long-established firms. For instance, companies can move straight to true client-server architectures which can be far more cost effective and provide better customer information than traditional mainframe-based systems. Open systems, and new information and retrieval systems also enable strategic leaps and present opportunities for competitive advantage. In the area of communications and multimedia, banks are at the pilot stage, as illustrated in Chapter 5, but this is clearly an area where information organisations with different expertise can overtake existing financial services companies which are focusing on a step-by-step approach to IT implementation. The dangers are obvious. The US Bank Administration Institute, in a recent report written with the Boston Consulting Group, warned that the online services, software, global entertainment companies and utilities have the network infrastructure and expertise which could enable them to erode the core retail business of banks unless they act with foresight and resolve to prevent it.

With regard to the developments in applications and services, there are major implications for the retail financial services company. For example, the growth of third party software suppliers means that applications such as the processing of life products will become a commodity which can be bought off the shelf, enabling any company with a client base to enter the market. In the same way modular programming will make it easier and quicker to develop niche applications for particular groups.

Conclusion

Companies in this sector are faced with two key issues in technology management: how do they deal with major technological discontinuities? and how do they introduce more advanced technologies which are often incompatible with the current status quo?

In the past, the sector has not had to face the kind of discontinuities which are on the horizon. When it comes to replacing old technology and introducing new ways of doing things, the financial industry is relatively conservative. For example, it was only in 1995 that all the main banks were able to introduce customer-based systems, and even these are fairly primitive tools for the kind of case handling needed to provide a comprehensive client service. New technologies such as open systems, client-server, document image processing are also being introduced gradually. This is understandable as a large percentage of their IT investment is still used to support an ageing, creaking infrastructure which makes it very difficult to bolt on new technologies. In telecommunications, most companies in the sector are at the pilot stage. Software development is also lagging behind.

These new developments – client-server, modular programming, and multimedia – open up the market to competitors from other sectors, and although this would not have mattered in the past because the whole industry has followed a similar trajectory, it matters very much today. Acquiring the technology is now relatively easy and cheap for any of the major retail financial services products – it can be bought off the shelf and any competitor can come in and set up a new company quite quickly. Companies with existing, well-established customer databases from outside the sector can easily enter the market. The main entrants at the moment tend to be brand names and companies in the motor manufacturing and retail sectors. But the new information industry, which is being created from four previously separate sectors – telecommunications; computing and software; consumer electronics; and entertainment, media and publishing – also poses an ever-growing threat.

7

MANAGING THE IT FUNCTION

This chapter focuses on the sector's response to the challenges faced as it affects the management of the IT function in the UK financial services sector. It begins by describing key features of the growth of the centralised DP department from 1970 to 1990. Analysis of the findings of the 1993 (IT2) survey identified five interrelated trends which summarise developments in the retail financial services sector. These trends, which characterise reorganisation of the IT function, match those described by Galliers and Sutherland (1991) in their 'revised stages of growth model'. It concludes with an analysis of the current situation in 1997 based on research in the banking sector and current consultancy and teaching experience across the retail financial services sector.

Background: the growth of the DP department (1970–1990)

The development of IT systems in the organisation has taken place in a period of monopoly markets for IT-based services and skilled labour shortages (Friedman, 1989).

Monopoly suppliers and centralised DP departments

Suppliers of the early computer systems not only employed the skilled staff required to install them, but also employed and supplied staff to train the operators, to provide on-going support and to maintain the systems within the user-organisations. Their support was crucial since the early mainframes were unreliable, requiring frequent maintenance of hardware components. Programs too required maintenance in the form of amendments and adjustments to meet user needs. Usually, only those who had designed the systems had sufficient expertise to do this kind of work.

As the demand for computer-based systems grew, the availability of support for systems development in the organisation became increasingly scarce and expensive. Consultants filled the gap for a time, but user-organisations soon realised that loss of self-reliance was leading to loss of power over their own processing operations and control over costs. They began to recruit their own computer personnel. They aimed to recruit people with computer skills and sufficient understanding of the business to ensure that the systems selected and developed met the current and future needs of their particular business.

Since early systems were located in the department which took the initiative to computerise, usually the accounts department, the new computer staff were located there too. In order to spread the responsibility of cost and development, to make more effective use of the system and offset high purchase costs, the computer manager looked for new applications in other departments. This led to the emergence of a centralised DP department with control over systems throughout the organisation. The DP department took on a mediating role between suppliers and users and, during and after installation, between the computer systems core and the users. The monopoly powers once held by the suppliers shifted to the DP department.

Problems of recruitment in the DP department

The scientific and academic fields were the main source of computing expertise from which experienced staff were recruited. Few had business experience. Trainees with an aptitude for computing were recruited from outside but also from within the organisation with the aim of building up a DP department with a balance of business and IT skills to suit its mediating role. This balance was difficult to achieve since the analytical and detailed character of systems development work tends to attract people whose interests and talents are introspective rather than communicative. After a very brief period of formal training, DP staff were expected to gain the skills and experience necessary for the work 'on-the-job'. The atmosphere of intense specialisation and individualism fostered close ties between like-minded people and a 'them and us' attitude which led to the emergence of a strong DP departmental culture with its own jargon. Continued shortages of computer-skilled labour reinforced this climate and a distinct culture gap emerged.

The growth of the culture gap

The DP department came to be staffed by computing enthusiasts whose loyalty to their profession and peer group surpassed their allegiance to the organisation and its needs. Although the DP department took great pride in the systems it developed, it seemed to have little interest in their effects on the working practices of the users who were expected to adapt quickly to the changes thrust upon them. Staffed by systems developers with little knowledge of business, the DP department became increasingly remote from the users who could not understand its work or its jargon. Whilst the DP department held the balance of power, it held no responsibility for the effects of the systems it produced.

A shift in the balance of power towards the user

Measures were introduced to dampen the demand for computer systems by spreading the costs of IT development amongst the user departments through charge-out systems. Such measures sharpened user awareness of the real costs of the services provided by the DP department. This new awareness of costs and their own growing technical sophistication gave users the confidence to take up the option of alternative sources of supply either by developing their own 'go-it-alone' systems using PCs or by outsourcing to external agents.

By 1990 the companies in the retail financial services sector had gone through stages which can be likened to the 'adhocracy' and the 'starting the foundations' stages identified by Galliers. They were in the third stage, the 'centralised dictatorship' stage (see Survey IT1), dominated by the large centralised DP department. In this stage most systems are centrally developed and installed, operated and controlled by the DP department with top-down, well documented IT planning. The Head of IT tends to be a technical professional and the whole department has a technical rather than a business focus. Although the DP department has considerable power it does not take responsibility for the systems it develops and it attracts increasing criticism from both the business users and senior management. Business users increasingly develop their own PC-based systems or buy in services from outside.

Senior managers had seen substantial leaps in technology investments in the late 1980s and were growing increasingly concerned about adequate returns. Galliers points out that the situation had arisen in part because senior managers had in the past 'reneged on their responsibility to manage and control IT'. Both business users and senior managers wanted more control and were dissatisfied with IT being run as an 'overhead'.

It is against this background that the management of the IT function in the retail financial services sector is analysed here.

Key changes and implications for managing the IT function

The 1993 (IT2) survey found that chief executives in the retail financial services sector were still facing major problems on how to manage the IT function. The powerful role played by the large centralised IT department, which characterised the past decade, was clearly under threat. The IT professional faced many changes with the movement away from large corporate IT departments to the provision of specific services tailored for individual business units and end-users and towards profit centres and outsourcing.

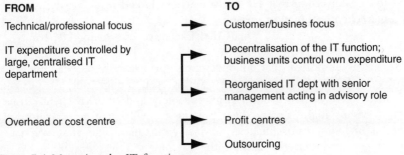

FROM

Technical/professional focus ➔ Customer/busines focus

IT expenditure controlled by large, centralised IT department

TO

Decentralisation of the IT function; business units control own expenditure

Reorganised IT dept with senior management acting in advisory role

Overhead or cost centre ➔ Profit centres

Outsourcing

Figure 7.1 Managing the IT function.

Figure 7.1 summarises the key changes which characterised reorganisation of the IT function in the sector. The five interrelated trends identified are considered here under sections headed:

> Towards a Service Orientation
> Towards Decentralised IT
> Towards An Advisory Role
> Towards Profit Centres
> Towards Outsourcing

Each section outlines the nature and extent of the changes identified by the 1993 survey (IT2), and considers some pros and cons of the management strategies adopted by the firms which took part.

Towards a service orientation

To determine how the IT departments of major financial services companies were responding to the needs of their customers and becoming more service-oriented, the survey looked at three areas:

- links between external customer satisfaction surveys and IT investment;
- IT mission statements;
- service level agreements.

The vast majority of chief executives were assessing their information technology investment along traditional lines with the emphasis on cost saving and increased productivity. The 1993 survey indicated a growing emphasis on monitoring business improvement and client satisfaction, and on using these measures as a basis for assessing the performance of IT investment and the IT function, for example:

> The emphasis at the bank will change over the next three years away from using technology to reduce the numbers employed,

towards ensuring that IT investments are linked to external custo-
mer/client satisfaction surveys.

(Chief Executive of a major UK bank)

The survey indicated that IT investment priorities were changing only
slowly in the majority of firms. However, even though only 10 per cent
of chief executives listed business improvement and external client satisfaction as having high priority, this represents a small but important minority
since it includes major financial services companies. The view was taken
by 10 per cent that the aim of the IT function was to provide a top
quality service to the business units within the firm and they prioritised
their IT investments according to levels of client satisfaction within the
firm.

Linking customer satisfaction levels to IT investment

We found that although nearly every organisation participating in the survey
regularly measured customer satisfaction, few measured the connection
between customer satisfaction levels and IT investment. Of those that did,
Birmingham Midshires building society, described in Case 7.1 is a typical
example:

Case 7.1: Birmingham Midshires

Birmingham Midshires, the 13th largest building society in 1994 with
both regional and some national presence, formed as a result of over
50 mergers through a 100-year period. In 1990 it employed 2,450
people. Although it had expanded dramatically in the 1980s, by
1990 it was facing major problems, in particular, a high cost structure
which was double that of its main competitors and arrears that were
double the industry average. The new chief executive, Mike Jackson
instituted a major change programme. This initiative, entitled 'First
Choice', set out to assess levels of customer satisfaction by measuring customer service on five different criteria: **F**riendly, **I**nformative,
Responsive, **S**ervice-oriented, **T**rustworthy. Prior to the implementation of an automated front-end system for handling mortgage business, the satisfaction score on these five criteria was 75 per cent
(1990), after implementation it rose to 88 per cent (1992).

IT mission statements

Of all the major service providers within large financial services companies, IT departments have been at the forefront in the introduction of mission statements. Many of the companies surveyed had both company and IT mission statements. 60 per cent of IT departments had IT mission statements (see Figure 7.2), though in contrast, few of the other major service providers such as personnel, marketing, and accountancy had introduced mission statements for their own function.

Mission statements vary from brief but effective to highly detailed statements covering two sides of A4. The newer mission statements, such as the following from Scottish Mutual Abbey National Life, emphasise the advisory/partnership role of IS in providing quality service to business divisions:

> To offer the company's business divisions at a cost and quality acceptable to them, professional advice, guidance and support in the evolution of reliable, flexible and responsive computer communications and applications facilities and provide agreed processing services.

(Scottish Mutual Abbey National Life)

Service level agreements

There is a parallel trend towards the introduction of service delivery contracts, based on measures of contribution between professional departments, such as information technology, marketing, personnel, and the business units they serve. Service delivery agreements are only a few short steps away from

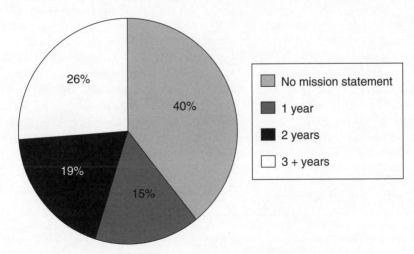

Figure 7.2 Mission statements: number of years in existence.

subcontracting the whole function to a third party. Once senior managers are confident of being able to measure the contribution and quality of a professional or business unit, they gain the flexibility to sub-contract the service, if and when necessary. Taken to its extreme this could involve such things as franchising the whole branch network of a major bank. It must be stressed that many IT departments still provide a 'take it or leave it' service and this was reflected in the priorities of departments with regard to their service level agreements (see Table 7.1).

This clearly shows that their first priority was to establish agreements with computer suppliers, then internal business customers and then, at a very poor third, the external customer of the financial services company.

In summary, the survey findings in these three areas – *Linking Customer Satisfaction Levels to IT Investment; IT Mission Statements; Service Level Agreements* – indicate that the IT function was becoming more customer-focused and that some of the more advanced companies were already measuring the way the IT function performs according to customer satisfaction ratings. Although few companies had gone this far, almost all had IT mission statements stressing service to internal customers, usually backed up with service level agreements. However, these agreements were based on relatively crude quantitative measures such as percentage of down-time etc.

Establishing a common understanding between business and IT/IS personnel about each other's area of expertise is seen as critical to the design, development and implementation of effective customer-focused systems, that is, systems which enable users to give customers the kind of service they want. IT managers and professionals must understand the nature of the business and customers' needs; business managers need some technical skills and awareness of the potential of IT. Good interpersonal and communications skills are needed to achieve a complementary level of awareness and to bridge the culture gap. Those who acquire the appropriate blend of skills take on a hybrid role, and it is argued that they play a central part in applying IT to improve business performance (Palmer and Ottley, 1990). Although little rigorous research into the business benefits exists, a comprehensive paper by Earl and Skyme (1992) which explores what is known about the hybrid role, cites cases where companies can relate the involvement of hybrid managers in system development to marked improvements in meeting and beating delivery deadlines within

Table 7.1 Service level agreements

IT dept. with suppliers	75%
IT dept. with internal business customers	60%
IT dept. with external customers	20%

budget: 'General Foods Bakeries', a case written by Kerr, 1989 and 'Esso UK', a case written by Meiklejohn, 1990.

Some suggest that the most likely candidate for the hybrid role is the IS professional (Keen, 1986), whilst others favour the line manager (Earl, 1989). Earl and Skyme's paper assesses the evidence and suggests that good hybrid managers could emerge from either source and may function in this capacity at many levels. It identifies key elements of the hybrid manager's skillbase and emphasises the need for appropriate education and experiential opportunities in IS projects within the company. It also stresses the need for more open career paths which facilitate and motivate the continual process of broadening skills for the IT/IS specialist as well as the general manager, who may choose to take on the hybrid role.

Towards decentralised IT

There is a strong resistance from many traditional IT departments to decentralising the IT function to business units. Traditionalists argue that decentralisation has three major disadvantages.

Lack of coordinated development

It is impossible to coordinate the different applications and the business information needs for the efficient running of the company without an authoritative, centralised information technology function. It must be able to set policies and standards in order to construct core systems for the benefit of the whole organisation. However, constructing core systems involves very complicated, long-term projects requiring huge resources, and the advantages may not be apparent for several years.

Over-emphasis on short-term benefits

Since the main objective of departmental divisions is usually to maximise short-term profits, they will go for IT applications which use proven technology and are relatively cheap, quick to install, and provide an immediate visible benefit. Line managers are primarily concerned with making their own profit centre efficient and effective. In many cases such motives are not in the interests of the business as a whole.

Inefficient use of IT

If all the divisions are doing their own thing, it will result in inefficient use of IT and a higher overall IT spend. Central IT departments have the advantage of economies of scale in such areas as bulk purchase, discounts of hardware, and in-depth expertise in systems analysis and programming. In addition, the

IT function should have an overall strategic, long-term view of the company's goals and its IT needs. However, these factors have to be balanced against the advantages of decentralisation which encourages exploitation of the latest technology and facilitates flexibility in terms of the speedy development of systems which can respond quickly to new markets and provide the sort of specific, detailed information required by business units. In addition, decentralised business units which set up their own new IT systems can avoid responsibility for the maintenance costs of the old systems at the centre.

In the past, the retail financial services sector was dominated by the large centralised IT department which typically controlled over 85 per cent of the expenditure. It also controlled all subcontracted IT functions. Of the companies surveyed, 90 per cent operated in this way in 1993 (see Table 7.2). However, 35 per cent predicted that they would decentralise IT services within three years, retaining only a centralised core consisting of a small number of senior, highly skilled IT professionals reporting at board level and responsible for setting policy and standards; and that IT budgets would be controlled by the business units.

For example, in Barclays Bank, the systems development function has been decentralised to the business units. It is now driven by their business strategy and needs within the overall framework defined by Barclays Systems Architecture (BSA) which comprises three complementary architectures: the application architecture; the data architecture; the technology architecture. There was almost 100 per cent agreement amongst the respondents that providing an overall IT framework would continue to be a vital role for the IT function.

This approach has much in common with the 'federal approach', one of five distinct approaches to IS management identified by Edwards, Earl and Feeny (1989) in large corporations. They describe the federal approach as one where:

> IS is a partly distributed function, with some business units containing and controlling some IS capability. There is, in addition, some central IS presence which has a defined responsibility for defined aspects of policy and architecture across the organisation. There is often central provision of some common or shared services, which may or may not be coincident with the central IS policy unit.
>
> (Edwards *et al.* 1989)

Table 7.2 Movement from centralised IT function to decentralised with centralised core

	% Now (1993)	% in three years' time (1996)
Centralised	90	65
Decentralised + Centralised core	10	35

They list three key reasons which justify this compromise approach:

- it helps to distinguish responsibility for IS strategy from IS policy;
- it allows decisions on applications and priorities to be made quickly at the point of need, whilst preserving corporate mediation on issues such as security, common systems, vendor selection and procurement;
- it provides a corporate framework for selected corporate provision, for instance, networks, data.

This approach, like the other four models – corporate services (centralised), internal bureau (centralised), business venture (centralised), and decentralised – has its disadvantages. Edwards *et al.* advise management that two key factors must be considered when balancing pros and cons to decide which approach/es to adopt:

- they must be consistent with the way the business works and is organised;
- they must take into account the IS heritage and traditions in the organisation.

Whilst stressing that the federal approach is not a panacea, their confidence in the stability and common sense behind it, leads them to conclude that:

> The federal solution has the merit that it is best able to cope not only with the typically continuous evolution of host organisation design, but also the ongoing experience of IS successes and failures, or 'IS heritage'. The federal approach provides a framework within which complex organisations can work out the most suitable balance of IS arrangements as events unfold – without catastrophic lurches between extremes of centralisation and decentralisation.
>
> (Edwards *et al.* 1989)

Towards an advisory role

Over the past decade there has been a considerable shift in the responsibility of the IT department. At the beginning of the decade, its main role was to produce complete solutions to data processing problems, whereas the current emphasis is on establishing core systems and designing and monitoring corporate IT standards. The person in charge of IT a decade ago was usually a technical person with middle management status, who had worked his way up within the department and who had been promoted for his technical excellence rather than his managerial experience. The person currently with overall responsibility for IT assimilation will have an understanding of both business and IT issues and will be at board level or in a senior management position reporting to the board.

The survey found that 36 per cent of IT professionals were at director level; respondents predicted an increase within three years (see Table 7.3) except at executive director level where they expected to see more hybrid managers, mostly general managers with IT knowledge.

With the slow breakup of large corporate IT departments, we are starting to see the development of smaller advisory IT functions as existing IT services are outsourced. The 1993 survey indicated that a third of IT departments in the sector would be managed in this way within three years. This trend is common amongst other professional groups and for the IT function in all industry sectors:

> IT is moving from a doer to a facilitator buying in the doing skills.
>
> (Price Waterhouse 1994)

Benjamin and Blunt (1992) predict that the IT function will continue to evolve in its hybrid role as a manager of infrastructure and staff adviser to senior executives and user organisations. Effective change will depend on their ability to work with all the stakeholders, including vendors, to retain a strategic role, which is the key to integrating new technology and processes. It will require a mix of technical, business, organisational, and consulting skills.

Research by Coulson-Thomas (1988) highlights the emergence of central 'professional' functions that are smaller, more professional and specialised, advisory in nature, and concerned with policy and strategy matters. He argues that professional status in the future will depend on the relevance of their contribution, rather than the position held in the organisation.

To summarise the points made so far, a slow but definite trend towards the breakup of the large, centralised IT department and its relocation as four separate functions is clearly evident in the UK retail financial services. We now see:

- a small, central core of high-level IT personnel acting in an advisory capacity;
- business units responsible for their own IT strategic planning and IT

Table 7.3 Level of senior IT personnel

	% Now (1993)	% Three years' time (1996)
Executive director	36	26
Director/senior management	58	60
Middle management	6	14

budgeting, some employing specialist IT project managers to liaise between the other functions;

- the remnants of the old centralised IT department set up as a profit centre offering IT services to the business units;
- most systems development undertaken by the business units or outsourced to contractors.

Next we look in more detail at the movement away from managing IT as a general overhead towards profit centre and outsourcing strategies. The arguments for and against each are considered.

Towards profit centres

There is a major trend towards profit centres in all industry sectors. Companies are splitting up into smaller business units, cost centres and profit centres. With the advent of better quality information systems, senior managers have far more information about where costs are incurred and where value is added, so the exact contribution of each department, branch or individual can be costed.

The survey results showed that IT departments were moving away from operating as a general overhead towards profit centre status. See Table 7.4 which shows the percentage of firms adopting and planning to adopt each of the five management strategies listed.

Organisations such as building societies were at a very early stage in the introduction of internal contracts, and they usually took the form of a service level agreement which was almost always quantitatively-based and relatively unsophisticated.

The arguments for and against each of the three main strategies adopted by firms in the survey are outlined below.

IT as a general overhead

Supporters of this strategy argue that it ensures the maintenance of good relations between the user and the IT department and avoids the bureaucracy

Table 7.4 Managing the IT department

	% Now (1993)	% Three years' time (1996)
General overhead	34	19
Cost centre	60	50
Profit centre	6	25
Independent co.	–	3
Outsourced	–	3

and paperwork associated with a charge-out system (cost and profit centres). It encourages innovation, experimentation and cooperation and makes the integration of the IT function with the business units easier. It also encourages long-term planning as opposed to a concentration on short-term results. On the other hand, there is no financial pressure on the users and they see IT as a free resource. They may therefore make unreasonable, inadequately thought out requests for services and information. If IT departments do not have to justify themselves financially, operational inefficiencies will be hidden rather than revealed. Also end-user managers are not forced to think out clearly what their needs are and how much they are prepared to pay for them. A building society, one of the top ten most profitable financial services organisations in the world, runs its IT department of 90 staff as a general overhead. Both the chief executive and his deputy, who controls the IT function, argue that this is the best strategy for their company because:

> With cost and profit centres you develop an unnecessary bureaucracy. We are confident that our IT investment is run both efficiently and effectively.

IT as a cost centre

This strategy has the major benefit of clarifying the IT cost structures of an organisation. However, unless they are carefully managed, cost centre charge-out systems tend to discourage both innovation and long-term planning. User managers will tend to go for tried and tested technology which results in short-term rather than long-term solutions and investment for future profits. Charge-out systems need a bureaucracy to administer. The way costs are worked out must be seen to be fair and reasonable on all sides otherwise it causes much friction.

A major insurance company currently operates its IT department, with over 500 staff providing services to both the general insurance and life insurance businesses, as a cost centre:

> Our aim is to recover all costs. IT services are charged out in the same way as consultancy fees, at X pounds a day. It is essential that the charging system is linked to the general ledger so the costs of the IT department can be clearly seen. Profit centres are a recipe for institutionalised conflict.
>
> (Director of a major insurance company)

IT as a profit centre

It is argued that the main advantage of a profit centre approach is that it brings the pressures of market forces to bear, and the IT function becomes accountable for all its actions. It is encouraged to hold costs down through efficiency and to market itself more aggressively within the company. It is easier for senior managers to control and to assess IT in terms of performance, quality of service and effectiveness in support of key business objectives. A drawback to guard against is the fact that profit centres may give preferential treatment to outside customers, leading to an erosion of services to internal customers. However, in practice, many profit centre arrangements help IT departments to retain monopoly powers because the complexity of core systems is such that going to outside suppliers is just not feasible.

One major bank, in common with many others, felt that a drastic decision was needed in its computer division. Some rivals decided to contract out computer management so that they could concentrate on banking activities, but it took the view that if the computer side could pay its way, then it was worth developing as a profit centre:

> We started to consider making the computer division into a profit centre at the beginning of last year. We made a decision to invest heavily in the division not only to drive costs down but to turn it into something that would add to the profits at the bank. Now we have to go out and win profitable business.
>
> (A major bank)

The computer division was made stand-alone and relocated in new premises in March 1993. The survey showed a clear trend towards the management of IT on a profit centre basis. The fact that this major bank's IT division is managed in this way and that a five-year projection shows that it could grow into one of the most profitable parts of its business, is adding impetus to this movement.

Companies are becoming more sophisticated in their use of charge-back systems such as these. With more detailed information on costs they are able to exercise tighter management control over the IT function, directing IT investment where it is needed most. However, tighter control can be counter-productive when searching for new responses to new opportunities. Research by VanLengen and Morgan (1993), albeit a small sample, supports concerns that charge-back systems might tend to limit the innovative uses of IS technology that are most likely to provide strategic advantage. Their results suggest that they inhibit effective long-term planning in IS and may make it more difficult to win approval of strategic uses of IS technology. Companies which adopt the 'federal approach' (Edwards, Earl and Feeny, 1989) are able to allocate new innovative developments to corporate overheads, for instance, the Mondex electronic cash card developed by NatWest bank.

Towards outsourcing

Price Waterhouse's recent survey of 1,000 companies across the UK in all sectors, including 85 companies in the finance sector, records a major increase in outsourcing since 1988 (Price Waterhouse IT Review, 1993/94), as shown in Table 7.5.

Our survey showed that although relatively few companies (only 3 per cent) were currently thinking of outsourcing the whole of their IT function within three years, almost all companies anticipated a major increase in outsourcing for all aspects of IT development including hardware and software maintenance, software development, operations, disaster recovery and networks. Here is a typical response to the question on outsourcing in the survey:

> I think the whole of the technical side of running our network could be subcontracted to a third party. It is no longer cost effective for the bank to manage and maintain its own telecommunications network.
>
> (IT Director of a major bank)

Among the reasons put forward for outsourcing were the following:

- it removed fixed costs and as such was a very good method of cost control;
- it could provide expertise not available in-house;
- it allowed IT departments to focus on key internal developments.

Most IT directors interviewed were reluctant to reduce the size of their departments but realised that outsourcing was inevitable as senior management develop the expertise to cost and evaluate the contributions of the various parts of the IT function. Effective management of outsourcing requires new skills in such areas as contract negotiation, evaluation of quality, project management, and detailed specification.

Takac's (1994) evaluation of outsourcing highlights the fact that little is yet known about its cost-effectiveness and that it will be another decade before any useful assessments can be made. In determining suitability for outsourcing, organisations where IT has a competitive service focus will

Table 7.5 Growth of outsourcing as percentage of IT budget

	1988	1993	1997
Hardware	3%	7%	13%
Software	11%	19%	28%

consider cost and operational effectiveness; those where IT is valued as a strategic resource will consider important priorities such as security, immediate access and control – issues that they will be more reluctant to delegate to an outsourcing vendor. Takac analyses the prerequisites for establishing a successful long-term outsourcing relationship (see Table 7.6) and covers key issues relating to setting up and documenting of outsourcing contracts (see Table 7.7).

Table 7.6 Prerequisites for successful outsourcing

Vendor requirements	User requirements
Track record	Strategic focus
Financial strength	Senior management support
Highly qualified and experienced staff	Linkage between outsourcing function and planning process
Good staff retention programmes	Alliance formulation skills
Compatible cultures	Alliance management skills and infrastructure
Industry and application, knowledge and experience	Middle management commitment
Well developed infrastructure	

Source: Takac 1994 (*International Journal of Technology Management*).

Table 7.7 Outsourcing: some contractual issues

Issues	Reason/approach
Specificity	As specific as possible.
Penalties	For failure to meet service level objectives.
Ownership	Clearly stated relating to assets and services. Specify conditions for transfer of staff or assets.
Liability	Clarity of user and outsourced responsibility.
Disputes	Process and procedures for dispute resolution.
Contingencies	In case of outsourced merger, take over or bankruptcy.
Confidentiality	Should be defined and penalties stated.
Responsibility	Individual organisational contact points should be identified and formalised.
Intellectual property	Ownership and conditions should be identified and outlined.
Period	It is in the customer's interest to have a short contract period unless the outsourced reduces fees substantially. Consider issues which may be revised or renegotiated at the end of the contract.

Source: Takac 1994 (*International Journal of Technology Management*).

Takac stresses that as the outsourcing relationship grows and evolves, the organisation in effect trades some of the problems of managing IT for the problems of managing alliances:

> By the time the vendor has learned enough of the business to be helpful in setting longer-term applications direction, the role of the outsourcing vendor will be more like that of a partner than a supplier.
>
> (Takac 1994)

As these partnerships based on trust and credibility evolve they must be backed by carefully worked out contractual agreements.

Partial outsourcing

Although relatively few companies are thinking of outsourcing the whole of their IT department, most large financial services companies typically spend between 10 per cent and 20 per cent of their IT budget on outsourcing.

As the West Life example illustrates (see Table 7.8), both the IT expenditure and numbers of IT staff have increased significantly over the past decade: the figures for 1994 show that IT expenses represent 25 per cent of group costs, and 450 IT professionals represent an increase to one in five of the workforce as compared with one in ten in 1985. Outsourcing has more than doubled over this period also.

Conclusion

In terms of Galliers' model, the 1993 (IT2) survey results show that companies in the sector were moving on slowly from Stage 3, the 'centralised dictatorship' stage, to Stage 4, the 'democratic dialectic and cooperation' stage. In the transition we see the large centralised DP department (now renamed the IT department) slowly replaced by a more federal structure. The role of Head of IT has more status, with more than 90 per cent of IT directors at senior management level, most recruited for their business knowledge as well as IT skills and their ability to work with the rest of the organisation at all levels. The number of IT professionals as a percentage of the total workforce

Table 7.8 Growth of IT expenditure in West Life

	1985	1994
IT expenditure	£8 million	£40 million
No. of IT staff	150	450
IT expenses as % of group costs	10	25
Outsourcing as % of total IT costs	8	17

has grown – in some top ten life companies we see increases of up to 20 per cent. Organisational integration is the main theme. Both the IT function and the IT professionals are more business-oriented in contrast to the techno-professional orientation of earlier years. The IT function is being made more accountable to both internal and external customers. Central IT budgets and systems development are devolved to the business units. Senior managers are developing more sophisticated approaches to managing the contribution of the IT department and cost and profit centres become the norm. Outsourcing the whole IT function is still rare but it is predicted to grow to over a third of the IT budget.

Present day

Findings of the 1995 survey (IT3) show that leading companies in the sector are moving to Galliers' Stage 5, the 'entrepreneurial opportunity' stage. During this stage the IT department becomes more outward-looking and starts to seek actively opportunities for the strategic use of IT. There is an increase in 'federal sophistication', that is, a growing competency and experience in this way of managing (Edwards, Earl, Feeney, 1996: 224). This may involve recentralisation of some activities, for example:

- to introduce a common IT infrastructure so that data integration or connectivity are possible across business units;
- to introduce the core IT competencies, both technical and managerial, needed throughout the organisation.

It may also involve further decentralisation of some activities, for example:

- devolving decision making on the development and implementation of IT applications to the business units which may control a majority of IT budgets;
- working in cross-disciplinary/function teams on the introduction of new business processes;
- the creation of strategic coalitions, both within the company, for example, mortgage lending and life insurance, and outside the company, either through outsourcing or strategic alliances.

Over the past decade there has been a steady improvement in the competencies in the IT functions. Increasing numbers of organisations in the sector have the necessary infrastructure (combining elements of both centralisation and decentralisation) to allow them to respond flexibly to changing environmental pressures.

8

MANAGEMENT STRATEGIES

Changes in the nature of technology and its uses and applications (Chapter 6) influence the way the IT function is managed in the organisation (Chapter 7), and the management strategies adopted, in turn, influence the pace and character of technological change.

An organisation's progress through the transition from automation to integration and business transformation depends on the skills of its managers and the appropriateness of their approach to management control and IT and business strategy. Whilst management theories in fields such as accounting, finance and production were well established by the 1930s, most conceptual frameworks for theories of management in the IT field have been developed only since the late 1970s. This lack of management theory meant a lack of management training and education and a shortage of management skills in the IT field. This has been exacerbated by the rapid pace of change. Concepts of effective management practice in computer systems development have changed dramatically since the early 1980s when the PCs first appeared and advances in communications technology were made (see Friedman with Cornford, 1989). More effective approaches to IT management are being developed as knowledge and experience with different systems and technologies grow, and as the dialogue between end-users, IT staff, and management improves. One important lesson learned is that management strategies must be flexible, open to review and continuous improvement if they are to keep pace with the kind of continuous change that the sector faces today.

This chapter focuses on three key IT management concerns highlighted in the findings of our surveys in the retail financial services sector. They are as follows:

- the need for different levels of management control at different stages in the assimilation of a technology;
- the need to align business and IT strategies;
- the growing emphasis on using IT to establish and strengthen effective links with organisations in the external environment.

Progress through the stages of IT development described in Chapter 5 depends on the organisation's approach to these three key concerns.

Matching management control to stages of IT assimilation

Whilst it is important for managers to control, it is equally important to know when to relax or slacken that control to encourage change and innovation in the organisation. In managing the labour process, managers create organisational environments which can be analysed in terms of a continuum ranging from control to slack (Cyert and March, 1956). This concept is relevant to the management of IT, and the implications influence the progress of IT development. Cash, McFarlan and McKenney (1992) propose that the management structures that are needed to guide the diffusion of new technologies into the organisation are quite different from those for the older established technologies. They recommend that firms must encourage innovation by IT staff and users with newer technologies, whilst focusing on control and efficiency in the more mature technologies.

In their book *Corporate Information Systems Management: The Issues Facing Senior Executives* (1992), they make use of ideas first proposed by Nolan and Gibson, in 1974, in arguing that the successful implementation of IT systems in the organisation can best be understood in terms of a life cycle with four key phases – innovation, learning, rationalisation and maturity.

Nolan and Gibson's 1974 theory was based on experiences with the implementation of large-scale DP technology. Cash, McFarlan and McKenney's refinement of these ideas can be applied to each new technology as it is assimilated into the organisation's 'portfolio of technologies'. The process is ongoing. The implementation of each new technology, for example, database, local area networks or new computer-aided design (CAD) workstations, goes through each of the four phases. Implementing a portfolio of IT systems projects built around continually evolving technologies is complex, and success depends on the early involvement of the users in their design and implementation. The four phases are summarised below:

A four phase life cycle in technology assimilation (Cash, McFarlan and McKenney, 1992)

Phase 1: Technology identification and investment
R&D type activities. A technology of potential interest is identified. A pilot project is funded to assess its value to the company in the form of useful and effective applications. The output of this stage is the development of knowledge and expertise. Expectations of profit pay-off are inappropriate. Today, such pilot projects may be initiated by user departments.

Phase 2: Technological Learning and Adaptation
Users are encouraged to experiment through a series of pilot projects to develop further insight into potential profitable applications. As learning occurs, user experimentation often reveals benefits as well as problems not anticipated in the initial trials and adaptations are made to ensure effectiveness.

Phase 3: Rationalisation/Management Control
This phase involves significant change in the organisations approach to the technology. End-user applications are reasonably well understood by both IT personnel and key user personnel and uses continue to evolve. The challenge is to develop appropriate support systems and controls to ensure that the new technologies are used efficiently and can be maintained over a long period. Formal standards for development and documentation, cost benefit studies and user charge-out mechanisms are all appropriate for technologies in this phase.

Phase 4: Maturity/Widespread Technology Transfer
By the fourth phase, organisational learning is well advanced with technical skills, user awareness and management controls in place. The experience gained is used to expand the use of the technology throughout the organisation. This process of technology transfer must be managed carefully before enthusiasm is lost.

As time passes, new technologies emerge which may offer opportunities which necessitate the restructuring of existing applications or which allow the opening up of new applications areas. At any one time the organisation may be adapting to, managing and assimilating several technologies, each in a different phase. Cash *et al.* argue that this approach emphasises the continual tension between effectiveness and efficiency in the use of IT. In the early phases, it is necessary to relax and let the organisation search for effectiveness, in later ones, it is necessary to focus on efficiency in order to control costs. Thus for organisational structure planning, they group the four phases into two broader categories: innovation and control.

The Innovation Phase which involves forecasting, assessing, learning, creating and testing. These activities are best managed by participating leadership (Hersey *et al.*) in an environment of organisational slack. Its chief concern is *effectiveness*.

The Control Phase which involves activities associated with general usage, acceptance, and support. It focuses on developing and installing controls for the new technology, and aims to define the goals and criteria for its use. The initial stage is best managed through directive leadership in a tightly controlled organisational environment. Delegation is possible later. Its chief concern is *efficiency*.

128

Friedman (1989) proposes that management strategies can be categorised in terms of a continuum ranging from *direct control* to *responsible autonomy*. The latter characterises the slack organisational environment which offers scope for creativity and innovation. Where direct control strategies, derived from an engineering view of labour management, are used, employees are treated as though they were no different from other inputs into the organisation. Managers try to limit the scope for independent initiatives from employees by closer supervision, by measuring and costing work, by concentrating on the purely financial means to motivate employees. Such strategies have rarely been applied in managing professionals in the past, primarily because of the difficulty of measuring their contribution to the organisation. However, with the introduction of internal markets and performance measurement, the 'direct control' approach to managing professional employees is becoming more and more common, both in the public and private sectors. For example, at Ford engineers are now required to become more business-oriented and customer-focused; in the NHS hospital, surgeons are being set performance targets; in state education, teachers are being measured on both the quality and quantity of their work.

The management of the IT function has oscillated between responsible autonomy and direct control strategies over the last thirty years. Responsible autonomy type strategies were prevalent in the early years of computing. In the 1960s and 1970s, automation of the systems development process allowed the continuation of strategies of this kind, but new techniques which simplified and standardised software development facilitated the introduction of direct control type strategies. In the 1980s, techniques which stimulated closer involvement of the end-user in computing led to a re-emphasis of responsible autonomy type strategies.

The trends described in Chapter 7 highlight the increasingly sophisticated approach to IT management in the large financial services organisations. The changes can be summarised as attempts to achieve a balance between control and slack to ensure the right blend of innovation/effectiveness and control/efficiency. Some initiatives emphasise increasing direct control, for example, through more accurate measurement of performance, and more accountability through profit centres and business units; others emphasise more autonomy, for example, through federal structures for managing IT support to the business units. Management is getting better at managing the IT portfolio, as described by Cash *et al.* (1992). For instance, some are now using different charge-out systems according to the stage of development of the technology. For example, innovative developments using new technologies such as multimedia are charged as an overhead, whilst activities based on well understood, mature technologies which have no direct competitive impact, such as credit card and mortgage processing, are outsourced. The end-user's growing awareness of the potential and limitations of IT, the IT professional's growing understanding of the needs of the business, the employment of 'hybrid' managers (Earl and Skyme, 1992) and IT personnel at board level are factors helping to improve understanding between the IT and business functions and the development of more appropriate approaches to management control.

Aligning business and IT strategies

The movement towards integrated systems has emphasised the need for integrated business and IS/IT planning, and the last decade has seen the development of increasingly sophisticated approaches to strategic planning. Business planning takes various forms: whilst a few organisations can survive with crisis management, most require varying levels of detailed yet flexible planning according to the market conditions in which they operate. For example, those with huge investments and project timescales, such as firms in the energy sector, require advance planning covering tens of years into the future; others with short life-cycle products require short-term plans subject to continuous review. Plans with in-built flexibility are increasingly important to facilitate responsiveness in today's volatile business environment. Even those in sectors formerly characterised by a relatively stable environment, for example, those in the life insurance sector, are currently having great difficulty developing business strategies and plans to cope with the rapid changes that are taking place. As we have seen, IT has an increasingly important role to play in managing this complexity and enabling responsiveness. Exploitation of this potential depends upon the alignment of business and IS/IT strategies. Alignment or integration is a dynamic, adaptive process which begins in the early stages of the business planning. It is achieved through successive refinements based on feedback involving consideration of all dimensions of the organisation. Integration cannot be achieved without high levels of inter-departmental cooperation and coordination.

The movement towards IT and business strategy integration in the organisation has been analysed by a number of observers, including Venkatraman, in terms of three stages: *Independent, Reactive and Interdependent*.

During the *Independent Stage* IT is used mainly in a support role and is regarded as an administrative expense. IT planning is focused on operational issues and the IT function has relatively low status in the organisation. In the *Reactive Stage* the importance of IT as a strategic resource is beginning to be recognised, IT/IS planning is derived from the business plan, the structure of the IT function changes so it can become more responsive to the needs of the business, and the status of the IT department increases. The aim of the *Interdependent* or *Integrated Stage* is a dynamic alignment between the business strategy and the information resource. In this case, the IT function is regarded as a critical resource and has a high status in the organisation, IT planning contributes and responds to business opportunities, and IT is regarded as a business investment.

Synott (1987) argues that it is only when the value of information as a key resource is recognised that the nature of integration is understood. He defines planning as the optimal employment of a company's key resources: capital, manpower, plant/equipment *and*, in a society where a high percentage of new jobs are information-related, *information*. Like any other key resources, information has value, costs money to collect, store, process, and disseminate, has qualities of timeliness, accuracy, and form, and can be accounted for and managed.

He claims that if business managers include information as a fourth resource in their planning, the potential contribution of IT to the organisation will be built into the planning process and the integration of business and information planning will be automatic. In other words, consideration of the value of information and the strategic uses of IS/IT in the strategic analysis phase of the business planning process will result in an integrated view of business objectives and IT capabilities, and will determine business relevant IS needs and priorities. Business and IT strategies are considered simultaneously and interactively. Venkatraman's strategic alignment model (SAM) provides one such framework for aligning business strategy, organisational infrastructure and processes, IS infrastructure and processes, and IT strategy.

The process defined begins with a clear statement of the business vision or direction, the business objectives and the strategies to meet those objectives.

Many organisations are finding that the transition to the integrated stage is hindered because of the complexity involved in defining objectives and communicating the overall vision, especially when rapid growth and diversification in the boom years has resulted in a wide spread of business activity. Rapid change, lack of information, lack of cross functional expertise, culture gaps and sometimes inter-departmental rivalry make the task even more difficult.

In the late 1980s retail financial services companies were starting to move away from the Independent towards the Reactive and Interdependent/Integrated Stages of planning. Chapter 7 has described how the role of the IT function has changed, adopting a federal approach and becoming more responsive, and how, at the same time, IT planning was starting to contribute and respond to business opportunities. This movement towards Strategic Information Systems Planning (SISP) and the SISP process is well described by Ward *et al.* (1990) in their book *Strategic Planning for Information Systems*

The SISP approach to integrated planning

Advocates of SISP stress the importance of the strategic business unit; a flexible, iterative approach; selection of the right people; and an integrated framework for analysis. These three key features of the SISP approach are discussed next.

Planning and the strategic business unit

Corporate organisations are made up of a number of business units, often grouped into divisions according to region or purpose, and each with a number of departments whose functions are performed by groups of individuals. Since each business unit has a distinct set of products or services, customers and competitors, its business and information needs, weaknesses and strengths can be defined quite clearly and distinguished from those of other units, some of which will have quite different objectives and strategies to achieve competitive success. If the integration of business/IS/IT strategy starts at this level of the organisation where business unit objectives can be clearly defined and distinguished, it is more likely that the unique needs of the different business units will be accurately identified since those most deeply affected by the results will be closely involved in the analysis. A higher, corporate level view of the individual strategic plans of all the business units will then reveal common needs and opportunities for cooperation and economy. The overall corporate IS/IT strategy will encompass strategies which meet the information and systems needs of the units, and the additional needs of the divisions, and the corporate body itself. A successful transition to full integration involves new levels of sophistication with regard to the nature and management of the planning process and the profile of the management team.

A flexible, iterative approach to planning

The traditional approach to planning – the annual planning cycle with both strategy and objectives reviewed only once a year – is clearly unsuitable in an environment of rapid change. Failure to review strategy and objectives as external circumstances demand means that companies are likely to be slow in responding to rapidly changing markets and hence lose competitive edge. Plans require an element of flexibility to enable the organisation to cope with the shifting perspectives presented by changing conditions. Therefore, the planning process must include some mechanism for ongoing evaluation, such as review cycles which continuously monitor and test the outcomes of the phases of analysis, design/proposal, and implementation. These review cycles reveal risks and new opportunities as conditions change, allowing adjustment or redefinition of objectives and strategies. The analysis needs to take into account all resources – business, IT and human – and their integration into an overall plan.

Although the strategic planning process is initiated by senior management, line management and middle management must be actively and continuously involved. The planning process, though based on formal strategic planning activities, must encourage input derived from creative, informal strategic thinking, especially in the search for new opportunities. Informal input from all levels of the organisation should be invited and can be communicated through the review and feedback mechanism to ensure a balanced approach.

During the last decade there has been an over-emphasis on the use of financial criteria to measure effective performance. This has resulted in the organisation losing sight of important indicators which measure levels of customer satisfaction, process flexibility or adaptation in response to changing needs. A strategy which concentrates on financial criteria is too closely related to short-term profit maximisation. Broader measures enable the organisation to establish longer term improvements which benefit competitiveness.

The right people to guide the planning process

Research has shown that strategy studies are more likely to produce useful results if the process is managed by an in-company team, led by an experienced and respected business manager. The knowledge required to develop an integrated business/IT strategy must be drawn from a number of people with a range of expert skills, hence a team approach is desirable. Selecting the right people, with the right approach and commitment is vital for the successful performance of such a team. Project management skills are essential in coordinating a fully integrated planning process with phases of analysis, design, and implementation which must be continuously reviewed and evaluated. The strategic planning team should be made up of people with cross functional skills as well as specialist expertise. It should include:

- a process expert, someone with knowledge based on wide experience in developing IT strategies, and with an awareness of all 'pros and cons';
- someone who has business knowledge, with an understanding of the business, and its current operational environment;
- an IT expert with an in-depth knowledge of the strategic and operational implications of IT;
- an organisation specialist who understands how the organisation can be adapted to suit changing circumstances, and realises the importance of gaining the commitment of the whole workforce;
- a financial expert, someone who sees IT as an investment, not just an overhead, and who can balance the costs, the benefits and risks to achieve an adequate return.

Strategic analysis the SISP way: scope, aims and objectives

The SISP approach to integrated business/IS/IT planning process stresses the need for a consistent but flexible framework for analysis which is understood by everyone in the organisation to ensure their full cooperation (see Edwards, Ward and Bytheway, 1991). The analysis is ongoing and iterative and must take into account the nature of the internal and external business and IT environments as outlined below:

- Analysis of the external business environment involves an assessment of the competitive, economic and structural forces that affect the industry sector in which the business operates; and the ways in which IS/IT is and can be used to influence these aspects to give the organisation competitive advantage and enable it to exploit new opportunities.
- Analysis of the external IS/IT environment requires an appreciation of key developments in IT; the economics of its use; its application to the business needs of the organisation; and the ways in which competitors, customers and suppliers are using it.
- Analysis of the internal business environment identifies information and systems needs by examining what the business does, how it does it, how it is organised and managed. It clarifies the mission and objectives; the business activities and linkage; the strengths and weaknesses; and the structure, culture and management style of the organisation.
- Analysis of the internal IS/IT environment involves an assessment of the organisation's IT resources, its current systems and those under development. It assesses strengths and weaknesses in terms of their contribution to the business and their potential. It lists current IS/IT assets and all resources including people, skills, management strategies and methods. It takes into account cultural differences between the IS/IT and business functions which must be reconciled to achieve a successful integration of business and IS/IT strategies.

The aim of the analysis is to determine information systems and IT applications which are directly relevant to business needs and can improve performance in terms of efficiency of operations, effectiveness of management control and decision-making, competitive positioning, and business scope. The objective is to produce a set of integrated plans consisting of:

- Business/IS strategies which define the information needs and priorities of the business.
- IT strategies which match applications to business requirements.

The scope of the analysis is wide and no single analytical technique can comprehensively cover all the issues involved. Edwards *et al.* (1991) recommend a number of high level tools which can be used in combination to do the job. Each offers a different perspective and their appropriateness may vary from firm to firm. An approach which makes use of an appropriate combination of such techniques, views the analysis and search for opportunities from different angles, offering a form of cross checking and a better chance of accurately identifying key factors including inter-linkages between the business units. Their intention is to offer a framework for thought which focuses rather than stifles creativity and expertise.

Whilst the logic of the SISP approach appeals to managers, the task of translating such complex plans into action is not easy. The implications of this, as discussed earlier in Chapter 1, are focusing research in the IS/IT field on developing an approach to the strategic planning process in which strategy formulation and implementation are more closely linked, iterative and informed by organisational knowledge. Galliers has summed up the kind of approach envisaged quite clearly:

> An approach that allows for both radical and evolutionary or incremental change; an approach that takes into account a range of viewpoints and allows for pluralistic outcomes; an approach that considers the role that IT might play, but does not necessarily place IT centre stage, and an approach that attempts to identify implementation issues as part of the very process of strategy formulation, would seem to hold considerable promise, particularly if the people aspects and the ethical considerations (Newell, 1995) are emphasised.
>
> (Galliers 1997)

He argues the case for a strategy process based on soft systems methodology (Checkland, 1995) emphasising that:

> the inclusion of multiple feedback loops helps to institutionalise learning so that change is informed by earlier change. Under such circumstances incrementalism is facilitated while at the same time not precluding more radical change.
>
> (Galliers 1997)

Using IT to facilitate links with external organisations

Whereas in the past the main concern of management in financial services companies has been the internal IT resource and its application, over the last five years there has been an increasing focus on improving communications links, especially with the external environment. Forrester Research (1994) predict that by the year 2002 financial services companies will spend 45 per cent of their IT budget on applications spanning company boundaries, creating links between a company, its partners, customers, suppliers and markets.

This new emphasis on external, as well as internal linkages, is growing as companies recognise the competitive potential of improved communications, and as recent developments make the potential realisable. Most are now well aware that:

- Developing products and services quickly in response to rapidly changing markets, requires fast reliable information exchange both within and between organisations. For example, Ford shortened its usual product development time by more than a year when it introduced its Taurus/Sable vehicle line. Achieving this required increased integration of information between departments such as design, distribution, engineering, purchasing and manufacturing, as well as between the various business partners, such as banks, design consultancies, retailers and parts suppliers.
- The new standards, guidelines and protocols now being introduced make it easier and safer for firms to establish and participate in inter-organisational systems.
- Major benefits, in terms of improved productivity and efficiency, are derived from linking the internal business processes of firms which do business together. For example, in the insurance sector, insurance intermediaries and companies have speeded up communications and reduced much duplicated effort by linking systems.
- The growth of home computing and developments in the Internet enable companies to link with customers at home and this presents major new business opportunities.

The strength of the new focus on linking up with the external environment can be assessed by asking three key questions:

- Are telecommunications being used as a business/marketing tool?
- Is the company participating in a range of IT-enabled strategic alliances?
- What is the company's level of commitment to networked relationships?

Each question is explained below and related to the retail financial services sector:

Telecommunications networks for business

The way in which companies manage their telecommunications networks appears to follow a three-stage evolutionary model as illustrated in Table 8.1.

During the *operations era* which lasted up to 1980, the main concern was to provide a reliable telephone and telex service for the organisation. In the *corporate utilities era* of the 1980s, telecommunications became increasingly complex with a proliferation of new products and vendors. This required the setting up of a separate telecommunications department to coordinate, plan, implement and operate this diverse range of facilities. However, these departments tended to be reactive, mainly concerned with technical issues and with controlling costs and supporting internal users. Telecommunications were not recognised as a strategic resource. A successful transition to the third stage,

Table 8.1 Stages in the development of networks

Stage 1 up to 1980	**OPERATIONS ERA** Concerned with providing reliable telephone/telex systems within the company.
Stage 2 1980–1988	**CORPORATE UTILITY** Setting up of separate telecommunications department to coordinate a range of facilities and systems. Reactive, concentrating on supporting internal users.
Stage 3 1988 onwards	**BUSINESS/MARKETING TOOL** Focus on supporting customers and suppliers. Telecommunications regarded as a strategic weapon.

where telecommunications networks are used as a *business marketing tool*, depends on management awareness of their potential for business applications. The focus changes from internal to external and towards supporting and linking up with customers and suppliers. To achieve this, the company's telecommunications strategy must be integrated with the business strategy.

Participation in information enabled alliances

There are four main kinds of information enabled alliances:

Partnership amongst companies with complementary services

This kind of partnership has major advantages for the customer and the company. Customers can obtain several services or products through a single channel, for example, the collaboration in the US between American Airlines, Citibank, Hilton Hotels and Budget Rent-a-Car offers the customer four interlinked services: flight, hotel, car hire and credit transfer at one point of contact. The company gains access to a wider customer base, cross-selling opportunities, and new distribution channels. For example, Citibank has gained a customer base of highly credit worthy clients through its involvement in the partnership. There are clearly massive opportunities for UK retail financial services companies but, in spite of the potential, such partnerships are relatively rare here. One clear example is the partnership between certain insurers and travel agents to provide travel insurance.

Partnerships among competitors from the same industry sector

This is potentially the most difficult to achieve because it involves co-operation amongst companies which are in direct competition with one another. In the UK there are examples of successful cooperation. For example, in the banking sector, CHAPS (Clearing House for Automated Payments) and BACS (Bankers Automated Clearing Service), which are jointly owned by the clearing banks, both increase the efficiency of the banking system; in the life assurance sector, the ORIGO initative has similar aims, see Case 8.1.

Case 8.1: ORIGO

Origo was established in 1989 by 20 leading life insurance companies with the aim of achieving a coordinated implementation of electronic trading in the UK life and pensions sector between major life companies and intermediaries who sell their products.

By 1998 it hopes to see the following in place:

- most of the major life assurers and intermediaries using electronic trading for all practical business applications;
- client and new business data captured once and then fed through to both intermediary and providers' systems electronically;
- quotations, proposals and acceptances produced electronically;
- proposal tracking from submission through to issue of policy and maturity (other valuation data is readily available electronically);
- electronic mail as the primary method for non-verbal, unstructured communication.

Steady progress has been made with the first six years devoted to creating a cohesive and cooperative infrastructure to enable partners to work together, developing a common trading platform, and agreeing standards.

Customer/supplier partnerships

This kind of partnership where networks link customers and suppliers is becoming more common. The much quoted case of McKesson Corporation (see Case 8.2) provides a good example of successful customer/supplier partnership.

Case 8.2: McKesson Corporation

McKesson is the largest independent distributor of drugs, toiletries and perfumes in the USA with over 50 distribution centres, dealing with over 50,000 supply items from 2,500 suppliers. It supplies over 14,000 pharmacies and over 2,000 hospitals.

Dealing with all the different suppliers and customers led to increasing administrative costs. In the late 1970s they decided to tackle this problem by giving pharmacists cheap computer terminals to enter their orders directly to McKesson's system. Fast order entry was backed by fast delivery, orders were delivered the next day in boxes arranged to correspond with the retail shelf layouts. This helped customers to keep lower stocks of drugs and also cut down considerably on clerical work. Consequently, many more pharmacists were persuaded to use the system.

McKesson then realised that they were gathering a lot of information on what drugs and in what volume their customers were buying. They took that information, analysed it and sold the analysis back to the pharmacists to help them manage their pharmacies more effectively and efficiently with regards to stocking, price labelling, rotating and displaying appropriate merchandise. Data from the pharmacists was also analysed by McKesson to gain control over its own stock levels. On the purchasing side the company set up direct links with drug companies which also cut down costs considerably. All the information collected from claims for drug prescriptions was analysed and sold as marketing reports for drug manufacturers, insurance companies and government agencies. By using telecommunications as a business tool the company was able to achieve spectacular growth and they were also able to develop profitable new businesses from information collected in their core business.

Networks which link suppliers and customers can be used to improve business performance in three ways:

- To increase efficiency either by lowering costs for existing levels of business or maintaining the same cost levels whilst expanding business.
- To increase effectiveness, for example, better customer service and more effective operations. At McKesson this included better management information, prompt delivery of products and information on the market for pharmaceutical products.

- To facilitate innovation. McKesson are using the data from their core business to set up new and highly profitable information intensive businesses.

Financial services companies are now starting to link directly with their customers through technology and this kind of partnership is becoming increasingly important, but progress in the sector is slow. For example, although the Bank of Scotland has introduced home banking via its Home and Office Banking System (HOBS) for small- and medium-sized businesses, and Barclays is piloting home banking with personal customers (since autumn 1995), this kind of service has not really taken off in the UK. It seems that customers are not yet ready for it.

Similarly, in insurance, a paper-based industry which involves considerable duplication of staff, buildings and technology and networks has the potential to make a major impact on both the structure and business procedures. However, little progress has been made since the first attempt to create an insurance industry network for personal lines general insurance in the UK in 1982. Today, in the personal property market, very few insurers have direct computer-to-computer links with the building societies from which they get the bulk of their business. This is purely a political decision because the technology to link the two has been in existence for over a decade. The same applies in the personal motor market where 75 per cent of insurance intermediaries have no direct computer links with insurers. Whilst other sectors such as retailing and manufacturing are well advanced with networked communications this is difficult to rationalise. Until 1993, for example, the AA, which is the largest personal lines broker in the country, had terminals in their three processing offices from the various insurers which constitute their panel and all data was re-entered and sent down the line to mainframe computers of the main insurers.

Partnerships with IT and software vendors

IT vendors have considerable expertise and resources for managing networks and they can provide several forms of partnership arrangement. The best example of this kind of network is provided by Tradanet. This was originally created in 1985, when a group of suppliers, such as Cadbury Schweppes, and retailers, such as Tesco, started swapping electronic orders and invoices over a network developed by the computer company ICL. By 1995 it had grown to over 6,200 companies including 78 of the *Times* 'Top 100', nine out of the 'Top 10' supermarket chains, and ten of the largest pharmaceutical companies. About 40 per cent of UK's groceries and 30 per cent of DIY goods are traded over the network. In 1987, it was taken over by General Electric Information Services (GEIS), a pioneer of EDI in the USA.

This kind of initiative could be threatened by the growth of the Internet but as yet there are doubts about whether it is fast enough, secure and reliable enough for electronic trading. The best example of this kind of partnership in retail financial services is that currently being set up between software suppliers Intuit Inc., developers of the 'Quicken' software package, and Microsoft, developers of the 'Money' program, and major banks in the US, to develop a home banking service.

Level of commitment to a network

Companies have several choices as to their level of commitment to a network ranging from simple exchanges of data to the linking of major processes. Whereas the first level involves very few organisational and systems changes, the final level requires major reorganisation. In all there are four main levels of commitment to a network:

Level 1: At the simplest level the exchanges are limited to transactions based on structured, standardised data relating to business activities such as orders or delivery.

Level 2: Inventory exchanges provide buyers with information on product availability and thus improve the effectiveness of relationships between buyers and sellers, for example, a broker being able to track an insurance policy in a major insurance provider.

Level 3: Expertise link which includes linking the services and expertise from two or more organisations. This involves linking people's expertise to problems needing this expertise which are beyond the scope and depth of expertise in any one company. Insurance underwriters in insurance companies and brokers would link up over networks to provide a proposal to a small company.

Level 4: Process linkage in which the business processes of two or more organisations are linked. In a process linkage there can be major cost benefits from cutting out duplicated or unnecessary processes and it can lead to collaborations which enhance joint capability. Details of customers would only be entered once at source, for example, at the insurance broker's.

Financial services companies today are in the early stages with regard to the development of networks. Most are moving to Level 3, as defined above, that is, using networks as a business/marketing tool. They are piloting a range of information partnerships in the four areas identified and gaining experience in various forms of networking.

Conclusion

Earl (1989) focuses attention on three phases through which organisations pass in managing their information systems. For example, from a predominantly isolated IT function to a competitive environmental focus; from ad hoc methodologies to structured methodologies; and from independent to fully integrated business/IT strategies. As organisations move through these phases, they use the expertise and knowledge gained to devise more sophisticated management strategies to develop the IT resource and to exert tighter management control over it. Senior managers are becoming more knowledgeable about information technology: they are exercising more control over the IT department through profit and cost centres; they are gaining experience of outsourcing key technologies. Management has begun to recognise the true potential of their information systems and their vital role in the business organisation. Financial services companies are moving to the Reactive and Integrated Stages of strategic alignment of business and IT strategies, as defined on page 130 by Venkatraman.

With the development of the 'Information Superhighway' and other communications networks, they are also beginning to look out from the organisation to create information partnerships with various competitors and external collaborators.

This chapter has focused on three key areas: managing the relationship between the IS function and the rest of the organisation; the strategic alignment process; and the development of information partnerships. In the financial services sector there is evidence in each area of a long-term commitment to an iterative process for building up organisational competencies in technology management and strategic capability.

Part IV

IT AND ORGANISATIONS

9

NEW STRUCTURES FOR TRANSFORMATION

As we have seen, the retail financial services sector in the 1990s is facing a period of intense competition, characterised by rapid changes in markets, technologies, and customer attitudes. There has been considerable discussion amongst managers, consultants and academics as to the most effective kind of organisational structures for companies competing in such an unstable environment. It is argued that the traditional, hierarchical organisational forms, so characteristic of the sector, have significant limitations and will not ensure survival over the next decade. They are criticised for being too slow to respond to a fast-changing business environment, for poor lateral communications, and for their functionally-based emphasis with large numbers of relatively unskilled staff working on fairly simple routine tasks.

In current market conditions, organisations need structures which facilitate the creation, communication, and flow of new ideas, allowing greater emphasis to be given to innovation, flexibility, and quick response to change. Different kinds of human resource strategies are needed to help those who work in them and those who manage them to adapt to new roles. In 'a learning organisation: an organisation which learns and which wants its people to learn' (Handy, 1989), the adaptation is seen as a two-way learning process in which managers and staff learn from one another and make mutual adjustments.

This chapter is in two sections. Section 1 outlines the key features of the flexible organisation, and the learning organisation – two popular themes of the early 1990s. Section 2 considers the development of new organisational structures, roles, and the human resource strategies required to manage change.

Section 1

The flexible organisation

All organisations, including the traditional hierarchy, are built on networks of relationships, some formal with long-term, regularised exchanges between members, others informal, shifting and changing, remaining viable in one form only as long as exchanges yield mutual benefits. The characteristic that differentiates the traditional, large corporate organisation from the highly successful small, entrepreneurial firms which emerged in the new technology sectors, is the flexibility of their internal and external networks. This, together with the growing use of new information and communications technologies to organise and accelerate production and distribution, and the 'maturing of network analysis as an academic discipline', has focused intense interest on studying the organisation in terms of the characteristics of its networks (Nohria, 1992). Large, traditional organisations, keen to emulate the success of these highly responsive new firms, are focusing on how to achieve the benefits of flexibility without losing the advantages that traditional, hierarchical structures offer.

The 'adhocracy' (Toffler, 1970), the 'dynamic network' (Miles and Snow, 1986), and the 'shamrock organisation' with three main strands in terms of human resources: a professional core, a contractual fringe and a flexible labour force (Handy, 1989), are all examples of organisations with flexible networks designed to enable rapid responses to changing market conditions. Miles and Snow's work describes three main types of network with varying degrees of flexibility:

> The *internal network* where market-like structures are introduced so that services are bought and sold within the organisation. Companies set up cost and profit centres and the contribution of departments and individuals is measured.
>
> The *stable network* typically employs partial outsourcing as a way of increasing the flexibility of the organisation. Non-core activities are typically outsourced.
>
> The *dynamic network* typically exists in an industry sector which is made up of a large number of small specialist firms with the sort of loose structures now common in publishing and the film industry. After twenty years of specialisation in the industry, films are now rarely made by a single major studio. Instead the major studio acts as a financial investor and the organisation of the film production is contracted out to an independent production company which may exist solely to produce one film. The production company contracts out the different film-making functions – set design and construction, sound mixing and mastering, film processing – to specialist firms. The dynamic network has evolved as the most efficient organisational structure for this particular industry because it has the flexibility to cope with a high-risk environment.

Examples of the 'internal network' and the 'stable network' are common in retail financial services, whilst the 'dynamic network' is found mainly in service and professional organisations involved in publishing and other media-based activities. It is also relevant to traditional activities which face similar risks, that is, risks associated with fluctuations in demand, and inefficiency in terms of cost and innovation as summarised here:

- *fluctuations in demand* – the risk associated with rapid changes in consumer preferences for increasingly differentiated products and economic cycles which have produced two major recessions in the last twenty years. These factors will play an important role over the next decade. For example, a major building boom in the 1980s followed by a severe recession in the early 1990s resulted in over a quarter of all architects becoming either underemployed or losing their jobs.
- *inefficiency in terms of cost and innovation* – the risk of not being able to compete because of high fixed overheads and the inability to devise innovative approaches to new products and processes which match those of their competitors.

The main advantages put forward for introducing *flexible networks* into a large organisation are as follows:

- *it facilitates risk-taking* – adhocracies are designed to deal speedily with the unexpected; teams of experts and other resources can be mobilised quickly and solutions designed interactively; risks can be taken because the power to make decisions, and change them quickly as the need arises and in response to changing conditions, lies with the team; decisions are not hampered or delayed by protocol and layers of command, hence response to the unexpected is prompt and timely, making fine-tuning of solutions possible;
- *it focuses on company objectives and contribution* – adhocracies are not without constraints, the team works as a network of responsible individuals within a framework of objectives which acts as a reference point for all; individual jobs focus on the objectives of the company and are defined in terms of their contribution to the objectives of the assignment;
- *it makes optimum use of new technology* – flexible networks enable the organisation to make full use of the latest technologies in ways not possible in traditional hierarchies. Nolan, Pollock and Ware (1989) argue that applying powerful technologies to obsolete organisational structures is like 'bolting jet engines onto propeller aircraft.'
- *it increases efficiency* – flexible networks are meant to be the most efficient way of connecting information, talent and resources.

The main *weakness* of an organisation based on flexible networks is its potential to exacerbate internal conflict (Eccles and Crane, 1987).

They are characterised by extreme differentiation resulting from high degrees of specialisation, and the effort required to integrate activities across all dimensions of this specialisation means that conflict is inevitable.

As highlighted in Chapter 1, the combination of improved connectivity and improved organisational knowledge gives managers more choice in how they design and structure organisations. Much more flexible structures can be set up. By considering IT at the design stage it is possible to build firms that can simultaneously increase size, complexity and responsiveness (Rockart and Short, 1989). New information technologies such as client-server will enable autonomous groups or enterprises specialising in a particular area of work to connect with each other over the Information Superhighway to form virtual organisations. In such organisations IT *becomes* the organisational structure because increasingly it is the principal source of information transmisssion (Sampler, 1996: 19).

The learning organisation

In today's uncertain markets, the organisation requires abilities to respond quickly to changing demands and to anticipate future developments in order to compete effectively. Short-term strategies for competitive advantage, such as cost-cutting and offering added value for money in terms of service and quality, are not enough and must be supplemented by longer term strategies which involve devising innovative products and marketing plans, and making preparations for the future which enable flexible and creative responses to new challenges. Such strategies place great emphasis on human resources as a source of competitive edge, and the organisation's responsibility for developing the capabilities, skills and talents which are needed to create wealth. Capability development extends to all those who work for the enterprise from its directors to its shop floor workers, as well as to those who support the company in other ways – the suppliers, dealers and even the customers. Planned investment is crucial, and companies with clear views of their long-term education and training requirements take on the role of the 'learning organisation'.

The 'learning organisation' tries to ensure that the conditions for learning and for responses to change are such that the aspirations of the individual, the team, and the organisation are in tune. It develops a learning culture where learning is valued and is seen as an integral part of effective performance.

'Learning organisations' devise new learning situations to develop capabilities for innovation, and examples of successful strategies can be found in much of the popular 'management of change' literature – *Megatrends* (1982) and *Re-inventing the Corporation* (1986) by Naisbitt and Arburdene; *The Age of Unreason* (1989) by Charles Handy.

Handy uses the metaphor of the 'learning wheel' to describe the iterative processes which characterise responsiveness to change and effective learning.

Like the learning cycle theorists such as Kolb (1974), he views learning as a cyclical process of continuous change with four key phases: question, theory, test, reflection. He argues that the same process is applicable in organisational learning as well as in individual learning since both learn by responding to the environment.

Learning is continuous as long as the 'learning wheel' keeps turning. If the individual or the organisation gets stuck at any stage then learning stops and fails to keep pace with change in the environment. If the gap between the two grows too wide, the ensuing crisis forces the organisation or individual to realise that something is wrong. By then the response required to put things right is a drastic and often painful one. Handy argues that the crisis can be averted if the 'learning wheel' is kept turning. He lists three variables of capability – he refers to them as the 'lubricants of change' – which must be present for the individual and the organisation to keep the 'learning wheel' turning. These 'lubricants of change' can be summarised as:

- confidence, motivation and acceptance of personal responsibility for one's own growth – setting one's own goals;
- the ability to reframe in order to view problems from new perspectives;
- the ability to live with doubt and uncertainty yet maintain a positive outlook; to accept one's mistakes and those of others as part of the learning process.

They represent an attitude of mind which allows a flexible approach to living and problem-solving. Situations or structures which limit their use effectively block change and learning.

The concept of the 'learning organisation' has been developed in organisation-specific terms in recent publications by Senge in *The Fifth Discipline* (1991) and by Pedler, Burgoyne, and Boydell in *The Learning Company – A Strategy for Sustainable Development* (1991). Peter Senge identifies five key characteristics or capabilities of the 'learning organisation':

- system thinking – formulation of conceptual frameworks within which the whole pattern of events rather than individual parts of the pattern can be viewed and understood;
- personal mastery – continual clarification and deepening of personal vision and mastery of relevant skills;
- mental models – continual reworking of mental models, exposing fixed mind sets to new influences;
- shared vision – a shared view of the future;
- team learning – integrative self-development and team-development activities feed the overall growth and learning of every member.

Pedler *et al.* (1991) list ten key characteristics of the 'learning company', as summarised in Table 9.1.

Barker, Camarata and Wen (1997) have identified four key areas where information technology has the potential to promote organisational learning and enhance the individual's capacity to learn.

These are:

Information distribution: E-mail, Groupware, Internet, Intranets
Information interpretation: decision support systems, spreadsheets, executive support systems
Knowledge acquisition: computer-aided learning, knowledge databases on CD-Roms
Organisational memory: organisational databases, hypermedia-based corporate memory systems

McKinsey is a good example of a company which recognises the important role that IT can play in developing its organisational knowledge. It is setting up a knowledge management scheme based on Lotus Notes to give online access to the expertise of the company to its consultants (see Peters, 1994). The aim is to leverage collective experience by developing and sharing

Table 9.1 Ten key characteristics of the 'learning company'

STRATEGY ...	STRUCTURES ...
• a learning approach to strategy and participative policy making – all stakeholders – employees, customers, suppliers, neighbours, owner – contribute to the development of creative solutions	• enabling structures – flexible role structures which allow for personal growth and experimentation
LOOKING IN ...	**LOOKING OUT ...**
• 'informating' – IT is used to inform and empower	• boundary workers as enviromental scanners – learning from contact with external customers
• 'formative accounting and control' – systems structured to assist learning;	• inter-company learning – benchmarking, learning from the experience of others, opportunities for mutual learning
• internal exchange – internal collaboration rather than competition – internal best practice comparisons	**LEARNING OPPORTUNITIES ...**
• reward flexibility – alternative reward systems	• learning climate – encourages experimentation, learning from experience, tolerance of mistakes as part of learning
	• self-development opportunities for all – provides access to resources and facilities and encourages individual responsibility for learning and development

Source: Pedler *et al.* 1991

organisational knowledge. Success depends on being able to persuade its hard-pressed consultants to make regular use of the system in their client work and to add their own contributions to the knowledge pool. McKinsey has adopted a particularly persuasive strategy – measuring contributions as a basis for performance evaluation.

In other words, McKinsey is building the willingness to share information into the culture of the organisation by making it one of the criteria for performance appraisal. It is clear that this leaves a very thin line between participation and coercion in encouraging cooperation.

Section 2

New organisational structures

Horizontal management structures

A number of writers question whether vertical management structures can support the kind of coordination needed to improve customer service, performance and competitive response over the next decade. They argue that organisations with flatter hierarchies or horizontal management structures respond much more quickly and flexibly to rapidly changing conditions characteristic of the new market environments. The key features and advantages of organisations with horizontal management structures as described by Ostrof and Smith (1992) and the BPR advocate, Hammer (1991), are summarised below:

- Hierarchies are flat with far fewer layers of command.
- Jobs are designed around the whole process rather than split into a large number of separate tasks.
- Responsibility for decisions is in the hands of the people who do the work; they monitor and control the quality of their own work – this contrasts sharply with work in hierarchical organisations where typically supervisors check and control work and managers deal with exceptions.
- Information is captured once at source and either dealt with at the initial point of contact or distributed in parallel: integrated systems and new technologies such as relational databases, workstations, image processing, bar coding, and electronic data interchange make it easy to collect, store and transmit information.
- Although rewards emphasise team performance rather than individual performance, individual skill development is encouraged so that each is motivated to expand their skills and engage in continuous learning.
- Customer contact is maximised and performance objectives and evaluation are linked to customer satisfaction.

These trends are speeded up by the introduction of new technology. For example, in their research in both the manufacturing and financial services sector, Rockart and Short (1989) found that the application of integrated technology could reduce the traditional multistage value-added chain to three major processes: developing new products; delivering products to customers; and managing customer relationships. This enabled the companies interviewed to respond quickly and effectively to market forces, to shorten product development time dramatically, to improve quality of customer service, and to cut costs at the same time.

Knowledge intensity

Toffler (1970), Masuda (1980), and Drucker (1988) argue that the transformation to a post-industrial society is characterised by changes in organisational structure which affect employment profiles in similar ways across most major sectors. For example, Drucker predicts that the typical business organisation of the future will be knowledge-based, consisting mainly of specialists who manage and monitor their own performance through feedback from colleagues and customers.

Organisations, increasingly dominated by knowledge workers and professionals, take on a characteristic 'diamond shape' structure with a high percentage of professionals in the wide, middle band and relatively few managers and clerical support workers. Information technology plays a key role in change of this kind, as illustrated by Venkatraman's (1991) case study of Batterymarch, which is summarised in Case 9.1:

Case 9.1: Batterymarch financial management

Batterymarch achieved dramatic growth from 1976 to 1986, increasing its investment funds under management from $1 billion to over $12 billion by making use of better information on stock movements contained in the company's database. It differs from the traditional investment firm (see Table C9.1) in that it has:

- 50 per cent fewer professionals;
- professionals working at a higher level making more intensive use of information;
- one sixth as many support staff.

Table C9.1 Comparison of staffing numbers in organisations using traditional and redesigned business processes

	Professionals	Support staff
Traditional investment management firm	36	108
Batterymarch financial management	18	17

As companies take up the challenge of innovation using IT in both support and enabling capacities, similar job reductions will be experienced and professional work will become more information-intensive leading to a demand for better qualified staff.

It is against this background that the progress made by financial service companies in adapting their organisational structures is analysed in Chapter 10.

New organisational roles

The introduction of rapid-response structures will have considerable impact on the work of clerical workers, and the work of professionals, and both senior and middle managers will also be affected. Research by Scott-Morton (1991), Zuboff (1988) and Rajan (1990) highlights the growing need in these new organisations for knowledge workers who can take decisions in the workplace based on information analysis; studies by Rockart (1989) highlight the main characteristics of the new organisations and implications for the workforce. Key issues raised by their research findings are summarised below:

Scott-Morton (1991) describes how IT can affect the production and coordination of products and services. He makes a distinction between information workers and knowledge workers: information workers process information without significant modification, for example, in tasks typically classified as clerical such as order entry; whereas knowledge workers are people currently in managerial, professional and technical jobs who in some way add value to the original information. He predicts that the demand for knowledge workers will increase as IT is used to automate more and more routine production tasks; and that it will also have a dramatic effect on improving coordination within and between organisations, as it speeds up the availability of reliable information. Coordination is also achieved by the use of databases which store information on different aspects of the company. As a consequence this improves the 'organisation's memory', for example, the use of personnel records to monitor training. In the future more people will be

153

involved in this coordination aspect of work and will need well developed personal skills to meet this new emphasis.

Zuboff (1988) coined the word 'informate' to describe what happens when automated processes yield information as a by-product. She predicts that workers will have to develop new skills to work with new information tools since they often involve new ways of thinking. The production worker becomes an analyst, a role involving a different level of conceptual skill from that needed before as a doer or machine-minder. Also new skills and information can be developed to a point where new market opportunities can be opened up.

Rajan (1990) lists the three key attributes, which are common in knowledge workers across a wide variety of city occupations, including technologists, solicitors, accountants and brokers, as:

- higher educational qualifications – showing ability to learn and amass knowledge;
- intellectual skills – showing ability to grasp new events quickly and respond effectively and creatively;
- discretion at the workplace – showing ability to assume multiple responsibilities and self management when discharging them.

Rockart (1989) highlights four key characteristics of new organisations and their impact on the workforce:

- *increased role complexity* – in the 1990s there will be continuous changes in products, markets, processes and organisational structures and managers, clerical workers and professionals must therefore have the right skills and attitudes to be able to deal with this and adjust more rapidly to new situations;
- *unclear lines of authority* – in a bureaucracy there are very clear lines of authority which have developed over a long period and there are set rules and well defined ways of doing things; in an adhocracy or a networked organisation there is an overall mission statement or business goal but no set rules on how to achieve objectives;
- *increased skill requirements* – knowledge workers are under constant pressure to improve their skills; problem solving, coordination, negotiating, persuasion and conflict management skills will be of particular importance over the next decade;
- *team work* – there will be a major increase in teamwork with task or project-oriented teams becoming the norm. This will lead to changed performance measurement systems. Measuring individual, team or profit centre success is difficult in an environment where co-operative work is increasingly the norm.

It is against this background that the changing roles of clerical workers, managers, and professionals in the retail financial services are examined in Chapters 11, 12 and 13.

New human resources strategies

For these new organisational structures to succeed, new methods of control and planning are needed. Of critical importance are human resource policies for developing new competences, motivation and coordination (McKersie and Walton, 1991). Nolan *et al.*'s management agenda for creating a knowledge workforce (1989) defines four stages in the process: worker blueprinting; right-sizing; equipping the workforce with IT; and encouraging a process of continuous learning (see Table 9.2).

According to this agenda, the first step many organisations must take, is to identify those members of the workforce who have either the requisite skills or the potential to attain them.

Major reductions in the workforce of up to 40 per cent, in organisations that have usually provided 'jobs for life', are bound to have a demoralising effect on those remaining. To then expect the 'survivors' to learn new

Table 9.2 Management agenda for creating a knowledge workforce

---

Stage 1: Worker blueprinting
Workers with the required skills, or those that are trainable within the timescales set, are identified.

Stage 2: Right sizing
Workers who don't fit the blueprint are 'outplaced'. This is a difficult task requiring a highly professional and caring outplacement programme. It usually involves major cuts, e.g. 40% in many large organisations which have undergone this process. New workers have to be acquired to fill the gaps. This whole process takes several iterations before a workable form emerges.

Stage 3: Equipping the workforce with IT
Staff are provided with access to the tools and sources of data needed to do the job:

* the workstation in the form of the PC gives the knowledge worker access to task enhancing tools such as WP, DB systems and spreadsheets and information sources such as the Internet;
* the workstation as a node in the infrastructure gives knowledge workers access to shared databases and global electronic networking. These enable the company to evolve from its traditional, functional hierarchy organisation structure to a faster, more responsive, flexible network organisation structure.

Stage 4: Continuous learning
The final stage ensures that skills are regularly updated to meet current business needs.

Source: Nolan *et al.* 1989.

information-based skills and to develop a continuous learning culture is a tall order. New human resources policies will, to some extent, smooth the passage by helping individuals adapt to new roles, skills and career patterns. New reward schemes which reward both individual and team contributions will also help. However, by far the biggest challenge, at all levels, is the development of a new mindset, one which is open to change and alternative viewpoints. Effective change requires a two-way dialogue between managers and workers to develop a mutual understanding of the benefits and risks for all parties. Worker participation at the design stage is clearly important – it will in the long run achieve quicker results than if the agenda is imposed from above without prior and ongoing consultation with those whose work is affected. Change cannot be driven through by charismatic leadership – coercion leads only to passive participation. Active, whole-hearted participation is only possible if there is trust between the parties involved. Without some kind of assurance on their futures with the organisation, it will not be easy for workers, at whatever level, to participate in the ways expected.

It is against this background that the human resources policies of major UK retail financial services companies are evaluated in Chapter 14.

Conclusion

Information technology can be a key enabler in the creation of new organisational structures. New developments such as client-server architectures, the Information Superhighway, and modular programming, together with more sophisticated strategies for IT management, make flexible networks and adhocracies viable options for large organisations. As we have seen, IT can facilitate organisational learning in four key areas: information distribution, information interpretation, knowledge acquisition, and organisational memory. Team working can be facilitated by information-sharing using electronic mail, leading to benefits, such as reductions in the time taken to bring new products and services to the market. Advances in IT and communications technologies can facilitate the trend to more knowledge-intensive work, new working practices, and flatter management structures. The knowledge-intensive organisation replaces unskilled clerical staff with self-managing knowledge workers reducing the need for middle tier management and changing the nature of the management processes needed to ensure success.

Are similar trends apparent in the retail financial services sector? Evidence drawn from our surveys in the sector, particularly Survey HR3 (1995), is discussed in Chapters 10 to 14 and related to the research outlined in this chapter.

Chapter 10 focuses on structural transitions and the impact of the trend towards knowledge-intensive work in the sector. Chapters 11 to 13 discuss the effects of these trends on the working practices of clerical workers, on professionals, and on middle and senior managers. Chapter 14 focuses on the need for new ways of motivating staff as their roles change, and the development of new kinds of reward schemes.

10

STRUCTURAL TRANSITIONS AND THE IMPACT OF KNOWLEDGE INTENSITY

This chapter discusses the progress made by financial services companies in adapting their organisational structures to enable them to respond to the challenges of a new environment. It summarises the changes which occur as an organisation moves through a transitional stage between bureaucracy and the more flexible adhocracy, and the findings of Survey HR3 conducted in 1995 (see Appendix) to determine the stage reached by firms in the sector. It then examines the trend towards knowledge intensity in the industry, looking in particular at the effect of IT.

Structural transition

The survey found that retail financial services companies are changing in response to the environmental and technological challenges described, though progress varies. Many of the firms participating claim to have reached a period of structural transition and our research aimed to chart their progress in four key areas: the shift from hierarchical to flattened structures, from function and procedure-orientation to process-orientation, from control to empowerment, and from administrative-focus to customer-focus. Many retail financial services companies are at a stage of structural development which Moss–Kanter (1983) calls 'bureaucracy in transition' (see Figure 10.1).

Towards more flexible structures

To achieve economies of scale, large companies have traditionally organised in a hierarchical way with business processes broken down into narrowly defined tasks or procedures and spread amongst several departments. In most sectors today, bureaucracies with rigid hierarchical structures are finding that their efforts to compete in new markets and to increase productivity are hindered by the functional barriers which separate decision makers from customers. As previously stable and predictable markets become more dynamic and

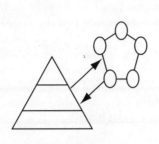

Bureaucracy In transition

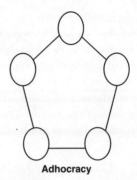

Adhocracy

Flattened hierarchy, few layers + parallel organisational structures, e.g. project teams.	A team is formed to work towards a solution to a specific problem; dismantled on completion of task.
Bureaucracy forced to change in response to an increasingly turbulent environment.	Developed to respond to fast-changing environmental conditions. Emphasis on flexibility.
Vertical and lateral communication between departments and between hierarchy and parallel organisations.	Technologies such as networks enable communications between Individuals. Importance of right connections and skills to be part of the project team.
Bureaucracy retained for administration. Parallel organisations developed to encourage innovation.	Jobs continually redefined through interactive self-management. The individual has to be motivated to produce high quality work.
Fewer middle managers and lower level operatives.	Large percentage of knowledge workers.

Figure 10.1 Towards adhocracy.

uncertain, many have begun to introduce new structures which allow greater functional flexibility in terms of multi-skilling and cross-functional capability.

These structures, with fewer levels of command, are designed to speed up communications between customers and decision makers ensuring that rapidly changing consumer needs, characteristic of today's market, can be dealt with more quickly and effectively. Though hierarchies are reduced, the best characteristics of bureaucracy are left in place to enable the organisation to continue ongoing administration and other routine tasks. Decision-making is devolved and, with fewer levels of control, there are fewer opportunities for promotion. 'Parallel organisations' such as profit centres, business units and project teams responsible for business development and special projects are set up.

These are the first stages in the creation of market-like structures within the organisation where individuals can trade resources, information, influence, skill, knowledge and ideas. Steps are taken to measure and cost the contributions made. There are far better information flows and the organisation becomes more knowledge-intensive with far fewer unskilled clerical workers.

Team working becomes the norm as process-based work replaces function-based work. The whole organisation becomes far more customer-led and far more adaptable to the changing environment.

Over the last five years some firms in the retail financial services sector have made changes to their organisational structures which place them between the two extremes of bureaucracy and adhocracy; others, depending on the type of work they do and the markets they serve are pulled in other directions, towards tighter control and greater standardisation.

Charting organisational evolution in the retail financial services sector

The survey sought evidence of how far this change process had progressed in the retail financial services sector. Each questionnaire included four outline graphs representing each of four key trends selected to summarise organisational evolution of the kind described here. Participants were asked to indicate the way they saw their organisations evolving by placing a cross to mark where they are currently, and a circle to pinpoint where they aim to be in five years' time on the lines on each graph representing the dimensions of change in each trend. On completion, the four graphs from each firm were combined to provide a useful set of visual organisation profiles for comparison. The trends selected as indicators of organisational evolution are those highlighted by authors such as Ostrof and Smith (1992) and Hammer (1991) as critical for success in the current climate:

1   *From hierarchical to flattened structures*
    Retail financial services companies have traditionally been organised as rigid hierarchies. In the past, a typical building society might have over twelve management layers. In many cases this has now been reduced – in one Top 10 building society, devolution has reduced this to four layers.
2   *From function and procedure-orientation to process-orientation*
    Business processes are sequences of inter-dependent tasks and functions, which together produce outcomes that contribute to the business success of an organisation. For example, a typical business process in a life assurance company would be application handling or new product development. Typically there are half a dozen such broad processes in any large organisation. In a process the execution of some tasks will be left to the discretion of the worker whilst other tasks will be defined in detail as procedures. A procedure defines the actions or decisions that workers must take under various circumstances. Procedures reflect detailed work design and leave workers no discretion to interpret what they should do. In the past, life company products – life insurance, pensions, unit trusts – were handled separately in discrete sub-businesses.

Each was run as an independent fiefdom, having its own strong cultural identity. This gave rise to a strongly bureaucratic and fragmented structure with separate functions, such as personnel, marketing and sales, and poor communications between them. Companies today are moving away from this to a process-oriented approach.

3 *From control to empowerment*
In traditional hierarchical structures there is considerable control over the way staff, especially clerical workers, work. In flatter organisations they are given more initiative and freedom to make decisions.

4 *From administrative focus to customer focus*
In the past, retail financial services companies have been accused of having a product and an administrative-focus as opposed to a customer-focus. The clerical worker would concentrate on the administration of the product and had very little contact with the final customer.

Organisational profiles from the retail financial services sector

Two examples drawn from the 50 profiles received are reproduced below. The first, Figure 10.2, represents a Top 3 UK bank. It indicates that the organisation is still very hierarchical with strong control mechanisms in place. However, it has recently completed the implementation of an integrated client management system and this will make the introduction of a process-oriented, customer-focused approach possible. It is planning a major transition over the next five years.

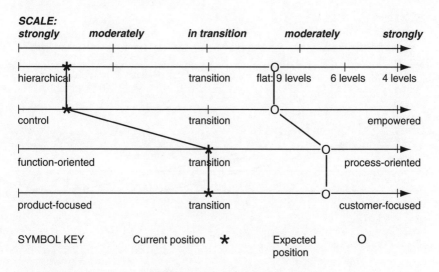

Figure 10.2 Organisational profile: a Top 3 UK bank.

The second example, Figure 10.3, is that of a Top 3 UK building society which is adopting a different approach. It aims to retain its traditional control structure but will place stronger emphasis on improving the customer interface through a quality approach which focuses on a thorough training in highly standardised procedures rather than empowerment. It is worth noting that this building society has a workforce with 25 per cent employed part time, mainly in the branch network.

Progress in achieving organisational change: survey results

Three broad conclusions can be drawn from the organisation profiles received from the fifty respondents, and these are summarised next:

- The process of change is underway with over 90 per cent of the companies surveyed claiming that they are moving in the direction of customer-focus, flatter structures, process-orientation and empowerment, though at very different rates. Almost all are expecting a major transition at some time, even the most traditionally hierarchical.
- The rate of transition varies from sector to sector. The majority of general insurance and finance firms having already made the transition. Banks, building societies and life assurers have been very slow to change and the building society profile, in Figure 10.3 below, is not untypical. However, the banks in the survey expect to make dramatic changes over the next five years, much of this change being facilitated by the intro-

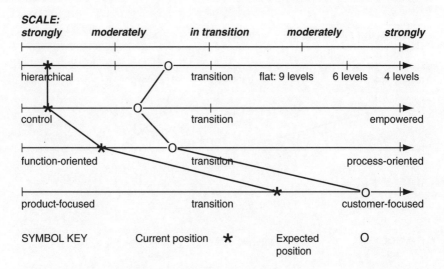

Figure 10.3 Organisational profile: a Top 3 UK building society.

duction of client-based systems and integrated technology. The building society sector is still relatively complacent, reflecting the fact that they are still making record profits despite eight years of recession in the housing market. Many of the major banks (see profile in Figure 10.2), consider the past five years of change and 'right-sizing' as the start of a major transition. The life sector is also expecting dramatic change, with more companies planning for drastic restructuring of the workforce.

- The rate of progress in each of the four areas of change also differs within the firm, in many cases. Some companies claim to have achieved the reduction of hierarchies and the shift to customer-focus well in advance of other kinds of change. For instance, many companies said that they had been able to reduce hierarchies fairly quickly (within a year) and it is not uncommon to find reductions of between four and six levels of staff in quite a brief period, particularly in the general sector. Also, almost all the companies reported that they were making a major transition in the area of customer-focus.

However, there was some recognition that the far reaching nature of change and the degree of coordination required between the different aspects had been underestimated. Ten per cent of the respondents indicated that they are pulling back and reviewing their plans for change in some areas, particularly with regard to delayering and management control. For example, Bank M thought it had cut back too many layers of management and is adding another tier and Company A, a financial services and estate agency, is reintroducing control into the business as it struggles to recoup losses incurred on being taken over by a major building society.

It is difficult to implement strategic change if the middle management layer is reduced too quickly and too severely, leaving inexperienced staff with insufficient training to cope alone. Without an effective redeployment strategy, redundancy may well be the talented middle manager's preferred option. Also recent studies by a major building society (1996) showed that over-drastic reductions in experienced personnel at all levels had an adverse effect on the business measured in terms of loss of corporate memory, reduced sales, and lower levels of customer satisfaction.

Further investigation in companies claiming great strides in customer-focus initiatives found that some had a more limited understanding of the concept than others and were introducing surface-level customer care programmes of the kind described below:

The package of proposals included training in telephone manner; a poster campaign around the office which proclaimed 'The customer is King' and exhorted staff not to leave their telephone for more than 30 seconds; a campaign to get staff to employ caring language; and a wide range of communications education in company broad sheets. Quality circles were also being used to punch home the message.

(Fincham *et al.* 1994)

Our research shows that most clerical workers currently employed in the majority of firms in the retail financial services sector still work on procedure-based rather than process-based tasks. Even the current trend to multiskilling tends to be based on procedures, with clerical workers now carrying out several procedures instead of just one. This is consistent with the findings of research on flexibility in the early 1990s in UK manufacturing which suggest that 'such initiatives have had more to do with the reassertion of managerial control over job mobility allied to work intensification' (Elger, 1991 in Mabey and Salaman, 1995).

Research in other sectors (Applegate and Cash, 1991) shows that the time taken to achieve change of this kind and to develop new functioning roles based on self-managing teams is, on average, between 24 to 30 months, though obviously progress rates vary from team to team. It also argues that IT is a critical factor in achieving the transition, and a re-evaluation of the IT infrastructure is vital to exploit its potential in a support and strategic role.

Few companies in our survey claim to have made much progress towards empowerment and process-orientation and many reorganisations are clearly lagging in these two areas. Becoming process-oriented is complex as this involves breaking down departmental barriers and changing old ways of doing things; empowerment too is a slow process which takes time to introduce and requires great clarity about purpose and intentions.

'Empowerment is imperative for the future, though in this organisation it may happen faster in some areas than in others. Some senior managers will be reluctant to let go of their decision-making authority. You need a totally failsafe framework so that people know what they are doing and know that it is right. There will still be a limit to decision making and the dividing lines between empowered work and non empowered work must be crystal clear. Currently we are identifying the decisions taken in each process so that senior management can then decide where to draw the boundaries for empowered staff. The implementation of empowerment would not be a Big Bang approach because the company already has a certain degree of empowerment – it will be more of a gradual, general move.'

(HR manager, major composite insurer)

'It is estimated that perhaps around 25% of staff are empowered and significant progress has been made in the Customer Service division. The effect of empowerment on customer opinion is very profound and positive. We are currently thinking through what empowerment means for managers. We have to understand their different contributions in an empowered environment; and the continuing importance of praise when people get something right.'

(HR manager, a Top 10 life assurance company)

Many companies in the sector could not fully implement a process approach because they also found that their current IT systems were inappropriate.

'IT is holding everything back. Being one of the first companies to use computers in the 1960s we have spent time building up lots of product-based databases but we are now looking to move into more customer-based work and this is causing problems of transition. There is a huge number of existing customers but the databases are all surplus now. The company needs to develop more customer-focused systems. The IT system is bureaucratic and complex but there is no neat and easy way of changing it. We have a team of IT consultants from the US working on this full time.'

(HR manager, a Top 10 life assurance company)

'IT can empower, but staff here have difficulty at present because the current IT systems prevent them from responding quickly and effectively to certain questions. They need much better access to information. We could use IT to provide details or guidelines which would give empowered staff more confidence to make decisions, though we would not want to introduce scripts for staff to follow verbatim when dealing with customers.'

(HR manager, Top 10 building society)

Towards knowledge intensity

Child (1986), in his research on the effects of IT on the service classes, identifies 'the nature of the task' as a key factor determining the extent to which information technology changes the job content of the 'white collar' worker. The nature of the task can be defined in terms of three features: the level of complexity, the extent of the knowledge base required, and the degree of risk involved in making the decisions necessary for a satisfactory result. Tasks with low levels of each are most suitable for automation, whilst those with high levels are not.

In the banking sector there is a direct correlation between job losses at clerical level and automation of routine low level tasks. For instance, a clearing bank cut 700 jobs after installing a £17 million automated cheque and credit handling system. Banks now have over 18,000 ATMs and it has been stated that each one can eliminate half a job.

At a higher level, the application of IT can change the work of professionals such as bank managers, as shown by Rajan (1988). Rajan's analysis of the task of credit rating of bank customers, once a key role of the bank manager, uses Child's criteria as outlined below:

- complexity – the collection and analysis of data regarding the personal characteristics and credit history of a large number of bank customers is a simple task which can be carried out much more quickly, and accurately, by computer;
- knowledge content – to make a yes/no decision based on the information gathered requires little expert knowledge.
- risk/uncertainty – with credit rating, reliable conclusions can be made on a statistical basis thus reducing risk and uncertainty.

The use of computer-based credit rating systems, which analyse customer details to determine their level of credit worthiness, has altered the job content of the bank manager. He or she now spends less time on this kind of administrative work and more on entrepreneurial work, staff selection and management (see Figure 10.4).

A similar process is occurring across a wide range of jobs and services in the financial services sector.

Sveiby and Lloyd (1988), in their research on managing the services organisation, categorise services according to the degree of complexity and knowledge intensity of the work involved. Their 'Services Spectrum' (see Figure 10.5) distinguishes between traditional service companies and 'know-how' companies.

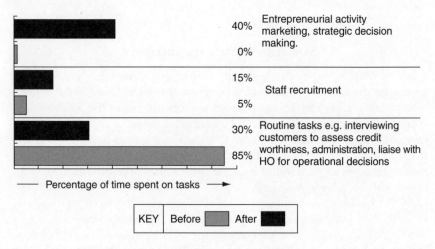

Figure 10.4 The effect of the introduction of a credit rating system on the job content of bank managers.

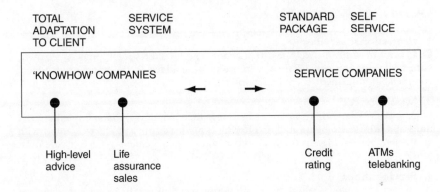

Figure 10.5 Financial service firms in the services sector spectrum.
Source: Adapted from Sveiby and Lloyd 1988.

Within the traditional service companies, they distinguish between firms offering self-service, such as provided by ATMs, and standard financial packages, such as car insurance, mortgages and personal loans. The 'know-how' firms are organised along similar lines to professional firms and range from companies which are highly systemised, such as auditing firms, to those which provide highly individualised advice and services tailored to the exact needs of the client. Figure 10.5 shows the positioning of financial services products in the services sector spectrum.

IT is affecting work throughout the retail financial services spectrum, as it is used to automate the less skilled parts of each job. At the top end, much of the work of a professional financial adviser can now be done by an associate level professional with a portable computer for basic financial calculations. The financial adviser is forced to move into more knowledge-intensive work such as tax and investment planning. Credit scoring of loan applications, once a managerial job, is now automated and can be sold as a package by a relatively unskilled clerical worker. Running a bank account, which used to involve human contact of some kind, can now be carried out automatically by talking over the phone to a computer, although this is still at an early stage.

Others have analysed this movement to knowledge-intensive work using more detailed models. For example, the Service Process Model put forward by Silvestro *et al.* (1992) correlates six service characteristics – people/equipment orientation, length of contact time, degree of customisation, level of employee discretion, value added at front/back office, process/product orientation – against the number of customers processed by an individual service unit per day.

The model defines three service archetypes, as listed in Table 10.1: professional services, mass services and service shops.

As an example, Figure 10.6 categorises eleven retail financial services (in italic text) according to this model.

Table 10.1 Three service archetypes

---

1. Professional services

Organisations with relatively few transactions, highly customised, process-oriented, with relatively long contact time, with most value added in the front-office, where considerable judgement is applied to meeting customer needs.

2. Mass services

Organisations where there are many customer transactions, involving limited contact time, and little customisation. The offering is predominantly product-oriented with most value being added in the back-office and little judgement applied by the front office staff.

3. Service shops

A categorisation which falls between professional and mass services with the levels of the classification dimension falling between the other two extremes.

Source: Silvestro *et al.* 1992. By permission of MCB University Press.

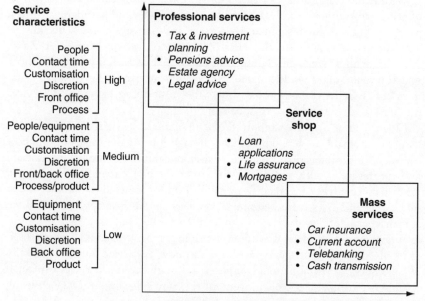

Figure 10.6 A service process model.
Source: Silvestro *et al.* 1992. By permission of MCB University Press.

As IT is applied to more sophisticated tasks, mass services become more and more of a commodity and companies are forced to move into higher level services, and as a result a range of changes occur:

- focus of activity becomes more people- than equipment-oriented;

- customer contact time lengthens;
- the degree of customisation is greater;
- employees use more discretion in their work;
- value-added moves from back to front office;
- focus moves from product to process-orientation.

Whichever model is used, there is a clear shift in the retail financial services sector towards more knowledge-intensive work, as represented by Silvestro *et al.*'s 'professional service' company and Sveiby and Lloyd's 'knowhow' company. In most banks, for example, the income from fees has grown to almost 50 per cent and has almost overtaken income from the traditional lending activities, as represented by the net interest income (NII). Table 10.2 charts the rise of fee income in the Top 6 UK banks by comparing the proportion of other income, mainly net fees and commissions receivable, to net interest income.

As the percentage income from fees grows, banks are starting to compete directly with the professions in the business services sector. For example, by offering will-making services, investment advice and tax planning services, they are competing with solicitors, investment advisers, and accountants.

At the other end of the spectrum, the massive automation of core banking activities has resulted in 50 per cent of all branch business in UK banks being done automatically via the ATM networks (see Table 10.3). This includes cash withdrawals, 70 per cent of all withdrawals, credits and deposits, direct debits and standing orders (various sources 1993).

There is clear evidence, provided by published statistics from the banking world, that the sector is moving to more knowledge-intensive products, and

Table 10.2 Major banks source of income

	1989	1990	1992	1994
NII	62	60	55	52
Other	38	40	45	48
Average of top six banks				

Source: Annual Reports 1994.

Table 10.3 Percentage comparison of the numbers of customer visits to ATMs and branches 1980–1995

	1980	1985	1990	1995
Branch	85	68	60	50
ATM	15	32	40	50

Source: From various sources 1993.

these two examples – the growth of fee income (Table 10.2) and the auto-mation of branch banking (Table 10.3) – are indicative of this shift. The specific examples of the effect of ATMs on clerical work and of credit analysis systems on the job content of bank managers, described on page 166, highlight the role of information technology in job restructuring.

Given the level of IT investment over the past decade in the banking sector, one would expect dramatic changes in the employment profile of the sector, including major job losses, and a significant increase in knowledge-intensity, as measured by the numbers of professionals and associate profes-sionals employed. The models proposed by Sveiby and Lloyd, and Silvestro *et al.* suggest a fairly dramatic change in employment patterns with a shift towards more employment in the 'service shop' and 'professional services' type companies.

The next section presents data which confirms these employment trends in the UK retail financial services sector.

Employment trends in the retail financial services sector

The numbers employed in retail financial services, which includes banking, insurance, mortgage lending and consumer credit operations, increased sig-nificantly from 1985 to 1990 from 737,000 to 883,000. The workforce in banking increased by 61,000; in the insurance sector by almost 40,000; and in the 'other financial services' sector, which includes the building societies and consumer credit operations, by almost 50,000 (see Table 10.4). Even during the recession 1989 to 1993, one of the worst in twenty years, employment in the insurance and 'other financial services' groups remained constant or increased slightly.

The job losses which have occurred, particularly in the banking sector with a reduction of almost 70,000 since 1990 and to a lesser extent in the general insurance sector, have received considerable press coverage. Commentators argue that they herald the beginning of a massive shakeout which will change the structure of the sector completely. However, compared with the massive job losses in the manufacturing sector, they are as yet relatively small scale. Job

Table 10.4 Employment in the retail financial services sector

	June 1985 '000s	June 1990 '000s	June 1994 '000s
Banking	393	454	387
Insurance	224	261	269.4
Other financial services	120	168	168

Source: Employment Gazette.

losses in the banking sector, since 1990, are approaching 25 per cent, whilst job losses in the steel industry have amounted to almost 90 per cent since 1970.

A comparison of the numbers employed in clerical, professional and managerial occupations across the subgroups in the financial services sector (see Table 10.5) reveals a marked difference between the retail banking sector and other groups within the financial services sector (Rajan, 1990; Watkins and Bryce, 1993).

In the retail financial services sector, banks have over 80 per cent of their workforce in clerical grades and only 16 per cent in middle management/professional and technical jobs; the life assurance sector has a more highly educated workforce with over 30 per cent of employees at graduate and A-Level as compared with 20 per cent in the banks or building societies. In contrast, in the business services sector, firms giving investment advice and those in accountancy, management consultancy and software services have a high percentage of professional/technical people and relatively few clerical workers. The City of London also has a large percentage of professionals.

The models proposed by Silvestro et al. and Sveiby and Lloyd would suggest a movement towards more knowledge-intensive work and the employment of more professionals, as typified by the business services sector.

Tables 10.6 and 10.7, based on 1993 figures from the Census of Employment and Labour Force Survey (University of Warwick, 1994), indicate how the employment structure has changed over the last decade. These figures show a 4 per cent fall in the number of clerical and secretarial staff and a

Table 10.5 The distribution of clerical, professional and managerial occupations in the UK financial services sector

	% Clerical	% Professional	% Managerial
RETAIL FINANCIAL SERVICES			
Banking	83	7	10
Building Societies	75	14	11
Life Assurance	63	24	13
CITY OF LONDON			
Banking	50	40	10
Insurance	25	60	15
BUSINESS SERVICES			
Legal Services	45	44	11
Investment Advisers	20	70	10
Accountants/Mngt Consultants	20	74	6
Software Services	13	76	11

Source: Rajan *et al.* 1990; Watkins and Bryce 1993.

Table 10.6 Overall employment in banking and finance 1981–1993

SIC		'000s 1981	'000s 1991	'000s 1993
1.1	Corporate administrators	21	42	43
1.2	Managers and proprietors	40	53	50
2.0	Professionals	9	14	14
3.0	Associate professional	10	17	17
4.0	Clerical and secretarial	355	468	433

Source: Labour Force Survey, University of Warwick 1994.

Table 10.7 Overall change in knowledge intensity 1981–1993

SIC		% 1981	% 1991	% 1993
1.1	Corporate administrators	4	6	7
1.2	Managers and proprietors	8	8	8
2.0	Professionals	2	2	2
3.0	Associate professionals	2	3	3
4.0	Clerical and secretarial	72	69	68

Source: Labour Force Survey, University of Warwick 1994.

corresponding rise in the numbers of corporate administrators and associate professionals. The corporate administrators include large numbers of the so-called business professionals, such as marketing, information technology, accountancy, human resources, as well as professionals traditionally associated with banking, such as the Institute of Banking, Treasury Management etc.

Over the same period companies have been increasing the number of employees in the more knowledge-intensive activities. For example, in 1990, the Royal Bank of Scotland had fewer than 10 per cent of its staff working outside retail banking, but today that figure has reached almost 25 per cent (Annual Report, 1995). Again the jobs created were in higher-value activities such as selling insurance packages and high-level financial advice.

There have been job losses in the banking sector but not to the extent one would expect given the massive investment in technology and there is little correlation between degree of automation and numbers employed. For example, whilst the percentage of bank branch work automated with no human contact rose from 25 per cent to 40 per cent between 1980 and 1990, the numbers of employees in retail banking rose from 393,000 to 454,000.

Conclusion

The results of the survey indicate that financial services companies are adapting their organisational structures but that some companies are moving faster in some areas than others. Most are cutting back on the number of layers in the hierarchy, though this is occurring more slowly in the larger companies. Almost all companies are becoming more customer-focused, for example, banks are cutting their back-office staff and a far higher percentage of staff are now in contact with the final customer. In life assurance companies, staff are allotted a number of customers to look after. Most companies are having difficulty in two key areas: in switching to process-based activity, though in many cases this is because the technology is simply not available; and in 'empowering' their staff. (The term 'empowerment' is regarded as problematic since it is too vague to have any real meaning. It is discussed more fully in Chapter 11.)

There is a definite trend towards the employment of knowledge workers and professionals, and an associated shift towards the kind of services characteristic of 'service shops' and 'professional services' as defined by Silvestro *et al.* There is also evidence that the professional workforce is growing rapidly in the business services sector. For example, rather than employ full-time specialist IT professionals, the banks are taking on subcontractors from the business services sector or setting up specialist divisions which are categorised as business services, such as specialist investment advice. However, the employment profile, as measured by the Standard Industrial Classification (SIC), has changed relatively slowly over a 12-year period. The figures do not tell us whether the clerical workforce is becoming more skilled and moving from low-level routine tasks to more skilled roles.

The implications of the changes described are far reaching and are explored in detail in Chapters 11 to 13, which focus on the changing roles of clerical workers, managers and professionals, and in Chapter 14, which considers the need for new ways of motivating and rewarding staff as their roles change.

11

EFFECTS ON CLERICAL WORKERS

This chapter determines how the roles of clerical workers are changing as organisations aim for greater flexibility, and contrasts the effects of IT for job enrichment and job specialisation. It summarises the views of focus group members on what they see as the main changes occurring in clerical work overall. It focuses on three main trends towards: skill and status differentiation; customer-based processes; and team work. It relates this analysis to the retail financial services sector and provides case histories of typical examples.

As described in Chapter 10, there is a continuing reduction of the clerical workforce, ranging from relatively small reductions in some sectors, such as building societies, to major reductions of over 40 per cent in other sectors, such as general insurance. The introduction of IT has cut out numerous routine, paper-based activities, enabling the remaining clerical workers to accomplish much more and to concentrate on other activities such as customer service.

The liberal view is that IT is neutral and can be used either for job enrichment or to increase job specialisation. It is very much a managerial decision which route is taken. Managers in financial services companies have tended to opt for functional specialisation with, for example, large numbers of staff employed as keyboard operators whose sole task has been to input data for payment based on number of words keyed, speed and accuracy. This approach has led to the creation of 'white-collar factories' as seen at the Bank of Scotland's VISA Centre in Dunfermline (see Fincham et al. (1994) 'Expertise and Innovation', Case 7: 46–7).

The VISA Centre was set up along factory lines with a combination of functional specialisation and with strict management control systems in operation. The labour force consists of a large number of part-time women doing unskilled work and a small number of permanent managers with career jobs and responsibility for planning, coordinating and managing the work. The work of the clerical staff is heavily monitored with, for example, supervisors being alerted if an incoming call lasts longer than 30 seconds. The clerical workers have very little autonomy or task variety, and they are subject to a highly intensive work system as made clear by this interview comment from a senior manager:

> It cost between half and three quarters of a million pounds to put that system in place. If staff are away yattering or wandering around the building, then we are not using the machines. So we do make sure we have a reasonable throughput.
>
> (Senior manager at VISA)

However, in some companies there are also examples of job enrichment for some of the remaining clerical staff. Even the implementation of relatively simple IT tools, such as spreadsheets, can have a marked effect. For instance, in one medium-sized life company, secretaries taught to use spreadsheets and database packages were able to take on many of the functions of middle managers such as routine operational decisions, budgeting, producing statistics and simple reports.

At a more sophisticated level of the technology, many more routine tasks can be eliminated. For example, an EDI network eliminates the need to duplicate input of data, releasing clerical staff to work on more interesting, varied tasks such as business development, advisory work and client contact:

> The clerical function is changing. Technical knowledge, social and diagnostic skills are now increasingly required of clerical staff who are expected to answer customer enquiries, liaise with brokers, process new applications and undertake underwriting. They are also responsible for an allotted number of intermediaries and are able to provide these customers with a personal service resulting in a major increase in productivity, sales and customer satisfaction.
>
> (Personnel Director, major insurance company)

Focus group members were asked to list key features which they believe characterise change in the clerical worker's role over the current decade (see Table 11.1).

Our survey highlights three main trends which are emerging as automation leads to a reduction in the number of clerical workers and changes in the nature of their work. These are:

- the growing differentiation between the highly skilled permanent employee and the low skilled often part-time employee;
- the focus on customer-based processes rather than inward-looking procedures;
- the new emphasis on the contribution of the team rather than the individual specialist.

Table 11.1 Clerical workers – changing roles 1990–2000

1990	2000
• large numbers	• fewer
• paper-based tasks	• IT based
• routine, basic skills	• more highly skilled, knowledgeable
• specialist	• generalist
• full time	• more part-time
• internal focus	• customer-focused
• procedures	• process
• individual	• team
• no responsibility, taking orders	• empowered
• low productivity	• high productivity
• low job satisfaction	• greater job satisfaction
• badly paid	• well paid

These three trends are discussed next under the headings: Skill and Status Differentiation; From Inward-looking Procedures to Customer-based Processes; and From Individual to Team Work. Two case studies are included in the discusssion on the last two trends to illustrate the main problems associated with these changes.

Skill and status differentiation (low/high skill; part-time/full-time status)

Whilst some of the remaining, much reduced, clerical workforce find that their jobs are broadened and enriched as they take on a wider range of tasks, others, like those at the VISA Centre at the Bank of Scotland are confined to more tightly controlled and specialised roles (see also the example of a Top 3 UK building society mentioned in Chapter 10 and illustrated in the organisational profile, Figure 10.3). There is evidence of a growing differentiation between full-time career clerical workers with interesting jobs, and part-timers in some of the more routine jobs remaining after automation. This confirms earlier research by Rajan (1988) which concluded that, although functional specialisation is occurring and will continue to occur, overall the future demand will be for higher level clerical workers with knowledge based and problem solving skills instead of task specific skills.

From inward-looking procedures to customer-based processes

In the past, to achieve economies of scale, most retail financial services companies have been organised in a hierarchical way with business processes broken down into narrowly defined tasks or procedures and spread amongst several departments. The use of integrated technology to reduce the multi-stage value-added chain to just three major processes, developing new products; delivering products to customers; and managing customer relationships, as described by Rockart and Short (1989) is only just beginning in the retail financial services sector, with a few large organisations leading the field.

For example, Company S, a Top 10 life assurance firm, has started restructuring one part of its business — the customer support section. A massive review of the company was undertaken in 1991 following the appointment of a new Chief Executive Officer, formerly an accountant in industry with experience in the financial services but not life assurance specifically. As a result of this overhaul, the number of products being sold was reduced from 50 to 25 and the organisation focused its attention on those sectors of the business which were expanding and developing, cutting out areas which were outdated and unprofitable. The company also undertook a major business process re-engineering project in the customer services department which resulted in the company moving from a function-oriented work pattern to a process-oriented approach where staff are formed into teams and there is a strong customer-focus. This creates a situation where different teams are responsible for certain processes and are represented at a single point of customer contact.

In order to persuade the rest of the employees that they needed to face the upheaval head on and with enthusiasm, researchers produced a set of statistics to demonstrate to the staff that the function-oriented pattern meant that production rates were slowed down by a lack of cohesion between the various units dealing with a certain piece of work. One statistic showed that it took 63 days to produce one policy, which staff found surprising as their individual contributions to the process might only take one or two days, but the communication between units slowed down overall production. Figures like these raised awareness amongst staff of the extent to which operations needed to change and speed up, if the organisation was to survive the coming turbulence. This made it easier for pilot programmes to be introduced, the results of which showed that process-oriented teams could produce dramatically improved results. Company S also recognised that it is not feasible or sensible to attempt to change the processes and stop at that; if change is to be introduced, a holistic view needs to be taken. Therefore changing the processes sparks off the need to redefine roles, redefine the reward strategy, retrain people, develop greater customer services skills in staff etc. With the redefinition of roles comes the creation of a new set of competencies for each new role, and new training programmes need to be designed to support these new roles.

From individual to team work

As rigid job boundaries are broken down and employees are expected to do more and to do a wider range of tasks, roles expand vertically within a single function or specialism and/or horizontally across a range of functions or specialities. As the boundaries shift, duties overlap making coordinated team effort based on sharing of some resources essential. Core teams are involved in the ongoing, day-to-day work of the business; ad hoc or temporary teams are assembled to tackle special, project-based tasks. One of the key features of National & Provincial's transformation is its emphasis on teamwork. It began through restructuring in the late 1980s when it split its monolithic hierarchy into a group of smaller hierarchies, each based on a different financial services product. By 1990, it found that this separation resulted in image inconsistency, duplication of support functions and increased overheads. They were becoming detached from the requirements of their customers and service deteriorated. It realised that its business was about giving the customer advice on the most appropriate financial service rather than selling individual financial products. It therefore adopted a modified TQM approach to rebuild traditional customer loyalty, transforming itself from a hierarchy to an innovative, process-driven organisation (O'Brien, 1993; O'Brien and Wainwright, 1993). Its three and a half year-long change programme introduced team working and the concept of team play through a sporting analogy.

Work is organised on a 'team of teams' basis which operates at four levels with managers, coaches, captains, and players. O'Brien and Wainwright (1993) argue that this approach helps in achieving the appropriate behavioural change for teamwork and consistency in the way different teams work, which makes it easier for them to work together. The Direction Management Team (DMT) sets the direction and identifies what is required to achieve it. Each member of DMT leads an Implementation Management Team which agrees requirements and determines resources. Similarly, each member of this team leads an Implementation Team which implements the appropriate activities for that process and measures performance against agreed targets. In November 1990, all current jobs were abolished, people were given roles according to competence, and teams were left to work out how best to implement them.

N&P stress that every individual member of the team must have a clear understanding of what their own and other teams in the organisation are trying to do and how they fit into the overall mission of the company. A team without a clear purpose is not a true team but simply a collection of individuals with different agendas.

N&P has experienced difficulties, some due to the fact that the current IT system is not yet capable of supporting all aspects of teamwork.

In the two companies studied, a Top 10 life assurance company and a Top 10 building society, the time taken to develop functioning, self-managing teams was, on average, between 24 to 30 months, though obviously progress rates varied from team to team and a number of set-backs had to be overcome. Although it was agreed that IT was a critical factor in achieving the transition, it was felt that a re-evaluation of the IT infrastructure was vital to exploit its potential in a support and strategic role.

The experience of leading companies such as these, like that of GE Canada (Applegate and Cash, 1991), suggests that the process of effective team building has four key phases: planning and preparation; orientation; transition; and operation. Features of each stage are summarised in the case history that follows. The trend towards effective team building of this kind in the retail financial services sector overall is at an early stage, as it is in most companies in most sectors today.

Stages in the development of self-managing teams
(Based on Applegate and Cash, 1991)

1: Preparatory Phase
Top managers, middle managers and employees are educated on the need for significant change in the organisation to ensure survival. The change programme is backed by research-based evidence to substantiate demands.

Plans for self-managing teams, and strategies to manage and support change and new working practices are announced.

Redundancy offered to managers who do not want change – typically up to 20 per cent will leave at this stage.

2: Orientation Phase (6 to 9 months)
Continuing dependency of the team on the current manager – current supervision remains in place.

Decision-making – achieving team consensus takes time – problems of knowing where the responsibility of the team ends and the responsibility of the coordinator begins.

Teams re-design/modify organisational roles – job design based on three general areas – job-related or technical work; team administration – planning, organising, integrating; and team process tasks – participation, facilitation; conflict resolution.

Coping with the additional administrative workload causes concern.

Confusion over how quality and productivity improvements are reflected in rewards and compensation.

Potential for conflict great – must be resolved or will lead to lack of commitment.

Reorganisation of physical environment – small group work areas set up to promote flexibility, openness and improved communication.

Training needs clarification; important to have human resources specialists to work with the teams; need for formal training courses in team skills such as meeting skills and interaction skills including conflict resolution.

Employees ranked on a variety of skill levels – loss of up to 40 per cent of staff possible at this stage.

3: Transition Phase (12 and 18 months)

Concept of shared management emerging; team taking over scheduling of work.

Clarification of team roles; cohesion developing.

Decision-making still an issue.

Many hard decisions being made, including termination of some employees, changing job roles for all, and new reward structures.

4: Operation Phase (24 and 30 months)

Structural changes are established with:

- clarification of coordinator's role, team coach, player;
- well organised team procedures;
- compensation and reward schemes linked to evaluation systems;
- work evaluated re: quality, productivity, risk-taking, management skills, initiative, group cooperation, team skills;
- career progression reflects the acquisition of advanced skills/ responsibilities in general areas which define the job;
- continuous learning to acquire the skills required in these general areas.

Many of the traditional managerial responsibilities such as planning, budget setting, hiring, firing, monitoring, and managing are now undertaken by the team; leadership, organisation-wide strategic direction, and assistance with integrating and coordinating the work of the separate teams is provided by a Coordination Team.

Conclusion

In the retail financial services sector, the role of the clerical worker is changing only slowly in the three areas investigated. As far as skill enhancement goes, many companies are undecided about the direction to take. Do they move towards functional specialisation and strict management control as seen at the VISA centre, or towards multiskilling as described in the two case histories – Company S and N&P? However, our research shows that most clerical workers currently employed in the majority of firms in this sector still work on procedure-based rather than process-based tasks, the movement to customer-based processes is hindered by inadequate information systems. Although the movement to team work is underway this can be a long-term process which may take up to three years to achieve, as Company S and N&P have both found.

As more and more of the basic procedures are automated there will be a big switch in the number of clerical workers from the back office to dealing directly with customer. The extent and speed of the change envisaged is highlighted in this recent quote from a major bank:

> Currently a minority of our staff are dedicated to dealing directly with customers face-to-face or over the telephone but this will change substantially. By the year 2000 it will be almost two thirds of the workforce.

However, as many academics have pointed out, even though clerical work in many companies is becoming more customer-focused, demanding and complex and team working is becoming more common, this does not mean that the power structure of the organisation has changed or that they are moving on from automating to informating as defined by Zuboff. For example, although Direct Line has many of these features, that is, team working, customer-based processes and multiskilling, it maintains a ruthless separation of the processing of information from its interpretation (Scarbrough, 1996). Of the hundreds of new jobs created, most require clerical, telesales and data handling skills and few require high-level skills involving the exercise of judgement based on specialist knowledge. Whilst telesales staff can provide a set answer to a query, the framework or script they use is designed by senior managers. Questions which cannot be answered are referred to supervisors, who hold the knowledge needed to answer questions not anticipated or too complex to be covered in the script. Telesales, in effect, is still a data collection job. However, as Zuboff (1988) makes clear, to move from the automating stage to the informating stage entails the development of analytical and interpretative thinking skills in those at the 'coal-face'. In other words we need to see the clerical workers using their new information skills to contribute to and develop these frameworks.

This is not happening to any great extent in the retail financial services, instead we see, as Zuboff and others have warned, the very systems which help broaden the clerical function being used to closely monitor their activities and performance. The system is providing detailed feedback on sales achieved, speed of response and accuracy of information input. Although new technology has the potential to informate staff, it is being used as a tool for even greater management control rather than for 'empowerment'.

12

EFFECTS ON PROFESSIONALS

This chapter examines the changing role of professionals in the retail financial services sector. It begins with a short overview on the growth of professional groups in general. In common with many other industry sectors, there has been a large increase in managerial staff, professionals and associate professionals in the retail financial services sector between 1981 and 1990. The sector employs large numbers from both the traditional professions, such as actuaries, solicitors, bankers and accountants, and from the newer professional groups, such as marketing, human resources, information technology, and financial advice personnel. Additional information included in this chapter is from a series of surveys over five years looking at the future of the professional workforce (see Watkins and Drury 1992; 1993; 1994).

Background: The growth of professional groups

Today the term 'professional' is used to describe the activities of a wide range of people across many occupational groups. The current Standard Occupational Classification defines a professional as one who has a professional qualification or a degree plus a postgraduate professional qualification. Professionals defined thus represented approximately 15 per cent of the workforce in 1990 and this is expected to reach 30 per cent by the year 2000. It is predicted that the UK employment pattern will follow that evident in the USA. According to the US Bureau of Labour Statistics Survey, of the 2.2 million new jobs created in 1995, more than 72 per cent were in managerial and professional, mainly in health care, education, financial services, business services, the media and telecommunications. By the end of the decade there will be over 10 million workers in the UK who can be classified as managers, professionals or associate professionals. Almost all of these will be involved in knowledge-intensive work and they will require a high-level education and continuing professional development throughout their careers.

Growth of professionals in the retail financial services sector

The number of managers, professionals and associate professionals in the retail financial services sector grew rapidly between 1981 and 1990, though since 1990 growth has fallen slightly. As the figures from the Labour Force Survey (IER, University of Warwick, 1994) indicate, the growth has been particularly noticeable amongst the sector's corporate administrative group, which includes the new business and management professions which evolved in the 1980s, for example, marketing, advertising, information systems, and personnel (see Table 12.1).

The numbers of information technology professionals in the sector have increased dramatically over the same period and the whole retail financial services sector employs over 30,000 IT professionals. The growth of IT employees in a Top 10 life assurance company, as shown in Table 12.2, exemplifies this trend.

However, there are signs now, especially in the banking sector, that their numbers are being reduced as IT services are outsourced to the business services sector.

The trends which affect professional working practices in RFS

Professionals working in the retail financial services sector, like those in other sectors, face major changes in working practices as new organisational structures of the kind described in Chapter 9 are introduced. Several focus groups

Table 12.1 The growth of professionals in the financial services

	Insurance 1981–1993 '000s		Banking and finance 1981–1993 '000s	
Managers and proprietors	12.21	13.70	39.70	49.80
Corporate administrators	13.71	26.39	20.54	42.61
Professionals	8.33	11.36	8.97	13.61
Associate professionals	12.08	17.57	10.25	17.06

Source: IER.

Table 12.2 The growth of IT employees in a Top 10 life assurance company

	IT staff	Total employees
1985	120	1,600
1990	180	1,900
1995	370	2,000

of managers and professionals currently working in the retail financial services were asked to identify the main changes in job roles, status, and employment patterns that would affect the work of the professional over the next decade. The key changes highlighted by the groups are shown in Table 12.3.

Although there is considerable overlap between them, this analysis indicates six key trends and provides a useful framework for summarising key issues and implications for professional roles in the sector. Key points are summarised under the following headings:

- Towards knowledge-intensity and increased use of IT;
- Towards value-added and business-linked;
- Towards team working, functional flexibility and customer-focus;
- Towards a smaller, centralised function which is advisory in nature;
- Towards greater accountability and performance measurement;
- Towards contracting out and consultancy.

Towards knowledge-intensity and increased use of IT

Many of the routine aspects of a professional's work can now be done more efficiently by computer, leading to important productivity gains in these areas and a concentration of professional expertise on high-level, more lucrative, work. The routine work can be devolved to support staff, an associate or paraprofessional with vocational and computer skills, thus increasing the range of work of which they are capable. IT which is harnessed to free the professional from the mundane so that he or she can make fuller use of higher level skills and potential is an obvious opportunity to those able to take advantage of it. To others it is a potential threat in terms of loss of income

Table 12.3 Trends in professional working practices 1990–2000

1990		2000	
• high percentage of routine work with limited technology	→	• routine work taken over by IT and associate professionals	
• service to organisation using knowledge for mainly routine problems	→	• value added to the client or customer	
• functional focus	→	• customer-focus and cross-functional teamworking	
• highly specialised in professional area	→	• specialised professional expertise, business advice + management skills	
• autonomy based on trust	→	• accountability and performance measurement	
• full-time employee	→	• consultant	

184

and loss of status. As the lower level work is taken over by computers and associate professionals, the professional spends an increasing amount of time working at a higher level on more complex tasks. Handy (1989) predicts that in the future there will be far fewer professionals in larger organisations, but that those who remain will be paid more but will be working harder and more effectively.

This has certain attractions in that this more demanding work is interesting and stimulating, but there are problems too since working at this level consistently often results in high levels of stress and early burn out. Surveys conducted by Gallie and White (1993) and by Fotinatos and Cooper (1993) found increases in occupational stress at all levels in the organisation. Gallie and White found that high levels of stress were reported most frequently by professionals and managers, and that the increase in stress over the last five years has been greatest in the professional/managerial and the technical/supervisory groups.

Both studies found that although job insecurity is very relevant to the growth of stress at work across all levels, the intensification of work effort is a major factor. People are expected to work harder and longer, to take on more responsibility, to work to higher standards and to update their skills more frequently.

Professionals in the focus groups agreed that their own experiences of change and occupational stress closely echoed the findings of these surveys. They too were working harder and longer and were being expected to achieve higher standards and to take on more responsibility without additional pay:

> In the past, Mutual Life was a company where lots of well-paid people worked their whole lives without necessarily contributing a great deal. Those days are gone. Each individual now has to take on more responsibility, to work to a higher standard, to meet set performance targets, and generally be more accountable. If they don't, they won't survive in the company.
>
> (Marketing professional)

As more of the routine work is taken on by associate professionals, focus group members found that the long periods of concentration needed to complete increasing loads of highly complex work were leading to exhaustion. As one focus group member pointed out:

> Thinking at this level makes life interesting, but when you have to do it all the time it's exhausting and sometimes painful.

Towards value–added and business–linked

In the past professionals were considered mainly as service providers who gave impartial professional advice. Over the past five years this role has changed: the professional is now expected to spend more time working in management teams, where he or she shares responsibility for business decisions and the design of value-added services to the customer. The role of the professional now has to be integrated into the business strategy of the organisation. This trend is apparent in a wide range of professional functions including lawyers, accountants, solicitors, human resources, marketing and IT.

Case study 12.1 illustrates the trend by describing the accountant's growing involvement in value-added/business-linked decision-making in the organisation.

Case 12.1: Accountants in retail financial services

The majority of the staff in finance departments of large organisations today are engaged in the *traditional/operational* duties of recording and reporting – see the bottom-left quadrant in Figure C12.1.

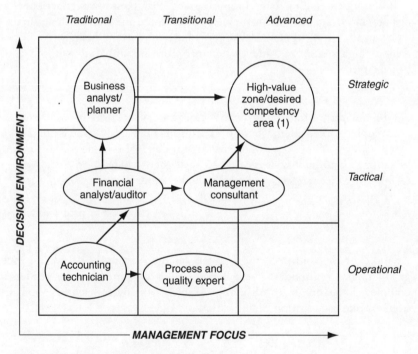

Figure C12.1 Competency model for finance professionals.
Source: Redrawn from Sidney Lee 1994.

Whilst important, these activities have limited value-added potential. Most of the tasks involve a large proportion of routine procedures which could be automated or reduced through technologies or reengineering. Only a small percentage of staff are currently working in high value-added activities. Finance must plan to move away from its traditional/ operational area of work towards the higher value work zone – see the top-right quadrant in Figure C12.1 – with advanced business-focus in order to achieve its vision and goals.

The transition from an information provider role to that of a business adviser and decision maker would require different skill sets as illustrated in Table C12.1. The executives have to be more proactive in sponsoring staff training and organisational development in this process.

Table C12.1 Roles, value-added content and required skill sets

Role	Value-added	Primary skill sets
Information provider	low	Technical skills e.g. finance, accounting, control
Business adviser/ information provider	medium	Interpretative skills, business functions, decision support systems skills
Decision maker/ business adviser	high	Management skills, consultative skills, strategic decision making, understanding organisations

Source: Sidney Lee, 1994.

The long-term result is a more productive, flexible and adaptive workforce able to carry out finance's mission. Not every staff member would be successful nor expected to go through all the stages. The objective is to facilitate the shift and to maintain a balanced and dynamic workforce able to respond quickly to the business needs of the enterprise.

Towards team working, functional flexibility and customer focus

Enhancing customer-focus is a key aim of restructuring the organisation for functional flexibility. It is argued that, if decision makers are not separated from the customer and from each other by functional barriers, their response to the customers' changing needs will be communicated and dealt with more quickly and effectively. Organisations are changing to encourage flexible working patterns. Rigid job boundaries are disappearing and professionals are expected to do more and to do a wider range of tasks – roles expand vertically within a single function or specialism or horizontally across a range of functions or specialisms. As the boundaries shift, duties overlap making coordinated team effort based on sharing of some resources essential. Core teams are involved in the ongoing, day-to-day work of the business; ad hoc or temporary teams are assembled to tackle special, project-based tasks.

This new method of working is being facilitated by the introduction of integrated systems, communications technologies such as electronic mail, computer conferencing, and the development of computer software to support teams and group working. For example, see the case study of French Life.

Case 12.2: French Life

French Life is a Top 10 Life company and one of the market leaders in providing investment products for the A B customer group. In 1994, a new integrated IT system was introduced which was customer-based and allowed management information from different departments to be combined. In the past, product development was a very slow process with products being developed sequentially, that is, each section, for example, market research, actuarial, IT, administration and sales, worked on it independently in turn, then passed it on to the next. With the advent of integrated systems professionals were able to work across functional boundaries in a 'simultaneous' approach to product development. That is, cross-functional teams of employees, from product development, design, production, sales and marketing, working concurrently on a new product. This approach, also known as 'concurrent engineering', is rapidly replacing the old sequential development methods.

The responses from focus groups make it clear that there has been a major increase in group and team working for all kinds of professionals. Although professionals have always made contributions in groups, effective team work requires much more commitment to the group, and trust in the ability and contributions of other team members. Experience of making contributions in cross-functional or multidisciplinary teams was quite common amongst focus group participants. The need to have sufficient knowledge outside their own range of expertise to enable them to communicate with others and collaborate on a multidisciplinary project was keenly felt. The need to learn from one another in a team situation and for that experience to be customer-focused was felt to be particularly important, especially for those not usually in the front line:

> I now see every profession in the company: accountants, the legal profession, marketing, statisticians and IT people, taking a much more active business role. When accountants and lawyers are part of the team, they have to get involved in the problem. They get much more satisfaction out of taking part in providing the solution. If you take a lawyer along to a customer with a problem, they learn an awful lot themselves.
>
> (Manager in large computer company)

> When you deal directly with customers, you get a better view of their needs in relation to the business objectives. When things start getting out of sync you're aware of it and can suggest some changes.
>
> (Senior administrator)

Towards a smaller, centralised function which is advisory in nature

As some of their more routine functions are devolved to line-management and in some cases to associate professionals, the professional will spend more time working in management teams, where he or she will share responsibility for business decisions, and will act in an advisory role.

These new roles demand greater business involvement, higher levels of work, devolved decision-making, high-level communications and negotiating skills and offer rewards based on measures of contribution. These changes are meeting resistance from many professionals, but the uncertainty bred by the current economic climate is hastening an acceptance of the need for change.

To survive in these new structures, a professional must have tradable skills which can be measured, costed and bought and sold within the organisation. Since communication and negotiation are key aspects of successful networking, the possession of social and personal skills is increasingly important. See Case 12.3.

Case 12.3: The human resources professional

In the retail financial services sector, as both the structure and the role of human resources departments change in response to external business pressures, the roles of its employed professionals change too. The personnel professional is taking on a new role as a member of a management team which shares responsibility for business decisions.

Our research indicates a major movement between 1994 and 1996, away from the large centralised function to a more devolved human resources function (see Table C12.3).

Table C12.2: Changing structure and role of personnel departments

	Now *1994*	*Two years'* *time 1996*
Centralised Large centralised HR function with complete control over all corporate HR activities	53%	30%
Devoted HR function devolved to divisional and line managers with different HR policies to deal with different environments	29%	30%
Core Reduced HR function with responsibility only for core tasks e.g.: policy formation, succession planning.	18%	28%

The large centralised function is becoming far more service-oriented – major organisational clients are provided with a personal service, for example, allocating a personnel professional to cover a whole range of personnel issues for that division such as industrial relations, job evaluation, training and manpower planning. The general trend is towards devolution; a smaller more professional human resources function which is far more strategic, less bureaucratic and linked with the business.

New technology, in freeing line managers from administrative tasks, gives them more time to take on some of the functions previously carried out by personnel professionals:

In the future the role of line-managers as decision makers, motivators and salespeople will far outweigh their declining role as administrators and their involvement in and responsibility for recruitment and personnel issues will increase substantially.

Chief Executive in a major building society

This is turn frees the professional from lower level tasks allowing him or her to take on a consultative role and to become involved, as a member of a team, in new complex areas such as business process redesign, quality management and project management as the following comment from the banking sector illustrates:

> Our role as a facilitator and adviser to group and individual business units is concerned with organisational development – re-engineering of work and management processes and focusing on quality issues and the flexible, cross-functional deployment of multi-skilled staff.
>
> Senior Personnel Profession

Many human resources professionals are not prepared to change their traditional roles and adopt these new ways of working. Without change they will be marginalised and the strategic aspects of their work taken over by other members of the senior management team or in some cases by a breakaway and more dynamic training unit:

> The traditional role of the Human Resources Department – job evaluation, appraisal – is shifting to an organisational development and facilitating role. In our company, senior management is taking on that role because the personnel professional is still playing the old game and does not actually have the ability to contribute on the organisation development type of facilitating role. He is being marginalised.
>
> Human Resources Director in a major building society

Towards greater accountability and performance measurement

Some professional functions are given cost or profit centre status, and services are sold to internal customers at cost or on a profit basis. There may even be negotiation of internal service contracts. In some cases services are also sold on the open market.

- With the advent of better quality information systems, senior managers have far more information about where costs are incurred and where value is added, so the exact contribution of each department, branch or individual (in some cases) can be costed.

- There is a parallel trend towards the introduction of service delivery contracts between professional departments such as information technology, marketing, accountancy, personnel and the business units they serve.
- Service delivery agreements are only a few short steps away from subcontracting the whole function to a third party (see page 122 in Chapter 7). Once senior managers are confident of being able to measure the contribution and quality of a professional or business unit, they gain the flexibility to subcontract the service, if and when necessary. Taken to its extreme this could involve such things as franchising the whole branch network of a major bank.

Towards contracting out and consultancy

A major feature of the 1980s and early 1990s was the growth of the business services sector which includes areas such as consultancy, law, accountancy, insurance intermediaries, surveying, advertising and leasing. During this period, the numbers working in the business services sector increased from 973,000 to 1,850,000 as major companies subcontracted out many of their professional services. Many of these people were engaged in activities which support retail financial services, for example, in the insurance sector the number employed in major insurance companies has fallen but the number employed in associated areas such as brokers, independent life intermediaries, loss adjustors and consultant actuaries offering services to the big insurance companies rose to over 100,000, of whom 32,000 are working on a self-employed basis.

The trend for organisations to shed professional staff and employ them back on a fee basis is predicted to continue through the 1990s. Many professionals are now required to provide specific advice on a periodic basis rather than work in a salaried position. They have become sub-contractors working for a fee for a particular service.

How can professionals respond to these trends?

These trends have major implications regarding the skills and competences required by professionals. As the useful lifespan of knowledge gained in an initial degree or professional course declines, the need for continuing education becomes more urgent. Education and training becomes a continuous lifelong process to keep abreast of change. In addition to their vocational skills, professionals need managerial skills to survive in an increasingly commercial environment, and cross-functional skills to enable them to negotiate and communicate with other professionals.

In a flattened hierarchy with fewer management levels, teams become self-managing, taking on and sharing the responsibilities of former managers, and reporting to a senior coordinator. Team members have to extend the breadth and depth of their existing skills and knowledge and learn new skills, including the interpersonal skills so crucial for effective teamwork.

As well as high levels of technical and professional knowledge, these additional skills – intellectual, people, coping, and commercial skills – are increasingly important (see Figure 12.1).

Writers such as Quinn (1992) emphasise the contribution of professional intellect to wealth creation and value-adding innovation and the need to encourage the development of new and more wide-ranging skills.

In his 1996 paper on managing professional intellect, Quinn argues that there are four developmental levels. At the first level, 'cognitive knowledge', professionals acquire the basic knowledge of a discipline through extensive training and certification. At the second level, 'applying knowledge', they are able to apply book knowledge and advanced skills in the workplace. Whilst most value-creating professionals work at this level, organisations are trying to develop their workforces to reach the two higher levels defined by Quinn. These are: 'systems understanding', that is, a deep knowledge of the 'web of cause and effect relationships underlying a discipline' which enables the professional to solve larger and more complex problems; and 'self-motivated creativity' which depends on will, motivation and adaptability.

Research in the UK (Watkins, 1996) uses a similar value-added continuum defining a four-level model of professional knowledge where the higher levels are labelled 'integrated knowledge' and 'dynamic knowledge'. The professional with 'integrated knowledge' (Level 3) has a deep understanding of the organisation's structures and systems and is able to work across disciplines, in teams, making use of the latest technology; those with 'dynamic knowledge' (Level 4) are able to apply and adapt the knowledge gained in the first three stages to find creative solutions in fast-changing environmental conditions.

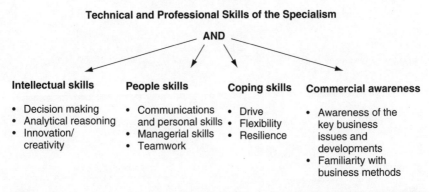

Figure 12.1 Competencies required by financial services professionals in the 1990s.

This model differs from Quinn's in that it highlights the importance of management in motivating and helping the professional to develop these higher level skills. It also stresses the importance of collaboration rather than the traditional view of the professional as an individual.

Conclusion

Financial services organisations are undergoing significant changes – making greater use of IT, adopting flexible working patterns to enhance responsiveness to rapidly changing market conditions, and becoming more knowledge-intensive. The six major changes described here – the trends towards greater knowledge-intensity, value-added and business-linked, team working and customer-focus, advisory roles in a smaller centralised function, performance measurement, and outsourcing – are beginning to have a profound effect on the professional workforce. Many professionals are facing levels of occupational insecurity and stress not encountered by members of this group before. They are also facing new challenges and opportunities which can only be met if new skills are acquired and if the facilities to develop and maintain their potential are available to them. Although the individual professional has a personal responsibility to ensure that his or her knowledge is updated and new skills and ways of working are acquired, the employing organisation has a responsibility too. Financial services companies need to consider new, more effective ways of supporting continuing professional development and training, of reducing stress levels, and encouraging professional employees to take responsibility for developing their own career plans. Their awareness of these issues and the strategies being adopted are described in Chapter 14.

13

EFFECTS ON SENIOR AND MIDDLE MANAGERS

Senior managers

In a time of rapidly changing markets, an industry sector as conservative as the retail financial services sector requires a new blend of administration, management and leadership skills in order to survive and prosper. Corporate transformation requires a shift in emphasis from administration to management and leadership. For many companies, especially if they have been successful in the past, the transition can be very difficult. Many senior managers are more concerned with the status quo than change and transformation. Yet this kind of change is vital if financial services firms are to reflect the new business conditions, which require a new approach to risk, whilst at the same time maintaining their image as a safe place for people to invest their money.

> The industry is receiving two contradictory messages. It has to maintain its image of being safe, stable and conservative whilst being dynamic, entrepreneurial and flexible at the same time.
>
> (Focus group participant)

Senior management in the UK retail financial sector has been, and to a large extent still is, dominated by professionals from a particular industry sector, many of whom have spent their entire working lives in the same field, often in a single company. Although there has been some movement into the sector by outsiders, particularly at CE level, as seen at Barclays Bank, N&P, Sun Life over the past five years, it does not represent a widespread trend, as it is not easy and there is some resistance from existing senior personnel:

> Senior management tend to believe that the necessary skills do not already exist within the company and that there isn't time to develop them internally. Bringing in new people from outside the company often to high levels has further destroyed the career path, trust and the old culture.
>
> (Focus group participant)

195

It is no easy task to change the skill structures of decades or even centuries. Dominant core skills are institutionally embedded and cannot be eliminated by regulatory or market change.

(Fincham *et al.* 1994)

Overall, senior management positions are still dominated by managers who have worked their way up within a particular financial service company. Recent research by Fincham *et al.* (1994) found this to be the case when they looked at the backgrounds and qualifications of senior managers in three Scottish financial institutions: in the Bank of Scotland, 7 of the 8 general managers were Fellows of the Institute of Bankers of Scotland; in Mutual Life, a large Edinburgh-based life and pensions company, 17 out of 29 senior managers on the executive were actuaries; in home and auto, a general insurer, of the 6 senior managers, 2 were from the Chartered Insurance Institute, 2 were chartered accountants, and 2 were from the Institute of Chartered Secretaries and Administrators.

The focus groups (see Appendix) identified six main changes which they believe characterise the changing role of the senior manager over the next decade (see Table 13.1).

Key issues on the changing roles of senior managers as characterised here are discussed next under two headings: Towards Leadership and Towards Information Coordinators.

Towards leadership

It has been argued that where radical transformation is the goal, an entirely new definition of the business is needed. This is not something that can be administered or managed, it must be led by a senior figure with a new and inspiring vision of the future of the company (see MIT90s research). Current senior management in the sector came in for considerable criticism in the focus groups for their lack of strategic direction, for example:

Table 13.1 Senior managers – changing roles 1990–2000

1990	2000
• dictatorial and autocratic	• more democratic
• tactical focus	• setting strategic goals
• no IT skills	• IT literate
• top of hierarchy	• information and people coordinators/ marketeers
• management	• key business drivers, visionaries
• filtered information	• able to deal with fragmented reporting

At a senior level in the industry, the majority of board members are not thinking strategically. Chief executives tend to prefer the routine or technical aspects of their work.

How can the next generation of leaders be developed? At the moment we have managers but not leaders. We need to get past one or two generations and drag in new leaders.

Criticism also emphasised the lack of suitable interpersonal, leadership and business skills, as indicated in this focus group comment:

Life companies are dominated by actuaries who have a very narrow view of the company and are traditionally poor at people issues. They cannot communicate with staff or motivate them – in the past they did not need to.

However, it was also recognised that the visionary, charismatic leadership style is not always appropriate or popular either. Where companies in the sector have brought in new visionary leaders to help transform their organisations, they have been heavily criticised by existing managers for their unwillingness to compromise, their single mindedness and, more importantly, their lack of sensitivity about when to go ahead or when to stand back and consolidate the gains made. Focus group members emphasised the need to avoid what one called the 'change junky syndrome'. Whilst making it clear that not every company wants or needs intense, charismatic leadership of this kind, they stressed the need for new qualities. Four main attributes were identified as essential indicators of appropriate leadership quality in senior managers:

- *conceptual abilities – handling cognitive complexity*
  The ability to create sophisticated mental maps of strategic and operational interrelationships over time; to conceptualise complex and ambiguous situations; to be comfortable when dealing with managerial dilemmas; to combine rational and intuitive knowledge.
- *well developed inter- and intra-personal skills*
  Interpersonal skills such as the ability to understand the feelings, attitudes and motives of others; persuasion skills to influence a wide range of people; mediation capabilities to resolve and defuse conflict. Intrapersonal skills embodied in a high-level of self worth and self belief; knowing one's strengths and weaknesses; physical and emotional resilience; capacity to reflect and learn from experience.
- *political sensitivity*
  In highly complex, dynamic organisations such as large financial services firms, a high level of political sensitivity is vital. This includes the ability to manage and influence both the formal and more importantly the

informal organisational networks, to understand the nature of power relationships and appreciate the need to establish alliances and build coalitions.

- *ethical consistency and professional credibility*
A person of principle – what is said is done; a track record of success in the particular field of professional activity and the respect of one's peer group.

Where the business environment is characterised by substantial and continuing change, middle and lower managers also need training and encouragement in leadership skills for team management.

Towards information coordinators

Managers at the most senior levels deal with unstructured problems and decisions which have a strategic impact on the future of the organisation. Poor decision-making at this level could be disastrous for the entire company – it demands great experience, knowledge, discretion and political skills and is heavily dependent on the ability to obtain and use valid information. The findings of Macleod and Jones (1986) are consistent with those of Moss-Kanter (1983) who found that much of the energy of successful executives was devoted to two main areas: *agenda setting* and *network building*. In gathering information to set their agendas effectively, senior managers rely more on discussions than on either executive information systems or computer reports and books or magazines. For them, the network of relationships throughout the organisation at all levels and with people in other organisations is of prime importance. At first they set broad agendas which become more and more specific and focused as they continuously sift information from this network. They do so by using their knowledge of the business to formulate specific direct questions rather than broad general questions, so that within their workday they need only ask a few critical questions to keep up to date.

Senior managers, who must coordinate the process of integration and the later stages of transformation require an understanding of the nature and value of the information that businesses create and use; of the technology infrastructure of the firm; of the needs and responses of the people who use the information and the technology; and of the ways the internal and external environments of the organisation influence its application. The influence of corporate culture, the values of senior management and their approach to corporate planning is key to the management of information technology and the organisational environments that support it.

Many organisations are finding that the transition to integration is hindered because of the complexity involved in defining and communicating the overall business vision, especially when rapid growth and diversification in the boom years has resulted in a wide spread of business activity. Rapid change, lack of information, lack of cross-functional expertise, culture gaps and sometimes inter-departmental rivalry make the task even more difficult.

Middle managers

Many pundits have predicted massive job losses amongst the middle management ranks. In 1991, Peter Keen in the USA predicted a 20 per cent reduction in middle management as a result of the delayering effect of information technology.

As well as coping with this kind of job insecurity, middle managers are expected to change their working practices very quickly. With this in mind, focus group members were asked to list key features which they believe characterise change in the middle manager's role in the current decade (see Table 13.2).

The changes identified for middle managers are discussed next under four headings: Fewer Traditional Middle Managers; Professional/Portable Skills; New Competences; Career Development.

Table 13.2 Middle managers

up to 1990	2000
• typically 10% of organisation	• far fewer traditional middle managers
• not well trained/low skills	• professionalisation e.g. MBA/highly skilled
• not portable skills – organisation specific skills	• more portable skills
• supervision/administration	• facilitator/coach/teamworker/business driver
• contribution difficult to assess	• performance assessment/no hiding place
• internal focus	• customer-focus
• limited decision making	• more responsibility/decision sharing
• clear career paths	• unclear career paths/no jobs for life
• titles	• no titles

Fewer traditional middle managers

Keen (1991) and others have argued that clerical workers have taken on much of the work previously done by middle management. This is changing the nature of middle management jobs and, at the same time, reducing the number of layers in the organisational hierarchy, a process known as 'delayering'. Of the many reasons put forward for this reduction in managerial jobs, the following have had the most impact:

- clerical workers are assuming more responsibility and taking over much of the routine decision making formerly done by supervisors and managers;
- the use of integrated systems, company-wide databases and modern communications networks cuts out duplication, improves integration and facilitates information sharing between departments and various levels in the hierarchy;
- the use of Management Information Systems provide aggregated data formerly provided by middle managers.

In his paper, 'Information Technology and the Service Class', Child (1986) discusses various factors that affect the extent to which information technology threatens the employment and work content of managers. Among the most important factors identified by Child were the nature of the task; strategic location in the workplace; and the nature of the service relationship. The effect of the first factor, the nature of the task, on managers has been discussed in Chapter 10. The second and third factors have major implications for the changing roles of middle and senior managers. Middle managers in charge of routine core operations, for example, administrative managers in charge of policy processing in an insurance company, are in a weak position to resist job changes driven by technology. In contrast, senior managers are hardly affected, for while IT can be of value to them, it cannot yet take over their key function, that of making balanced judgements based on incomplete data using their own intuition, expertise and experience.

Those who provide a direct service to the client are less at risk of technological displacement than those who are concerned mainly with processing information, organising work schedules, etc. For example, accountants whose work once involved a large element of bookkeeping now find that clients expect a complete business service. In addition to understanding the technicalities of cash flow forecasts and balance sheets, accountants need wide business experience and good inter-personal skills for successful face-to-face negotiation with the client. Their work is now more advisory in nature.

However, the results of the Labour Force Survey (Warwick University, 1994) covered in Chapters 10 and 12, point to an increase in managerial jobs rather than a decrease. The HR3 survey confirms this view to a certain extent. For example in Table 12.2, the number of IT professionals increased from 120 in 1975 to 370 in 1995, and a whole new set of managers was required to manage them. As work in the financial services sector becomes more knowledge-intensive and team-based, there is need for more managers to coordinate the work of professionals and more highly educated clerical workers. However, they will require quite different skills to their predecessors who were managing in a far more structured environment.

Professional/portable skills

In the past retail financial services companies were dominated by managers who had worked their way up through the organisation. This has major benefits in that they got to know the company very well, but times are changing:

> Traditionally, we use the Hay grading system: up until five years ago the people who got to the top of their department did so through being there the greatest number of years; now increasingly people are being recruited into these positions from outside the company. Previously there was no formal training but more of a conveyor belt system, so you could arrive at a certain senior position regardless of whether you had the appropriate skills, knowledge, experience, etc. to do the job in question. This meant managers were often unsuitably qualified for the job of managing. Now professionals are being recruited from outside who have been trained up in another organisation. I think that this shows that the organisation is starting to value relevant qualifications more and focus on core competencies, getting the people with the right competencies to do the jobs which need those skills. And there will be a rapid rise in the number of professionally qualified managers, for example, people with MBAs, MSc in Management, or professionals who have obtained management qualifications.
>
> (HR director of a Top 10 life company)

Clearly, 'learning on the job' strategies are no longer enough and supplementary formal management training is deemed necessary. Recruitment policies now emphasise the possession of professional management qualifications or competences, and where this is lacking, suitably qualified candidates are brought in from outside.

New competences

Competences required by middle managers will vary, and will have much in common with those required of senior managers. They include information coordination, leadership, and inter-personal skills so vital for a successful facilitator, coach, teamworker and mentor. The need to update business skills continually is especially important. Advocates of performance measurement argue that the use of assessment against objectives techniques will reveal the lack of such skills. Participants in the survey argued the need for a blend of old values and new competences in times of rapid change, and stressed that the methods of achieving an appropriate blend must be chosen carefully:

The company is only just starting to identify what it wants from its managers, and to identify the competencies they need to develop. They have spent a lot of time working on the identification of competencies and thus the type of manager they will need to take us forward. These managers will be different from previous managers who were generally people just moving through the system. The company acknowledges a need for more risk-takers, yet senior management must accept the implications of this, and the organisational culture will need to change to accommodate this. If risk-takers are recruited and senior management refuse to accept the risks they want to take, this is bound to lead to conflict – any new model within an organisation requires a painful transition from old culture to new.

(HR director of a Top 10 life company)

Companies have to handle the introduction of managers with new ways of doing things carefully. It is important to have management teams with an appropriate blend of skills – it is no good having a company full of risk-takers and entrepreneurs. In the transition phase, many long-serving managers find they cannot adapt and leave. Fortunately, in our case, this kind of skill depletion has been kept to a minimum and has been balanced by the introduction of fresh ideas from new people, some of whom, in the past, might not have reached a management position.

(Senior manager, major UK bank)

In order to implement any changes successfully, the commitment of these people was essential and the management therefore had to overcome the negative and defensive attitudes of the customer services personnel. At this point the organisation offered managers over the age of fifty the chance to leave on favourable terms if they felt that they could not accept the changes that were to be implemented, and around one quarter of them chose to go. As a result a new breed of managers was brought in, some of whom would not have qualified for this promotion in the past because the hierarchy would have demanded that they should have attained a certain level first. The new management included more women, and the attitude was less risk-averse and more exciting, in keeping with the changes in the sector overall.

(Head of Training and Development, Top 10 life company)

Career development

Restructuring to produce flatter hierarchies results not only in job losses for traditional middle managers but also in fewer opportunities for promotion and career development. This presents serious problems for both employee and employer. When layers of command are removed, the few remaining levels are further apart, and differences in job specifications at each level are much greater. It will obviously take longer to acquire the higher level skills and competencies required for promotion to the next grade, opportunities are fewer, and competition is stronger. Many employees become discouraged because they can see no obvious route to follow in terms of their individual career development, and high flyers, impatient for recognition of their skills, are tempted by offers of better prospects from employers who prefer to poach rather than train their own staff. Thus employers, who invest in training, run the risk of losing this investment unless they offer some kind of interim reward which encourages loyalty.

To avoid this situation arising, management will need to find ways of refocusing organisational culture on the acceptance of new kinds of reward and greater personal responsibility for career development. Many companies now stress that individual employees must take more control of their own career development plans.

Employees are advised to aim to guarantee their employability in the field, if not in the particular company and role in which they are currently employed, by continuously updating their skills on a broad front and maintaining a keen awareness of alternative opportunities.

Conclusion

The MIT90s research highlights the role of senior managers in altering entrenched beliefs and organisational cultures to achieve successful transformation.

However, in most of the companies interviewed, senior managers are still concerned with maintaining the status quo and ensuring that change is relatively gradual. Although their view is that the best way to retain the loyalty and trust of their customers is to focus on a safe, conservative image, current competitive pressures also demand a more dynamic, flexible and entrepreneurial approach. Companies need senior managers with the new competences described here, but also with the ability to combine the best of the traditional/conservative and the flexible/dynamic approaches to managing business growth.

The current senior management focus is on the traditional remedies usually applied in a mature industry sector: rationalisation through mergers and acquisitions, major downsizing and overhead reduction. This combined with further automation will result in a shrunken industry sector dominated by relatively few companies. Rationalisation is occurring over a ten-year period and senior managers are being rewarded for hastening the process. What is not so apparent is whether or not these organisations are building their strategic capability as defined by Quinn (1989) (see Chapter 1). To do this involves a leadership style which:

- capitalises on the combination of improved connectivity and improved organisational knowledge;
- gains the cooperation and commitment of the workforce through the integrity of their aims;
- ensures that jobs are not so tightly managed that individuals and teams have space to innovate or time to think and reflect.

Some of the IT competencies required are being built up as highlighted in Chapters 7 and 8 to enable the creation of new information businesses. Most now have executive team members who are familiar with the potential of IT, and include an IT professional at senior management level. They have experience of piloting new businesses using the latest technologies; of setting up new strategic information alliances whilst retaining the status quo. However, it is difficult to build up organisational competencies when the workforce is tightly controlled and overworked and when trust has been broken through continual downsizing. Without this kind of strategic capability it is hard to see where new business growth is going to occur and how new replacement jobs can be created.

The trend to greater knowledge-intensity is fuelling the demand for better qualified managers with experience and skills in information coordination, mentoring, and leadership. It was clear from the in-company interviews that there has been a reduction in the number of traditional middle managers. However, there has been an increase in 'managerial type jobs' as measured by the Standard Industrial Classification (SIC). This trend, which is also apparent in many other sectors of the economy, is being driven by a number of factors, as discussed earlier, but may be distorted to some extent by changing job definitions within organisations. For example, in the health service ward sisters are now nurse managers, and generally all members of self-managing teams have 'managing and coordination' featuring in their job descriptions. Both the SIC and the traditional workforce classifications used by large companies are clearly outdated as jobs are more frequently redefined to accommodate complex changes in the nature of the work.

Over drastic reductions in experienced personnel at all levels particularly at middle management level can have an adverse effects on business, in terms of loss of corporate memory, reduced sales and lower levels of customer satisfaction. Many companies interviewed were losing talented middle managers who were either taking early retirement, redundancy or being poached by competitors.

14

EFFECTS ON MOTIVATION
AND REWARD SCHEMES

The MIT research (1991) highlighted flexible human resource practices as one of the essential requirements of organisations wishing to succeed in business transformation. This chapter examines the ways in which organisations are changing and developing new strategies to motivate their employees. It outlines the views of respondents and focus group members on the changing nature of the psychological contract. It looks at the effects on motivation, and the need for alternative career paths and opportunities for self-development to support continuing employability and rebuild loyalty and trust in corporate governance. It examines retail financial services firms' efforts to introduce new forms of remuneration and performance management systems.

Changing the psychological contract and creating new career paths

The 'psychological contract', a concept first defined by the organisational psychologist, Chris Argyris in 1960, describes the outcome of the ongoing but partially hidden process of negotiation and renegotiation between employee and employer concerning performance and rewards. It is to do with forming a relationship where exchanges between those involved are characterised by some degree of trust and loyalty. Most of the terms negotiated are implicit, resting on the value of assumptions about the future as well as on what actually happens as the career develops. Although this leaves the situation ambiguous, the psychological contract is real in the sense that both parties expect tangible results after the potential of the relationship has been explored and confirmed in the early phases of employment.

With the trend towards flexible labour, the idea of a lifetime career in a single organisation and even in a single occupation becomes unrealistic, and the reality of short-term contracts with explicit terms of commitment must be faced by both parties. It is argued that in today's modern workplace there are only three basic rules, and these reflect the change from guaranteed employment to guaranteed employability (see *The Economist*, 28.10.95). These rules are as follows:

- no company can guarantee a worker a job for life;
- the most important asset for both worker and the company is knowledge;
- as technology and working methods change ever more swiftly, a worker continually needs to learn new skills.

In organisations that have recruited and retained staff on the strength of their commitment to long-term employment, sudden and massive job cuts amongst all ranks have had a devastating effect on the confidence and motivation of those who remain. Generous redundancy payments have failed to revive morale, and in many cases have had the effect of encouraging the most talented, those with tradable skills, to leave first.

Almost all focus group participants agreed that the terms of the psychological contract were being eroded in their organisations. Having seen friends and colleagues made redundant overnight from apparently secure jobs, the trust they had in the implicit promise of long-term employment in return for unswerving loyalty had evaporated. This is giving rise to increasing indignation and lowered morale. In certain sectors, for example, retail banking and life assurance, the clerical workforce has been subject to the most wide-ranging and profound change.

The retail financial services has in the past attracted people who want a safe, secure job for life, but today this is no longer on offer, as made clear by this leading life assurance and pensions company:

> In this firm, the breaking of the psychological contract over the last few years has caused an immense and painful culture change. The organisation has existed for around 170 years and for 165 of those the culture of the organisation has been highly paternalistic, providing a career structure, health care and other benefits. Employees joined the organisation with a view to remaining with it for the whole of their working lives, and the company encouraged this viewpoint. Now the ethic is very different, and it is made clear that 'you're only as good as your last decision' and it is expected that most employees will stay for around five years.
>
> (HR director, large, traditional life assurance company)

Many members of the focus groups, disconcerted by deep levels of demoralisation amongst clerical staff in their organisations, felt that the rapid pace of change was leading to chronic inertia and lack of commitment:

The typical clerical worker is a demoralised individual in an industry in crisis. There is widespread inertia – resistance would be better and easier to cope with.

Even where commitment and loyalty were strong, constant change and the lack of reward for sustained effort had undermined motivation. One focus group member, an assistant bank manager quoted a typical response from a long-term, extremely capable and loyal employee in customer services, an area where staff numbers, mostly experienced people, had been cut by 20 per cent. Struggling to learn new systems, and constantly being urged to improve quality, this employee, having reached a peak of exhaustion, finally admitted serious misgivings about her position and future with the firm:

This is just too much! Even if I get over all these problems and do a really good job, what is the point? They've not just cut the staff, the chances for promotion just aren't there any more!

The assistant manager felt that too much reliance on self-motivation and too little appreciation of loyalty and effort had affected morale at the bank, and was beginning to affect the performance of the most capable and committed front-line staff:

The unwritten contract has been broken at this bank. What do you replace it with? Managing your own career may be OK for managers and professionals, but what about the vast bulk of employees who are clerical workers? How do you motivate them?

The trend is leading to a hardening of attitudes in both the individual employee and the organisation:

At the moment job security is more of a liability than an asset to the firm.

(Personnel director)

The employment contract reflects the reality of what I expect from my company, no more, no less.

(IT professional)

Increasingly, employees measure their loyalty to the firm and match it to the rewards on offer; their loyalty to their craft or profession becomes a priority. They look for ways to guarantee their 'employability' in the field; they update their skills continuously on a broad front; and they maintain a keen awareness of employment opportunities in other firms and in other areas.

In view of this change in attitude, how do employers retain or rebuild the

loyalty and trust of their employees? Although our survey revealed an awareness of the dilemma and slightly more emphasis on opportunities for development, it found few, apart from some leading-edge firms, had made much
progress in establishing alternative incentives. A scheme, devised by one that
had, is summarised in the Case 14.1 at the end of this section. The survey
results on staff motivation and non-cash incentives, and key issues on the shift
from 'guaranteed employment' to 'guaranteed employability' are discussed
next.

Motivation and non-cash incentives: survey results

Our survey questionnaire asked respondents to rank five main ways of
increasing staff motivation – job security, opportunities for career development, opportunities for personal development, promotion, and pay increase –
in order of importance on a scale from 1 to 5, where 1 is the most important.
The results are summarised in Table 14.1.

It will come as no surprise, at a time when people are looking for some
certainty in an uncertain world, and need to finance long-term commitments
such as mortgages, that 'job security' is regarded by most employees as a
priority. It is rated by questionnaire respondents as being the main motivating
factor for the bulk of their employees. Promotion and pay increases have
lower ratings than opportunities for development.

Participants were also asked to indicate which non-cash incentives they
offer as rewards for good performance and to rank them according to effectiveness in their organisation as shown in Table 14.2. The responses indicate
that most of the companies taking part in the survey are pursuing fairly
unimaginative ways of motivating employees. The non-cash incentives
ranked 1 and 2 require only minimum levels of effort and are the kind of
schemes that any company should be running as a matter of course. Whilst
secondments and work-related courses are used by over a quarter of the
respondents, other effective ways of motivating employees through the provision of personal development opportunities, for example, non-work-related
courses, giving people time off either as a sabbatical or extra holidays, are
rarely used. Initiatives which encourage creativity, for example, the freedom
to pursue personal projects for say 10 per cent of the time, as practised in
some research companies in the pharmaceutical sector, are increasingly
important at a time when competitive success depends more and more on
innovation, yet not one company in the sample claimed to have made any
headway in providing this kind of opportunity.

Further in-depth interviews with HR specialists from a mixed sample of
firms revealed a range of perspectives on motivation which reflect a growing
understanding of the issues concerning job insecurity and a new focus on
employability. Some argue that loyalty engendered by job security rarely
motivates exceptional performance, and that the provision of opportunities

Table 14.1 Staff motivation

Sources of staff motivation	Ranking
Job security	1
Opportunities for career development	2
Opportunities for personal development	3
Rise in status – promotion	4
Pay increase	5

Table 14.2 Use of non-cash incentives

Non cash incentives	% Companies using NCIs
Team event/social function	63
Employee of the month	44
Secondment	33
Work-related courses	25
Extra holidays/time off	16
Non-work related courses	8
Sabbatical	0
Freedom to pursue one's own projects in company time	0

for self-fulfilment, based on an understanding of the psychology of the individual, is the best focus for motivation:

> Job security is not necessarily a motivator and will not necessarily encourage people to perform better. If it did, it would have been the most successful bank for 300 years. What motivates people to perform well is challenging work, clear expectations and the feeling of being accountable and receiving regular feedback. . . . As I see it, most people are motivated by being able to compete, being rewarded when they do well, being given interesting things to do and the odd perk. Motivation is a question of finding out what makes the individual tick and finding ways of eliminating what doesn't.
>
> (HR director, a Top 3 retail bank)

Whilst some described an ideal and had a clear view of a new employment contract, they acknowledged difficulties in putting this into practice in a mutually beneficial way in firms which have grown to maturity with traditional loyalties and rigid hierarchies:

> Organisations should be looking more towards providing individuals with a rewarding career, fair pay, interesting jobs and projects and

development opportunities because the individual is looking to develop transferable skills; employees look on the employment contract as a transactional one, they are selling their skills in return for increased employability. A system whereby personal growth and development is the main motivator can be implemented and people could be better equipped to take control of their own careers but this is difficult in a formerly paternalistic organisation.

(HR manager, a Top 3 building society)

Others focused on the tensions that arise due to the influence of peer pressure on motivation when people work in teams. Job security is then more closely linked to team performance and team loyalty, and appraisal, motivation, and the decision to dismiss become team responsibilities:

The new contract between employer and employee at present seems to be based on discretionary effort for discretionary reward. This is the new organisational ethos. Previously you did not have to motivate people in this way because you could afford to offer job security even if it meant accommodating poor performers. It is now the case that there are teams of people working together within the organisation and if there is one low performer, the other employees are not prepared to 'carry' him/her. It is not always easy, however, for the management style to deal with this.

The degree to which this shift of responsibility for job security is a form of 'empowerment', or a new and disguised form of managerial control will influence the behaviour of the team and the quality of the business decisions it makes. Management must take care to find ways of ensuring that team loyalties focus on the best interests of the firm as well as those of the group of individuals who make up the team.

From employment to employability

In a period of major restructuring, with no guarantees for secure employment, what measures are organisations adopting to retain or rebuild the loyalty and trust of their employees so that they are motivated to perform well?

As layers and costs are cut in organisations, there is less emphasis on job security and motivating employees through upward promotion or incremental pay. With fewer levels of command, the difference in job specifications and skills at each of the remaining levels is much greater. It takes longer to acquire the higher level skills and competencies required for promotion to the next grade, opportunities are fewer, and competition is stronger. Many employees become discouraged because they can see no obvious route to follow in terms of their individual career development, and high flyers, impatient for recognition of their skills, are tempted by offers of better prospects from employers who prefer to poach rather than train their own staff.

Without some kind of interim or alternative reward which encourages loyalty and trust, the risk remains and this kind of attitude persists. Some firms in other sectors have started initiatives based on career planning, and the development of new career paths, where horizontal moves also confer status and where there are opportunities for self-development and job enrichment. The aim is to enhance employees' prospects of 'continuing employability'. This promises some chance for security in the wider labour market, if not life-long employment in the firm. However, success depends on being able to change perceptions of reward, and on honesty and openness about intentions.

Some of the leading-edge firms in the retail financial services sector are adopting this stance with training policies which aim to benefit both sides and which encourage individuals to take charge of their own career development plans, for instance:

> In terms of encouraging commitment in staff, today's employee must accept that there is no such thing as job security. The company also accepts that staff will move on, and strives to raise the standards of the industry as a whole by developing efficient, good people who can then take their skills to other organisations. Staff are given every opportunity to develop their current roles within the organisation and in ways which will benefit their future positions.
>
> (HR director, a Top 10 life company)

Individual employees in retail financial services are advised to take more control of their own career development plans. With the loss of job security, HR strategies which help staff to develop skills valued in the wider labour market have a positive effect on motivation, and can help to rebuild loyalty and trust.

New forms of remuneration

This section examines employee attitudes to PRP, and outlines the progress made by retail financial services firms in introducing PRP schemes and flexible pay structures which recognise individual differences. It summarises the pros and cons of different pay and grading systems, and the critical success factors. It includes responses from a number of leading-edge firms participating in the survey to illustrate the importance they attach to the new approaches they are adopting, as well as their concerns about the need for more effective and fairer ways of measuring performance.

Performance-based rewards

In many sectors today, the emphasis on performance, rather than years of service as a basis for reward, is driving the development of new kinds of reward systems based on more flexible pay structures. These include, for example, individually negotiated contracts, performance-related and profit-related schemes, employee participation schemes, and employee share ownership plans.

Survey participants reported that performance against objectives (80 per cent) and company performance (53 per cent) are the major factors in determining the size of pay increases. Only 7 per cent continue to use length of service in pay determination, while 30 per cent use cost of living. Performance-related pay schemes are now fairly well embedded in the financial service sector, for all categories of staff, as part of a drive towards greater competitiveness. More than two-thirds of managers, professionals and clerical staff are covered by performance-related pay schemes, typically introduced around the turn of the decade.

A non-executive director of a leading building society, a former HR practitioner with wide experience, stressed the point that PRP schemes take time to implement:

> The problem with some HR practitioners and line managers is that they introduce something like performance-related pay and expect a pay-back in the following year in terms of performance or behaviours. This is nonsense, the introduction of such pay schemes, when supported by sound performance management, takes three to five years as part of an integrated strategy. But if the mix is right then the pay-back can be significant in terms of increased staff focus on the key business issues, greater involvement of staff in the business, increased staff performance and changed behaviours.

Our survey found a number of organisations which had based their approaches to performance-related pay on business-focused performance management schemes. In these firms, performance and reward frameworks are designed to support business objectives and PRP forms a key component of the overall HR strategy. They felt that this approach to PRP contributes strongly to promoting the values of the organisation, focusing staff on the key measures and rewarding success.

Performance-related bonus

Nearly half of respondents reported operating bonus schemes for some of their staff, 40 per cent operate them for all staff. As with salary increases, the most important determinants of bonus payments are individual performance against objectives and company performance.

> There are a number of bonus schemes in place to support the business goals. Bonuses are decided upon subject to a personal grading process based on measuring performance in comparison with the individual's previous performance rather than hierarchical comparison with other workers.
>
> (HR manager of a general insurance firm)

The primary reasons respondents gave for operating bonus schemes were to provide incentives, to reward and motivate performance, to allow employees to share in company profits and to contain payroll costs.

Team working and performance-related pay

Twenty per cent of respondents have team-based bonuses and a further 10 per cent indicate that these are under consideration. This reflects a growing interest in the area of team-based remuneration as organisations in the sector seek ways of reinforcing and supporting team-based working methods.

> The team bonus runs on the understanding that if you can run your business unit at a lower cost whilst retaining the same, or greater, level of customer service, this will generate money which is then paid to the team as a bonus. Therefore there are various financial incentives to provide quality service and encourage teams to support the business goals.
>
> (HR director of a Top 10 life assurance plc)

Team-based pay is not sufficient on its own to encourage effective team work. However, an organisation's approach to pay provides powerful signals about how employees are expected to work. Where team working is important, the pay system should support its principles and values. Only one company in the survey had introduced team-based pay.

Case 14.1: Team-based, performance-related pay

This company introduced team-based pay in early 1993. A recent Institute of Manpower Studies survey on team-based pay (August,1994) found that most companies wanted to manage performance-related pay in a team context but only 4 per cent of companies were actually doing so – we were one of them. It has been well received here but it is recognised that individuals can be dragged up or down by the system and there is an element of unfairness in that. A high performer in a high performing unit will do better than a high performer in a low performing unit where the bonus is lower. Despite this it is generally perceived as fair and ensures that team members make more effort to work together as a team. Communications between them improve dramatically. On average every customer holds four insurance policies, and team work facilitates the development of customer-based rather than policy-based relationships. Customer-based work allows customers to have a single point of contact for all their insurance business. Here, policies are bar-coded so that the organisation can measure the productivity of individual teams. MORI conduct customer service reports on our behalf and bar-coding allows each customer response to be traced to a specific team.

The trend towards flexible pay structures

More and more companies in the retail financial services sector are moving towards the introduction of fewer, more flexible pay bands, and a few have either introduced individually-based salaries or are seriously contemplating it. The trend is especially evident in investment banks, financial advice and management consulting firms with a high percentage of professionals. Figure 14.1 illustrates the shift that is occurring as companies downsize, become more knowledge-intensive and entrepreneurial.

As the trend towards performance-based criteria has developed, individualised contracts have become more common for a wider range of managers and professionals, not only the 'star' performers or leading experts with exceptional talents. Many salaried professionals are now eligible to receive substantial performance-based earnings, such as commission on sales or merit bonuses, as a 'top-up' to their performance-related basic salaries.

Advantages and disadvantages of different pay and grading schemes

There are advantages and disadvantages to each of the differing schemes outlined above, as summarised in Table 14.3.

Most retail financial services companies, wishing to recognise individual differences, have moved, or are moving, towards flexible pay bands and benefits:

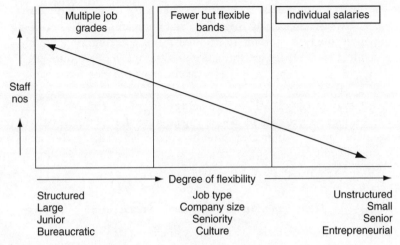

Figure 14.1 Multiple job grades vs. individual salaries.
Source: KPMG 1995.

Table 14.3: Job grades, flexible bands or individual salaries?

	Multiple job grades	*Fewer but flexible bands*	*Individual salaries*
PROS AND CONS	• Recognition steps • Internal relativities • Ease of control • Reference for external comparison • Promotion necessary to fulfil ambition • May drive wrong behaviour • Inflexible/ bureaucratic • Tied to hierarchy	• Suits flatter structures • Wide reward/ differentiation • Decreases grade fixation • Scope for growth within job • Limits personal recognition • Difficult to manage salary • Progression/internal relativities • Job sizing may be difficult	• Maximum flexibility • Maximum reward for performance • No recognition of hierarchy • Difficult to manage consistently • No public recognition • Can be inflationary

Source: KPMG, 1995.

Flexible benefits will be the key. This will encourage greater acceptance of the pay package and better staff satisfaction and greater job satisfaction. The biggest barrier at present is systems support, not just IT support. Satisfaction tends to vary from person to person. The company believes that the best way of satisfying people is to satisfy them that they are doing a good job and this can only come from customer feedback.

(HR director of a major composite insurer)

215

The organisation needs to recognise the value of each individual separately, acknowledging their skills and competence. It is becoming increasingly important to recognise the contribution of each individual to company performance as all employees are different.

(HR manager of a major retail bank)

They feel that this approach to managing rewards is consistent with the broader business objectives of flatter organisational structures with fewer management layers and greater 'empowerment' of staff. It also helps in facilitating more flexible deployment, allowing employees to develop along faster career streams.

More emphasis on performance management

Performance management is an approach which tries to integrate the management of human resources into the organisation's wider strategic goals by translating them into personal goals for individuals and groups of employees (see Mabey and Salaman, 1995).

Models of performance management generally describe a cyclical, iterative process with five phases – setting objectives, measuring performance, feeding back results, setting rewards, and amending objectives and activities; and the concept is underpinned by two theories of social psychology; expectancy theory, and goal-setting theory (see Figure 14.2).

Accordingly, a performance management framework or system must identify appropriate goals; provide information on how far the objectives are being met using appropriate measures; must include a means of auditing the process links, that is checking that the links between effort and performance and between performance and rewards are valid; and must have procedures for continuous review of the system itself. It is recognised that the current model of performance management and the theories which underpin it are based on assumptions about a level of rationality in decision making which rarely exists in practice. In designing a performance management system, difficulties commonly arise in the following key areas:

- *Setting goals*: it is not always easy for the company to identify clear strategic objectives, especially in times of rapid change.
- *Measuring performance*: there is a tendency to choose performance dimensions that are easy to measure, but many aspects of good performance, especially with regard to customer satisfaction and service, are difficult to measure in objective terms. Objective, quantitative measures need to be relevant, easily understood, free from external influence and manipulation, and cheap to collect. Subjective, qualitative measures require rigorous procedures to eliminate bias.
- *Rewarding performance*: managers must understand what motivates their

Expectancy theory	Goal-setting theory
(Galbraith and Cummings 1967; Vroom, 1964)	(Locke 1968; Mento *et al.*1987)
Individuals expect that:	Goals should be:
<ul><li>their performance will lead to a measurable outcome (expectancy);</li><li>the outcome will be rewarded in a given way (instrumentality);</li><li>the reward will be satisfying (valence).</li></ul>	<ul><li>specific;</li><li>demanding but attainable;</li><li>accepted as desirable by employees;</li></ul> Feedback on performance in attaining the goals should be available.

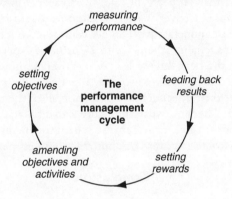

Figure 14.2 The performance management cycle.
Source: Based on Mabey and Salaman 1995.

staff before they can decide upon effective rewards, and since people vary so much in terms of intrinsic and extrinsic satisfactions, a range of rewards based on defined needs, subject to continuous review, is desirable.

- *Process links*: the links between effort and measured performance and between measured performance and reward must be clear to the employee. He or she must perceive that they are valid, that the performance and the rewards are attainable and achievable in ways that make sense to them, whether the performance management system uses a set formula or management discretion to determine the level.
- *Performance feedback and system review*: employees need feedback on their performance and advice on how improvements can be made – honesty and openness are crucial; the performance management system itself must be subject to review and amendment so that the strategic objectives and the means of achieving them are aligned.

Current research in other sectors is gathering evidence of a wide range of contextual factors, such as culture and values, type of organisation, structures, type of work, etc. which influence the effectiveness of performance management. Mabey and Salaman (1995) use some of these findings to explore the level of complexity which may need to be addressed when designing performance management systems, in their recent book *Strategic Human Resource Management*.

Performance management: survey results

Most respondents to our survey believe that their efforts in performance management form a very important part of their corporate HR strategy. The results show that 70 per cent rated performance management systems linked to corporate objectives as a very significant part of HR strategy and 20 per cent rated it as a moderate part. 86 per cent of respondents already have a performance management scheme with a further 10 per cent planning to introduce one in the next three years. Whilst overall, more than 50 per cent of companies rated them as *successful*, and 10 per cent as *very successful*, the rest had doubts about their effectiveness in meeting all of the objectives listed in the questionnaire. The most worrying figure is that only 10 per cent regarded their current performance management scheme as being *very successful* in achieving the key objective, that of improving business performance.

Conclusion

Many retail financial services companies, in the early stages of corporate transformation, are breaking the 'psychological contract', and as a result employees are dissatisfied. There is considerable danger that they will become demotivated and that firms will lose many of their best performers at a critical stage. Critics of the 'psychological contract', as it existed, liken it to a 'dependency culture', and argue that it has to be replaced with a new culture which says 'my job is safe as long as the whole company is successful'. The levels of distress observed make it clear that some new kind of 'psychological contract', which clarifies responsibiities and expectations, needs to be found. Experience in some companies suggests that an alternative based on the provision of opportunities for both personal and career development would be acceptable to both sides. As yet companies are only slowly introducing new human resource policies which support this kind of initiative. Performance-related pay is being introduced in the sector but companies are having considerable difficulty getting it to work and almost all pay is still based on individual results rather than team effort.

The risks of the shift towards tighter control have to be considered more carefully. In cases where there is an over stringent drive towards flexibility, there is clear evidence that it is leading to a loss of flexibility in terms of competencies, corporate memory, organisational learning and commitment. The knock-on effects on strategic capability could be serious.

CONCLUSION

This conclusion has two sections. **Section 1: An overview of the research findings** summarises the survey findings under the headings: **Technology** and **New organisations**. **Section 2: Transformation: an analysis** discusses transformation under the headings: **Phases of business transformation; The transformation process** and **Mindset**.

This study analyses business transformation in the sector by reference to a number of models which have their roots in rational planning/information processing theory, in particular, Venkatraman's business transformation model and Galliers' stages of growth model. Like all models they have their limitations. Doyle (1991) argues that most are unidimensional and simplistic and therefore fail to capture the dynamic nature of the interaction between the organisation, competition and technology. He warns of the danger of frameworks becoming 'cages' which force both the researcher and the user to think in one particular direction and to adopt predetermined classifications. Others, such as Farbey *et al.* (1995), argue that their strategic focus neglects operational and implementation issues which are the manager's main concern.

Although they have weaknesses, the models used in this study also have considerable strengths. They are based on years of in-depth research by teams of leading academics and provide a synthesis of their work. They offer valuable high-level ways of explaining key strategic developments clearly to both academic and management audiences and in so doing they create a bridge between theory and management practice. In particular they are useful in that they offer a 'big picture' perspective, an overview of the way an industry sector is developing. They provide a starting point for strategic analysis, a way of cutting through the complexity to develop greater understanding. Treacy (1986) puts the continuing popularity and endurance of such models down to the fact that they are 'more powerful than competing language systems for describing elements of the research.' In other words they are one of the most effective ways of explaining abstract theories and concepts to the practising manager. However, it is clearly important never to lose sight of the fact that the model used can never fully describe the 'rich picture' and that it is merely a tool, one of many tools to aid understanding.

Section 1: an overview of the research findings

Technology

In the 1970s and 1980s the retail financial services had followed a predictable trajectory, with all companies in the same subsector adopting similar technologies, and with different companies taking the 'pioneer role' at different times. In the past, the favoured position of most companies was that of the 'fast follower', that is, one where the technology is introduced only after it is proven by the pioneers who run the risk of the costly first-time user mistakes. As the case studies in Chapters 5 and 6 illustrate, most firms in the retail financial services sector are still following a well defined path based on proven, if older technologies. Companies have made massive investments in existing systems, and IT staff have built up their expertise over decades to support them, consequently, it is not surprising that the introduction of new technologies is gradual. The integration stage is being achieved with a combination of old and new technologies. The Foresight Programme report makes clear that there are several key trends occurring which make this strategy potentially dangerous, for example, client-server architecture, which allows companies far more flexibility and better price/performance, enables new companies and new entrants to cherry-pick profitable parts of the market.

Over the past decade the large centralised IT departments have changed gradually. They are becoming more decentralised, they are more customer- and business-focused, and they are being managed by professionals with a clearer understanding of both the business and IT issues. They are being managed in a more sophisticated manner with a wider range of strategies to suit the problems encountered. For instance, some are using a mix of over-head, cost centre and outsourcing strategies to manage the IT portfolio in the most cost-effective way; some are setting up federal type structures which aim to maintain a balance between centralisation and freedom for decentralised business units to develop individually. The IT department is taking on an advisory role as well as gaining considerable experience of new technologies in parallel start-up firms.

Senior managers are experimenting with information partnerships, as illustrated by the Origo case studies in Chapter 8. They are gaining experience of new technologies both through pilot schemes and through setting up new, parallel companies, often in competition with their own core businesses. Although such initiatives exist they are not widespread and, overall, their efforts are still mostly devoted to maintaining the existing technology.

The stages model put forward by Galliers and Sutherland (1991) offers useful guidance on the way the IT functions of large retail financial services organisations have developed up to the last five years. Most of the companies surveyed have characteristics which match those described in Galliers and

Sutherland's Stage 5, with some moving into Stage 6. The key changes in Stage 5 relate to the membership, knowledge, expertise and experience of the senior management team. Most now have executive team members who are familiar with the potential of IT, and an IT professional at senior management level. They have experience of piloting new businesses using the latest technologies; of setting up new strategic information alliances whilst retaining the status quo; and of a wide range of more sophisticated IT management strategies, such as the use of outsourcing.

The overall impression is of mainly large, relatively slow-moving organisations taking a long time to achieve the integration stage with old technology, but with senior managers who are gaining appropriate and valuable expertise in managing IT. Their current approach is based on planning major technological changes over a long period of up to ten years; gaining experience of new technologies through pilots and new, parallel companies; developing information partnerships to ensure the company is well placed to take advantage of radical new technologies, such as the Information Superhighway. The main danger of this approach is that, EITHER new entrepreneurial companies, using the latest technologies, will move in to compete aggressively in profitable areas, OR companies which have in-depth expertise with the new technologies such as client-server and the Information Superhighway, will go straight to the final customers, bypassing financial institutions such as the banks altogether.

New organisations

The evidence presented in Part IV, on the changes companies are making to their organisational structures and the effects on job roles and human resources policies, suggests that they are also adopting a gradual approach to the creation of a flexible, knowledge workforce. Although the process may be described as gradual, it is neither smooth nor even. As with all processes which involve learning to deal with new situations and developing new skills and attitudes, mistakes are made and setbacks must be overcome. The shift from hierarchies of command and control to one of empowerment involves changing organisational cultures, management attitudes, and employee perceptions. This takes time, careful management, and an awareness of the differing assumptions held by the stakeholders, that is, all those with an interest in the outcome both inside and outside the organisation.

The tendencies observed in the companies surveyed are consistent with the view that organisational change is iterative, cyclical, and driven by a wide range of processes, some of which are often unconnected and uncoordinated; that it is influenced by inconsistent assumptions about intentions, implementation, and interpretation; and that sometimes progress can be attributed to unplanned coincidental factors. However, as Van de Ven (1988) points out, the 'cumulative effect' of these very different kinds of change may result in radical transformation for the organisation.

Mabey and Salaman (1995) stress the need to be alert to the unintended consequences which may provide valuable learning opportunities. They cite the example of a medium-size insurance company (Kerfoot and Knights, 1992) where it was found that senior management strategy and rhetoric about 'team spirit' had less real impact on teambuilding than the slow incremental change negotiated at team level, amongst team members, and the incidental recruitment of mature and experienced entrants, whose positive influence resulted from their personal initiative to ease the transition by taking on, what was described as, a 'matriarchal' leadership role in the early stages.

This does not mean to suggest that change can be left to chance, rather it strengthens the argument for an integrated approach to strategy formation, one based on continuous review, analysis of results and adaptation, and one which is flexible enough to cope with a range of unforeseen variables and outcomes.

Although the nature of the changes revealed in the HR surveys indicates uneven progress, there is clear evidence in the sector of a definite movement in each of the following three areas:

The development of new organisational structures

Analysis of the 1995 survey findings on organisational change in four key areas – the shift from hierarchical to flattened structures; from function and procedure orientation to process-orientation; from control to empowerment; and from administrative-focus to customer-focus – indicates that change in the majority of the large companies participating has been slow and evolutionary. This comment from the chief executive of a major bank illustrates the kind of thinking behind this approach to change:

> It is clear that the numbers employed will decline, but the trick is not just to replace jobs with machines but to redesign the whole business, to do it gradually over time so that it creates as little pain as possible.

Although progress has been slow, flexible organisations with fewer layers of command, greater customer-focus, and multiskilled clerical workers are beginning to emerge.

Companies are slowly becoming more knowledge-intensive but there are massive pressures driving the industry to fragment. Their responses take the form of three generic strategies which focus on activities categorised by Silvestro et al. (1992) as 'professional services, service shop, and mass services' (see Chapter 10). Each approach needs very different organisational structures. Reference to Mintzberg's (1979) model of organisational structures suggests that it is likely that the 'professional services' firms will be pulled towards the professional bureaucracy or adhocracy type structure whilst the 'mass services' firm may be drawn towards a combination of a machine bureaucracy for the clerical staff who remain after downsizing, and a professional bureaucracy for the IT specialists running the IT infrastructure. However, since the 'service shop' is where most of the future employment opportunities will be, it is the current focus of concern for HR directors. The distinguishing characteristic of the 'service shops' is the provision of relatively low-level advice by technician-level individuals.

The development of new skills for new roles

Four key features of the flexible firm – unclear lines of authority; teamworking; closer customer contact; and knowledge-intensity – have a profound impact on working practices and skills. To survive in such organisations, all employee groups – clerical workers, professionals, middle and senior managers – require new skills. Although each group will have different skill needs, the HR surveys highlighted the growing importance of generic and transferable skills for maintaining employability and adaptability in the face of continuing change. Those who recognise this need for new skills, are redesigning training and development programmes so that they are:

- more focused and tailored to the needs of particular teams or individuals;
- linked to an external standard (57 per cent of companies are pursuing the 'Investors in People' award);
- linked to the company vision statement and to the overall communications strategy;
- integrated with the performance management system.

However, despite their efforts along these lines, many of the companies interviewed expressed concerns about the scale of change and the training needed. It is estimated that up to 40 per cent of the workforce will not be able to develop these new skills, nor adapt to these new structures. There is a danger of a massive skills imbalance developing.

The development of new HR policies to motivate the workforce

In a period of major restructuring such as this, when there are no guarantees for secure employment, organisations must find new ways of retaining or rebuilding the loyalty and trust of their employees so that they are motivated to perform well. The findings of the surveys undertaken suggest that some progress is being made, but that most employees feel that there is a long way to go before their needs are met.

Focus group interviews (1994–1995) with a cross-section of employees from the sector, revealed that the 'psychological contract' – loyalty in return for secure lifetime employment in the firm – has been broken. Human resource departments now face the difficult task of replacing the old contract with a new one which reflects the change from guaranteed employment to guaranteed employability. Few of their current initiatives, for example, non-cash incentives and career management schemes, are sufficiently developed, as yet, to make up for the loss of traditional job security.

The response from employees and HR professionals to the use of performance-related pay (PRP) was mixed: some thought it was divisive, others thought it had been very successful. HR respondents stressed that the changes needed to get PRP working properly took a long time; most cited three or more years. PRP schemes are now fairly well embedded in the sector with more than two-thirds of managers, professionals and clerical staff covered by them. The survey found that half the respondents were operating performance-related bonus schemes; 20 per cent have team-based bonuses; and only 2 per cent had introduced team-based PRP. Companies are also introducing more flexible pay schemes with fewer but more flexible bands.

Although almost 90 per cent of the companies have introduced performance management schemes, they too have had a mixed response. Half the respondents thought they had worked well and half thought they had limited value. The most telling figure was that only 42 per cent thought that their scheme had been successful or very successful at improving business performance. The two biggest criticisms were that:

- they are based on flawed or incomplete theories which try to simplify and mechanise human behaviour, and cannot accommodate the complexity and unpredictability that actually exists;
- they are too bureaucratic and have developed into a form-filling ritual which diverts effort away from more fundamental solutions, a pattern described by Senge as 'shifting the burden'.

Until these issues are resolved it is difficult to see how the process of change can be accelerated to meet employers' expectations.

Section 2: transformation: an analysis

Phases of business transformation

Since the research began, the focus of concern of the large companies which dominate this sector has been the first two stages of transformation: localised exploitation and integration of IT. Back office automation and the introduction of customer information systems which occurred in the banking sector in the early 1990s are examples of this focus. Case CL1 illustrates the major changes which occurred as a result of introducing such systems, including wholesale branch closures, major job reductions, the redefinition of the clerical role and a reduction in the tiers of management.

Case CL1: A major UK bank (1992/93)

The introduction of customer-based systems in this bank has been accompanied by major restructuring which involved wholesale branch closures. Before this system was introduced, it would have been impossible to close branches without losing a large number of customers. Much of the processing was done by hand at the branches and branch closure would have meant immediate loss of processing capacity and customer links:

> In the past we could not merge branches because of our back room operations. Now fortunately we are not 'making a motor car' in the back of every branch; new technology has killed these paper factories.
>
> Senior Manager

The introduction of customer-based systems at this bank was accompanied by regrading and the creation of a multiskilled clerical workforce in the branches. Prior to this, a bank customer, wanting a complete update of his or her current financial situation from a local branch, would be dealt with by perhaps five or more different clerical workers, one each for enquiries, overdraft, cheque book renewal, standing orders, credit card, paying in etc. Many of these activities were carried out manually and each was recorded on a separate policy-based system. With integration, this complete service can be carried out at one terminal by one clerk, working anywhere in the country.

Since a customer-based system can provide more information on each customer, it allows the banks to cut out several tiers of management and enables the remaining professionals and managers to concentrate on the fee earning part of their jobs. The introduction of integrated systems is also starting to redefine the clerical role with the clerical worker carrying out a wider range of functions.

Venkatraman stresses the importance of first successfully completing the evolutionary phase – automation and integration (Levels 1 and 2) – and building up the organisation's competencies before attempting to move on to the revolutionary phase. The competencies needed for revolutionary business transformation relate to new ways of doing business, the capacity to create fundamentally new products and services and the capacity to create new markets and eventually new industries. Organisations have to decide which of the three revolutionary options – BPR, BNR, BSR – are relevant or critical to their business.

The length of time required to achieve integration is often underestimated, as typified by a major Scottish bank where the process started in 1989 and predicted to end by 1997 has now been extended to the year 2000. This is not surprising when one considers the nature and scale of the changes required to develop the organisational competencies needed to tackle the revolutionary phase. The costs of integration are massive for these large, long established companies and because the timescales are so long there is a danger for some that the market and the technology will have moved on before full integration is achieved.

In most cases, Business Process Redesign (BPR) is only being introduced on a limited basis, as it is too risky for large, successful and well established companies to make the drastic changes required to achieve it over too short a period. New companies are being set up with BPR principles in mind but as yet they only represent a small, but growing percentage of the market.

Companies are piloting Business Network Redesign (BNR) initiatives to gain experience of information partnering. The evidence of the surveys suggests that the whole process of change, both technological and organisational, is being introduced in companies in the sector in a carefully staged and controlled way, as indicated in Table CL1.

Measures to phase in technology gradually over an eight to ten-year period are accompanied by measures to improve skill levels and encourage commitment.

As stated in the introduction, the term 'moving through stages or levels' is meant to signify the phased expansion of the focus of concern rather than a simple progression. As shown in Table CL1 and Table CL2, automation and integration will remain 'in focus' well into the next decade. As competencies are built up, for example, in information partnering, the focus will start to change. With the benefit of hindsight it is now possible to see that it would have been very difficult for companies to introduce full Business Process Redesign, as defined in Figure 5.1 (see Chapter 5), because the organisational competencies were not there. It will be several years before companies in this sector will be able to tackle BPR and BNR with a high chance of success and relatively low risk. But if and when they do, the 'second wave' of BPR and BNR will have a revolutionary effect on organisations and on the structure of the sector.

Table CL1 A phased approach to business transformation in the retail banking sector?

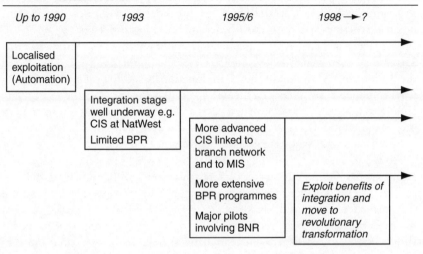

Up to 1990	1993	1995/6	1998 → ?
Localised exploitation (Automation)	Integration stage well underway e.g. CIS at NatWest Limited BPR	More advanced CIS linked to branch network and to MIS More extensive BPR programmes Major pilots involving BNR	*Exploit benefits of integration and move to revolutionary transformation*

Table CL2 A phased approach to developing the knowledge workforce

1990	1993–1995 *(Bristol University Survey Data)*	1998 ——> *Exploit benefits of integration?*
Peak of employment	Steady reduction of the workforce	*40% reduction in workforce*
Career managed by employer – guaranteed employment	Breaking the psychological contract Introducing structures for individual career management	*Employability, manage your own career*
Start of performance management schemes	Getting to grips with performance management	*Fully operational PMS*
Rigid pay structures	Steady introduction of flexible pay schemes	*Flexible pay structures*
Bureaucracy	Bureaucracy in transition	*Flexible organisational structures*

BPR is one of the more recent examples of an approach where its over-promotion as 'the right answer' and its use to meet the needs of the status quo in the short term rather than the fundamental long-term needs of the organisation have corrupted the original message.

Authors from the business process reengineering school, such as Davenport and Short (1990) and Hammer (1991), vigorously promoted the idea that the key to radical change and transformation was to replace rigid, hierarchical structures based on outdated business procedures, with new horizontal, flexible structures based on cross-functional business processes.

The fact that the BPR consultancy industry has become big business with a $50 million turnover in 1995 is indicative of the popularity of these ideas and the promotional activities of the IT multinationals and the media. It offered a way to reduce costs, increase efficiency, and make more effective use of new technology. Since it was concerned in part with basic procedures it seemed to offer an operational, rather than strategic focus which appealed to action-oriented managers whose main concern was cost-cutting.

However, Hammer and Champy (1993), two of the main protagonists, estimate that 50 to 70 per cent of organisations' BPR initiatives did not achieve the kind of dramatic results expected. This perceived level of failure (less than dramatic results may also be seen as evidence of partial success) indicates that BPR, as it has been practised, is very risky and that proposed BPR initiatives (and other change initiatives) need to be evaluated more in terms of balancing benefits and opportunities against risks.

Although the original BPR message had empowerment and job satisfaction at its heart, it is argued that it became distorted in its application by power groups in the organisation who used it to achieve their own short-term interests and goals (see Mumford, 1996). For some, the claim that restructuring and delayering would strengthen their organisation's chance of survival in the predicted global market provided an appropriate excuse for downsizing. It gave them the chance to cut costs, improve productivity and share price almost at a stroke through redundancies and expanded job descriptions. The long-term consequences, particularly the negative effects on motivation and morale and on organisational capability were ill considered. Staff, who are so tightly controlled, so focused, so overworked and so anxious about job security, as many are in organisations that have downsized to the absolute core, do not have the time, commitment or the motivation to maintain and develop the qualities that Quinn (1989) describes as essential elements of the organisation's strategic capability – sensing, awareness and responsiveness. The emphasis on using BPR to manage the short-term risks results in a much more serious long-term risk of damage to employee commitment, corporate memory and organisational capability.

Enid Mumford (1996) explores the theme of risk in relation to BPR initiatives in the paper 'Risky ideas in a risky society'. She describes the sequence of events which led to the distortion of the original BPR message; Deevy's (1995) claim that re-engineering consultancies had given poor advice which was causing irreparable damage to healthy organisations; Hammer and Champy's (1995) defence of their original thesis; and Davenport's (1996) which concluded:

As is always the case with any fad, there was a kernel of truth to reengineering. Over time that truth got lost. But that doesn't make it any less true. The most profound lesson of business process reengineering was never reengineering, but business processes. Processes are how we work. Any company that that ignores its business processes or fails to improve them risks its future. That said, companies can use many different approaches to process improvement without ever embarking on a high risk reengineering project . . . When the Next Big Thing in management hits, try to remember the lessons of reengineering. Don't drop all your ongoing approaches in favour of the handsome newcomer.

(Davenport 1996)

Mumford argues that BPR was presented to managers as a solution to the perceived threat of global competition, and that the inherent risk in the BPR idea itself only became apparent when they tried to introduce it for short-term gain. Since the global market hypothesis itself is now questioned and the idea of the 'open international economy' is advanced instead, the risk of the BPR idea for those with a short-term focus has turned out to be greater than the risk or problem it was meant to solve. The implementation of new ideas brings with it the risk of over dependence on experts and on groups with vested interests whose distortions, unintended and deliberate, create new and unexpected risks in their wake. These risks clearly need to be understood and balanced against the benefits sought.

Edwards and Peppard (1994), in a paper entitled: 'BPR: hype, hope or hypocrisy?' provide a critique of BPR initiatives studied over three years. They identified six main approaches to BPR each with a different focus: information technology; delivering business strategy; quality; operations; human resources; creating a new [parallel] organisation. They draw a clear comparison between BPR and other main change philosophies: TQM and JIT, based on a continuous and incremental approach; and simultaneous engineering, time compression management, like BPR, based on radical change. They conclude that in spite of the hype and hypocrisy that surrounds BPR, the fundamental principles are sound. They expect the name will die out but the kind of questioning and organisational rethinking it has inspired – 'Davenport's kernel of truth' – will live on. They also point out that the benefits of BPR may take more time to appear than anticipated in some organisations; and that more than one attempt is often necessary (feedback from partial success + commitment will eventually lead to success); and that the long-lived model of change: unfreeze, change, refreeze (Lewin, 1951) is counterproductive when what is needed is a new model based on 'unfreeze, change, then create a state ready for more change'. Or to use the terminology currently used in the popular change management literature, a state where a 'new mindset' can develop, thrive and continually challenge convention.

The transformation process
Integrating change across the organisation

The surveys provide evidence of a movement towards integrated approaches to IT management and organisational change and away from the kind of isolated initiatives that featured in the financial services sector in the 1980s.

These findings are consistent with the views of Murray and Willmott (1997) who also found evidence that organisations are entering a period where there is a convergence of structural, technological and cultural change strategies and that networking – linking systems, different technologies and people – is enabling this convergence:

> It is possible to detect a gradual shift in each of these three directions of organisational change that is indicative of a more holistic, strategic orientation to organisational transformation in which the dimensions are increasingly understood to be interlocking and independent.
>
> (Murray and Willmott 1997)

The integration of previously separate areas of organisational knowledge enables further innovation in product and service development which stimulates further change in the competitive environment. It is this combination of improved connectivity and improved (integrated) organisational knowledge which supports the transformation.

In persisting with a gradual, iterative process of strategic alignment of information systems, process capabilities, culture, human resources and control systems, the retail financial services sector is gaining the kind of experience and cross-disciplinary knowledge that makes this kind of convergence or integration possible.

Part II of this book has described how new information technologies are affecting the basis of competition in the financial services sector. Companies from very different sectors, such as retailing, telecommunications and manufacturing, have acquired the necessary core competencies (through their development and use of customer databases, improved customer interfaces, and information systems) to enable them to move into the financial services sector. Similarly, core competence development in the formerly separate sectors of retail banking, insurance and mortgage lending, has enabled their coming together, leading to wholesale rationalisation of the sector.

Parts III and IV illustrate how companies are moving to a position where the integration of organisational knowledge is leading to the emergence of new organisational forms. Our findings indicate that the length of time needed to achieve this kind of integrated organisational transformation is likely to be far longer than the management gurus are currently predicting.

CONCLUSION

Smoothing and speeding the process of change

The research findings indicate that the approach to strategy formulation in the retail financial services sector is still based on the rational analytical model and that strategy implementation is still incremental and evolutionary, as in the 1980s, but that the process is somewhat smoother. To use Handy's metaphors, the 'learning wheel' is turning faster; the 'lubricants of change' are being developed and applied. Experience and experimentation with a range of initiatives, particularly those which highlight the iterative and continuous nature of organisational learning, and the active participation of workers in redesigning structures, jobs and roles, has been especially important in raising awareness of the human and cultural issues which hasten, or hinder the change process. They are helping to smooth or lubricate the process of change.

The big danger of the evolutionary, incremental approach is that the organisations which proceed steadily, building up the core competencies may be overtaken by others making strategic leaps. It may be a great advantage to be a late-comer, not only can they avoid the mistakes that the pioneer organisations make, but they may be able to surpass them in effectiveness. Being unencumbered by the need to link new systems with older, incompatible ones, they are able to introduce the latest technologies and management techniques, new organisational structures and a more skilled workforce(as illustrated by the Direct Line case study on page 78) much more quickly.

However, the advantage of learning from the mistakes of others and of being able to introduce new systems 'cleanly' may be outweighed by another consideration. It may be that pioneer organisations, by learning from their *own* mistakes, and through longer experience with IT, may acquire certain capabilities based on tacit knowledge which cannot be easily transferred between organisations or generally reported in the field:

> Typically however, skipping portions of the model can only be successfully accomplished when senior management of the organisation have already experienced the conditions that effect performance in the earlier stages and thus understand the benefits/ advantages of following correct procedures.
>
> (Galliers and Sutherland, 1994)

In other words late-comer organisations which leap-frog older organisations in terms of techniques and technologies acquired may suffer from difficulties of implementation and ineffective use by not having the accumulated capacities of pioneer organisations. For example, at the moment many organisations which have moved to PC-based systems have discovered that control systems, of the sort developed by central IS functions around mainframes, are still required.

The other danger faced by companies adopting the incremental approach is that we are in a period of major technological discontinuity as represented by client-server architectures and the Information Superhighway. The explosion in the use of inter-organisation networking via the Internet, and the use of video discs for compact storage of data are examples of technological break-throughs which are driving progress in sudden surges (discontinuities) rather than steadily continuous advances. The convergence of computing and tele-communications poses major threats to the financial services sector. Compa-nies with a large customer base can use the emerging telecommunications and computing technologies as a cheap way of moving in on the financial services domestic market. So, for example, British Telecom's 'video on demand' should not just be seen as an attempt to provide an entertainment service but an attempt to master a critical new technology, a technology which has many more uses than that being considered now. In view of the size of BT's customer database, the potential is very wide indeed.

The overall picture is of an industry which is restructuring in a managed, orderly and logical manner. Low skilled staff are being laid off at around 5 per cent a year; companies are moving into new high-value areas, creating more professional and knowledge-intensive jobs; BPR is being introduced cau-tiously; and new parallel companies, based on BPR principles, are being set up in a whole range of new, higher value activities. BNR pilots are being implemented and a wide range of new information-based services are being established.

The retail financial services sector is part way through a ten-year restruc-turing initiative. Evidence from the surveys suggests that this is being carried out in a phased and controlled way. The major doubt about this strategy is whether they are moving quickly enough, as companies from a wide spec-trum of activities (for example, Microsoft – software services, Ford – car manufacture, BT – telecommunications, Marks & Spencer – retailing) already have sufficient expertise to use converging technologies with their existing customer bases to take huge chunks of this market. The key question remains – will the retail financial service sector be able to develop the kind of foresight and core competencies needed in time to set in motion a process which will achieve transformational change without the kind of crisis usually generated by revolutionary tactics? Or as Hamel and Prahalad (1996) have phrased it 'a transformation process that is revolutionary in result but evolutionary in execution.'

Mindset

Although the main aim of this study is to describe key changes in the financial services sector over the past decade, it can offer some comment on the wider debate about the emergence of the information economy. Since the publica-tion of the work of Bell (1974) and Porat (1977) there has been considerable research effort by economists, geographers and policy analysts to demonstrate the existence, importance and growth of an 'information economy'. This concept has been heavily promoted by governments in the industrialised countries with, for example, the USA, European and Japanese governments publishing labour statistics which reinforce the view that a large and increasing portion of the working population is involved in generating, recording, processing and transmitting information – the so-called information or knowledge workers. Writers such as Drucker and Masuda put forward the view that the 'information economy' is leading to unprecedented social and organisational changes. For example, in Drucker's (1988) article 'The coming of the new organisation', IT is identified as central in the process of transformation and radical change and he predicts that within twenty years the knowledge-intensive organisation will be the predominant organisational form.

The retail financial service sector, which is an information-intensive service industry, is one of the sectors where many of these changes will manifest themselves if the predictions prove to be true. The survey findings reported here seem to confirm some of the views of writers such as Drucker and Scott-Morton that there is a direct link between investment in new technologies and the creation of more knowledge-intensive organisations. Employment is moving, if slowly, to 'service shop', 'professional' and 'knowhow' companies of the kind described by Silvestro, and Sveiby and Lloyd. Clerical workers are becoming more multiskilled and carrying out more complex work; the number of professionals in companies is growing and their expertise is being leveraged; management is becoming more 'professionalised'. However, it should be noted that the current SIC definitions of clerical worker, associate professional, professional and manager are also clearly inadequate as categories to describe the differing kinds of knowledge worker. We agree with Bloomfield et al. (1997) on the need for far more precise definitions and for more critical evaluation of the concepts underlying the information economy.

Lyon (1988) points out that the current tendency for uncritical adoption of many of the basic assumptions and definitions which support the notion of an information economy, causes us to miss out on the deeper questions. For example, whilst much work has been done on changes as they relate to job content and apparently new categories of work, there is relatively little research on deeper issues such as their effects in shifting or strengthening the current basis of power.

As pointed out in Chapter 11, there is little evidence of the clerical workforce being informated and empowered, an essential feature of the predicted transformation, rather they are expected to learn more and do more in less time. Similarly, the professional workforce is also expected to develop a whole range of new skills and competences whilst being subjected to unprecedented levels of insecurity and stress and to intrusive control of their expertise. The number of traditional middle management jobs are being cut, as teams are trained to become self-managing, though the cuts have not been as ruthless as was predicted, apparently because organisations are concerned about the possible detrimental effects on organisational memory. There is little evidence of the 'fostering of trust' which writers, such as Webber (1993), regard as essential if there is going to be a sustained shift towards networked forms of organisation. The 'evangelical zeal' of much of the work on the 'information age' needs to be seriously challenged and qualified before rhetoric can be translated into reality. Our findings in the UK retail financial services sector confirm this cautionary note.

As we have seen, the methods used to introduce and manage IT in the sector are rooted in the rational analytical strategic planning and information processing schools of thought. The assumptions underlying this perspective are that problems can be analysed and broken down into their component parts and rational solutions can be devised and imposed on the organisation through managerial action. This approach tends to reinforce the current business paradigm where managerial action, driven primarily by the profit motive, supports the vested interests of the current status quo and power structures. Organisational transformation programmes have typically included major downsizing, overhead reduction and process reengineering with an emphasis on management processes to strengthen control and coordination. Concentration on such measures is increasingly regarded by many management theorists, for example, Pascale (1991) as a potential recipe for industrial extinction. They argue that the kind of thinking needed to shape and transform the futures of our organisations requires a new business paradigm or mindset to challenge the old traditions and cultures which permeate organisational activity today.

Short-term cost-cutting strategies such as 'downsizing' or 'rightsizing' will achieve little of lasting value unless there is parallel investment and coordinated effort in establishing long-term, but flexible strategies for development and growth.

The level of coordination and integrated effort required to benefit from flattened management structures, process-orientation, empowerment, and customer-focused systems has been underestimated, as a number of firms have found to their cost. In some cases over-drastic downsizing and delayering resulted in loss of corporate memory, reduced sales, and lower levels of customer satisfaction, and firms have been forced to re-employ experienced staff.

Stephen Roach of Morgan Stanley, argues that the pendulum is due to swing back from capital to labour and warns that:

> The slash-and-burn restructuring is not a permanent solution. Tactics of open-ended downsizing and real wage compression are ultimately recipes for industrial extinction . . . If all you do is cut, then you will eventually be left with nothing, with no market

share . . . If you compete by building, you have a future: if you compete by cutting you don't . . . At the end of the day, you can create wealth only if you've got a corporate sector that has its act together and takes a long-term strategic point of view . . . The debate itself is a healthy one. It goes to the core of what it takes to compete and boost standards of living. Do we get there by growing? Or – which is what we've been doing – by hollowing out companies?

(Stephen Roach of Morgan Stanley, *Independent on Sunday*, 12.5.96)

It is clear from the survey that some firms in the UK retail financial services sector recognise this point of view and perhaps have also glimpsed a future where employees, customers and shareholders will require assurances on corporate goals, ethics and responsibilities.

APPENDIX

Research methodology

Research approach

In a comprehensive review of academic research on the relationship between information technology and organisational structure over the past 40 years, Sampler (1996) makes several important points on the nature of research in this particular area.

He points out the need for research which:

- uses composite methods which both detect changes over time, for example, survey data, and those which try to follow and understand how these changes occurred, for example, case studies;
- takes into account the growing view that IT and organisation structure mutually influence and constrain each other. If this view is taken longitudinal or event studies research are a necessity;
- encompasses whole organisations as opposed to small parts of the organisation 'if one wants to make statements about the organisation as a whole then one must study information systems that impact on the whole organisation. There is a danger of studying small customer ordering systems for example and generalising to the whole organisation';
- which takes into account the changing nature and variety of information technology. IT capabilities have changed rapidly over the last 40 years and it is therefore very difficult to generalise from one form of technology, for example, the early mainframes, to current technologies such as the Internet.

When this study was first envisaged in the late 1980s there were very few academic surveys which focused on one sector of the economy, for example, the financial services sector, and which used composite methods over a period of time, which encompassed whole organisations, and which tried to take into account changing technologies. The research upon which this study is

236

based is attempting to do this over a ten-year period (1990–2000). This book covers the first five years of the research and the issues that are emerging as we approach the next five years.

Established researchers in the field argue a case for combining different research methods to obtain results which can be cross-validated, and meaningfully interpreted and generalised, for example, Fincham *et al.* argue that:

> Organisational research is particularly well suited to composite methods. Complex processes of organisational change are best suited to using a blend of data from multiple sources such as interviews, documentary evidence and survey data.
>
> (Fincham *et al.* 1994: 38)

The research methodology adopted for this study was designed with this in mind. It uses a number of approaches, including the traditional survey, and these are listed below:

- questionnaire surveys to obtain a strategic overview of the key trends;
- interviews to provide more detailed comments;
- focus groups so that information can be discussed in depth;
- case studies to illustrate key issues;
- secondary data analysis, for example, IT periodicals and journals, company documents, academic papers.

It makes use of action research involving an iterative process which constantly monitors the effectiveness of the approach adopted over a period of time and uses the feedback to improve it continuously. The surveys which provide the data for this study are being conducted over a long period, ten years in total, and the results are being fed back to practitioners in the form of publications, seminars and discussion meetings. This gives additional opportunities for respondent validation of the findings. The results are then used to improve further the relevance and focus of the research. So far seven practitioner research papers have been published and over 300 practitioners have attended the research seminars.

This approach has four key stages:

- carry out the research using the methods listed above (questionnaire survey, interview, case study, focus groups, and secondary data analysis);
- publish practitioner research paper;
- conduct interactive research seminars where results are challenged and discussed; also present case study material etc. to mature MBA students working in management positions in this sector for further discussion and feedback;
- review hypothesis to focus on key issues.

Key surveys

This study is based on the findings of a series of ongoing surveys which started in the late 1980s. The findings are supplemented by feedback from on-going senior management teaching at MBA level (as part of the Lombard scheme), by current consultancy and through the use of focus groups to obtain current views. The technology surveys were sponsored by IBM and the Britannia Building Society. The human resources surveys were sponsored by KPMG. Each survey since 1989 has been reported in a separate publication. The surveys are described and the publications listed below:

Survey set 1: the technology surveys

Survey IT1

The main focus of this survey was the alignment of business and IT strategies, the changing role of the IT function, and the speed of introduction of new technologies. It was conducted in three parts as follows:

1   An interview survey with IT directors of major retail banks participating (1990).
2   A survey carried out between October 1989 and May 1990 which included 72 interviews with IT directors of a representative sample of life assurance, composite and general insurance companies. This was sponsored by IBM and resulted in the publication:

    'Focusing on Business Success: A comprehensive study of the changing use of IT in the insurance industry' (1990)

3   A survey carried out between February and May 1991 which included a questionnaire survey of 96 members of the Building Societies Association (60 per cent response rate) plus in-depth interviews with a representative sample of IT directors of building societies. This resulted in the publication:

    'Focusing on Business Success: A comprehensive study of the changing use of IT in the building society sector' (1991)

Survey IT2

This survey was carried out between October 1992 and Spring 1993 and was sponsored by the Britannia Building Society. The results were reported in the publication:

'Managing the Transition: A Comprehensive Study of the Changing Use of IT in the Retail Financial Services Sector' (1994)

The survey was conducted by questionnaire and interview. Questionnaires were sent to the chief executives and IT directors of 300 UK-based retail financial services companies including banks, finance houses, life insurers, general insurers, mortgage lenders, insurance brokers and estate agents. There were 112 individual responses from 74 different companies, most of which are amongst the largest companies in banking, insurance and mortgage lending. In-depth interviews were conducted with 22 senior managers to clarify issues arising from the questionnaires, partly to make up for a low response rate from the large composite insurers and to detail some typical case studies.

The sample represents a good cross-section of the largest UK financial services companies but lacks representation from the smaller and medium-sized firms. The sample profile is detailed below:

- The retail branch banking sector in the UK is dominated by eight major and a further five smaller banks as measured by total assets and operating income. Ten companies took part in the survey.
- In the UK life and pensions sector, the top 40 companies account for over 80 per cent of premium income. Twenty Life companies took part, 17 of these were from the Top 40.
- In the building society sector there are 83 building societies; the Top 20 account for 92.5 per cent of the total assets of all UK building societies. Seventeen took part, 12 of these were from the Top 20.
- In the general insurance sector, the Top 20 companies have 85 per cent of the market as defined by premium income and the top 50 have 90 per cent of the market. Seventeen took part, eight of these were from the Top 20 and seven from the Top 40.
- Respondents also included three of the largest retail chains of insurance brokers, three of the largest finance houses, two large chains of estate agents and two of the largest mortgage lenders.
- There were 22 interviews carried out with senior managers in five banks, four building societies, five general insurers, four life assurers and four miscellaneous.

Survey IT3: focusing on retail banking, a follow-up to Survey IT2

This was carried out during 1995 and involved following up companies who had participated in the 1992/3 survey to see how they had progressed. In particular it looked in depth at the retail banking sector. The retail branch banking sector in the UK is dominated by eight major and a further five smaller banks, as measured by total assets and operating income. Ten banks took part in the original survey in 1993, and an additional six banks were interviewed in 1995 to determine their progress with integration in terms of the stages described by Venkatraman's model. General trends are reported rather than details.

Survey Set 2: human resources surveys

The main focus of this set of surveys has been to map changes over time in the following areas: the strategic role of HR, organisational structures, career development, new skills and performance management. Three surveys have been carried out so far and resulted in three practitioner publications.

Survey HR1

A survey carried out during 1991 which included a questionnaire completed by HR directors in 80 major UK retail financial services companies plus interviews and group discussions. This resulted in the publication:

'HORATIO: A survey of human resources ratios in the UK retail financial services sector' (1992)

Survey HR2

A survey carried out during 1993 and 1994 which included a questionnaire completed by HR directors in 70 major UK retail financial services companies plus interviews and group discussions. This resulted in the publication:

'HORATIO II: A survey of human resources practices in the UK retail financial services sector' (1994)

Survey HR3

This survey was carried out during 1995 and 1996 and was funded by KPMG Management Consultants and Bristol Strategic Publications. This resulted in the publication:

'People and Performance: A survey of HR issues in the Retail Financial Services Sector' (1996)

Total sample: 45 participants including 11 building societies and 1 mortgage lender. This represented:

- Six of the Top 10 building societies/mortgage lenders, a further three of the next ten, and two smaller building societies. Three of the Top 10 building societies were interviewed.
- Seven of the Top 12 retail banks took part, and interviews were conducted with two banks.
- Five of the Top 12 general insurers took part plus three others. One interview was carried out.
- Ten of the Top 20 life assurers plus a further three smaller companies took part in the surveys. This was the sector where most change was expected; five were interviewed.
- Two finance houses, three independent financial advisers and one major estate agency chain also took part. There were no interviews in this sector.

Focus Groups: 1994 and 1995

In addition six focus groups were run:

- Four on the changing competences of the retail financial services workforce. These were run as part of an MBA course for managers in this sector.
- Two on corporate transformation in the sector. These were run in collaboration with the Tavistock Institute.

Each focus group was made up of between 15 and 30 participants.

REFERENCES

Andersen Management Consultants (1988) *Changing Horizons for Insurance.*

Applegate, L.M. and Cash, J. (1991) Case Studies, Boston: Harvard Business School Publishing.

Applegate, L.M. and Cash, J. (1991) *GE Canada: Designing a New Organisation*, a case study for Harvard Business School (9): 189–38, Boston: HBS Publishing Division.

Association for Payment Clearance Services (APACS) (1993–1995) various research reports.

Association of British Insurers (ABI), *Quarterly Statistics and Research Review* (7), October 1995; and (8), January 1996.

Barker, R.T., Camarata, M.R. and Wen, J. (1997) 'Developing long-term strategic relationship advantage: a conceptual approach for transnational learning alliances', paper for SEMS 2nd International Conference, published in *Dynamics of Strategy*, University of Surrey, April: 55–74.

Barron, I. (1994) 'Systems Demographics', Section B in OST, H., Downing, (Ed) 'The Demographics Roadmap: IT & Electronics', Technology Foresight Programme, OST, August.

Bell, D. (1974) *The coming of post-industrial society: a venture in social forecasting*, Harmondsworth: Penguin.

Benjamin, R.I. and Blunt, J. (1992) '*Critical Information Technology Issues: the next ten years', Sloan Management Review*, Summer.

Bhabuta, L. (1988) 'Sustaining productivity and competitiveness by marshalling IT', Conference proceedings 'Information Technology Management for Productivity and Strategic Advantage', IFIP TC – 8, Open Conference, Singapore, March.

Bloomfield, B.P., Coombs, R., Knights, D. and Littler, D. (1997) *Information Technology and Organisations: Strategies, Networks, and Integration*, Oxford: Oxford University Press.

Brady, T., Cameron, R.,Targett, D. and Beaumont, C. (1992) 'Strategic IT issues – the view of major investors', *Journal of Strategic IS*, 4 (1) September.

British Banker's Association (BBA) (1995) Annual Abstract of Banking Statistics, Statistical Unit, BBA, London.

Cash, J., McFarlan, W. and McKenney, J. (1992) '*Corporate Information Systems Management: The Issues Facing Senior Executives*, Homewood, Ill.: Irwin.

Caulkin, Simon *et al.* (1991) 'The New Manufacturing' in 'Business Process Management', *Office 2000 Series*, Wang Laboratories Inc.

Central Statistical Office (CSO), The UK Service Sector, spring 1995.

Checkland, P. (1995) *Systems Thinking, Systems Practice*, Chichester: John Wiley & Sons.

Child, J. (1986), 'Information Technology and the Service Class' in the *Changing Experience of Employment*, London: Macmillan.

Churchill, N.C., Kempster, J.H. and Uretsky, M. (1969) 'Computer-based Information Systems for Management: A Survey', National Association of Accountants, New York.

Couger, J.D. (1982) 'Evolution of system development techniques' in Coufer, J.D., Colter, M.A. and Knapp, R.W. (eds), *Advanced System Development/Feasibility Techniques'*, New York: John Wiley.

Coulson-Thomas, C. (1988) 'The New Professionals', The British Institute of Management.

Council of Mortgage Lenders (CML) (1995) Research Summary, September.

Currie, W. and Willcocks, L. (1996) 'New Branch Columbus Project at Royal Bank of Scotland: the implementation of large-scale business process re-engineering', *Journal of SIS*, (5): 213–36.

Cyert, R.M. and March, J.G. (1956) 'Organisational factors in the theory of oligopoly', *Quarterly Journal of Economics*, February: 44–64, in Friedman, A.L. with Cornford, D.S., 'Computer Systems Development: History, Organisation and Implementation', John Wiley and Sons: Chichester.

Davenport, T. 'Why reengineering failed: the fad that forgot people', in *Fast Company*, premier issue, pp 70-4, January 1996.

Davenport, T.H. and Short, J.E. (1990) 'The new industrial engineering, IT and business process redesign', *Sloan Management Review*, 31 (4): 11–27.

Deevy, E. (1995) 'Get rid of experts not workers,' *The Boston Globe*, 24 October.

Doyle, J.R. (1991) 'Problems with strategic information systems frameworks', *European Journal of Information Systems* 1 (4): 273–80.

Drucker, P. (1969) *The Age of Discontinuity*, London: Heinemann.

Drucker, P. (1988) 'The coming of the new organisation', *Harvard Business Review*, January–February 45–53.

Drucker, P.R. (1991) 'The New Productivity Challenge', *Harvard Business Review*, September–October 69–79.

Earl, M.J. and Skyme, D.J. (1992) 'Hybrid managers – what do we know about them?', *Journal of Information Systems* 2 (3).

Earl, M.J. (1986) 'Information systems strategy formulation' in Boland, R.J. and Hirschheim, R.A. (eds), *Critical Issues in Information Systems Research*, Chichester: John Wiley & Sons.

Earl, M.J. (1989) *Management Strategies for Information Technology*, Hemel Hempstead: Prentice Hall.

Earl, M.J. (1994) 'Putting IT in its Place: A Polemic of the 1990s', in R.D. Galliers, and B.S.H. Baker, *Strategic Information Management: challenges and strategies in managing information systems'*, Oxford: Butterworth-Heinemann Ltd pp. 76–90.

Earl, M.J. (1996) 'Integrating IS and the Organisation: A Framework of Organisational Fit' in M.J. Earl (ed.) *Information Management: The Organisational Dimension*, Oxford: Oxford University Press, ch. 24: 485–502.

Eccles, R.G. and Crane, D.B. (1987) 'Managing through Networks in Investment

Banking', quoted by J.F. Rockart and J.E. Short in *The Corporation of the 1990s, Information Technology and Organisational Transformation*, Scott-Morton, M.S. (ed.) 189–219.

The Economist, (1995) 'Learning Organisations: Those who can, teach' 28 October 1995.

Edwards, B.R., Earl, M.J. and Feeney, D.F. (1989) 'Any way out of the labyrinth for managing IS?' in Galliers, R.D. and Baker, B.S.H. (1994) *Strategic Information Management: Challenges and Strategies in Managing Information Systems*, Oxford: Butterworth-Heinemann Ltd.

Edwards, B.R., Earl, M.J. and Feeney, D.F. (1996) 'Organisational Arrangements for IS: Roles of Users and Specialists' in M.J. Earl (ed.) *Information Management: The Organisational Dimension*, ch. 11: 231–46, Oxford: Oxford University Press.

Edwards, C. and Peppard, J.W. (1994) 'Business Process Redesign: hype, hope or hypocrisy?', *Journal of Information Technology* (9): 251–66.

Edwards, C., Ward, J. and Bytheway, A. (1991) *The Essence of Information Systems*, Adrian Buckley (ed.), Hemel Hempstead: Prentice Hall.

Employment Department (1991) 'The National Standard – Links to Assessment Indicators', Sheffield.

Ernst and Young (1994) 'Choosing the right path to virtual banking', Ernst and Young and American Banker Special Report on Technology in Banking.

Farbey, B., Land, F.F. and Targett, D. (1995) 'A taxonomy of information systems applications: the benefits evaluation ladder', *European Journal of Information Systems* (4): 41–50.

Farbey, B., Land, F. and Targett, D. (1995) 'IT Investment: A Study of Methods and Practice', London: Butterworth Heinemann pp. 122–33.

Fincham, R., Fleck, J., Procter, R., Scarbrough, H., Tierney, M., and Williams, R. (1994) *Expertise and Innovation: Information Technology Strategies in the Financial Services Sector*, Oxford: Oxford University Press.

Forrester Research Computing Strategy Report (1994) 'The new customer connection', September.

Fotinatos, R. and Cooper, C. (1993) Occupational Stress Survey, UMIST.

Friedman, A.L. with Cornford, D.S. (1989) *Computer Systems Development: History, Organisation and Implementation*, Chichester: Wiley.

Friedman, A.L. (1994) 'The stages model and the phases of the IS field', *Journal of Information Technology* (9): 137–48.

Gallie, D. and White, M. (1993) *Employee Commitment and the Skills Revolution: First Finding from the Employment in Britain Survey*, London: PSI Publishing.

Galliers, R.D. (1990) 'Strategic information systems planning: myths, reality and guidelines for successful implementation, *European Journal of Information Systems*, 1: 55–64.

Galliers, R.D. (1987) 'Information Systems Planning in the UK and Australia: a comparison of current practice', Zorkorczy, P.I. (ed.), *Oxford Surveys in IT*, 4: 223–55, Oxford: Oxford University Press.

Galliers, R.D. (1997) 'Business Process Re-engineering: The Fad that Forgot People', a paper for SEMS 2nd International Conference, published in *Dynamics of Strategy*, University of Surrey, pp. 1–13, April.

Galliers, R.D. and Baker, B.S.H. (1994) *Strategic Information Management: Challenges and Strategies in Managing Information Systems*, Oxford: Butterworth-Heinmann Ltd.

Galliers, R.D. and Sutherland, A.R. (1991) 'Information Systems Management and Strategy Formulation: applying and extending the stages of growth concept', in Galliers, R.D. and Baker, B.S.H. (1994) *Strategic Information Management: Challenges and Strategies in Managing Information Systems*, Oxford: Butterworth-Heinemann Ltd.

Gibson, C. and Nolan, R.L (1974) 'Managing the four stages of EDP growth', *Harvard Business Review* 50 (4), January–February.

Hamel G. and Prahalad, C.K. (1994) *Competing for the Future*, Boston Mass. Harvard Business School Press.

Hammer, M. (1991) 'Re-engineering work – Don't Automate, Obliterate', *Harvard Business Review,* July–August.

Hammer, M. and Champy, J. (1995) *Reengineering the Corporation: A Manifesto for Business Revolution*, New York: Harper Business.

Handy, Charles *The Age of Unreason* (1989) London: Hutchinson.

Harlow Butler Ueda Ltd (1992) *Butlers Building Societies Guide 1992: A Statistical Analysis of the Building Society Movement*, Hemmington Scott Publishing Ltd.

Hirschheim, R., Earl, M., Feeny, D. and Lockett, M. (1987) 'An exploration into the management of the information systems function: key issues and an evolutionary model', Conference proceedings, 'Information Technology Management for Productivity and Strategic Advantage', IFIP TC – 8, Open Conference, Singapore, March.

ICL's 'A Window on the Future' (1990) Massachusetts Institute of Technology's research programme: 'Management in the 1990s'.

Ireland, J. 'A Report to the Technology Foresight Panel on Financial Services', July OST (1994).

Johnson, G. and Scholes, K. (1989) *Exploring Corporate Strategy: Text and Cases*, Hemel Hempstead: Prentice Hall.

Kay, J. (1993) *Foundations of Corporate Success: How Business Strategies Add Value*, Oxford: Oxford University Press.

Keen, P. (1986) Rebuilding the Human Resources of IS' in *Information Management: The Strategic Dimension* M.J. Earl (ed.) Oxford: Oxford University Press.

Keen, P. (1991) *Shaping the Future*, Cambridge MA: Harvard Business School Press.

Kerfoot, D. and Knights, D. (1992) 'Planning for personnel – human resource management reconsidered', *Journal of Management Studies*, 29 (5): 651–68.

Kerr, S. (1989) '*The New Is Force*', Datamation, 35: 18–22.

Knights, D., Noble, F. and Willmott, H. (1997) 'We should be total slaves to the business: Aligning IT and Strategy – Issues and Evidence' in B.P. Bloomfield, R. Coombs, D. Knights and D. Littler, *Information Technology and Organisations: Strategies, Networks, and Integration*, 2: 13–35.

Kraft, P. (1977) *Programmers and Managers: The Routinisation of Computer Programming in the US*, New York: Springer-Verlag.

Kumar, K. (1995) *From Post-Industrial to Post-Modern Society: New Theories of the Contemporary World*, Oxford: Blackwell.

Land, F. (1996) 'The new alchemist: or how to transmute base organisations into corporations of gleaming gold', *Journal of Strategic Information Systems*, (5): 7–17.

Laudon, K.C. and Laudon, J.P. (1994) *Management Information Systems: Organisation and Technology*, New York: Macmillan Publishing, p. 513.

Laudon, K.C. and Laudon, J.P. (1994) *Management Information Systems: Organisation and Technology*, New York: Macmillan Publishing, pp. 222–23.

Lee, Sidney (1994) MBA Thesis on the changing role of the accountant in a retail financial services company, University of Wales.

Lewin, K. (1951) 'Field Theory in Social Sciences', New York: Harper & Row.

Lindblom, C.E. (1959) 'The science of muddling through', *Public Administration Review*, USA, (19): 82–8, Spring

Lyon, D. (1988) *The Information Society: Issues & Illusions*, Cambridge: Polity Press.

Mabey, C. and Salaman, G. (1995) *Strategic Human Resource Management*, Oxford: Blackwell Business.

Macloed, R. and Jones, J. (1986) 'Making Executive Information Systems More Effective', *Business Horizons*, September–October.

Martin, B. R. (1995) 'Foresight in Science and Technology', in *Technology Analysis & Strategic Management*, 7 (2): 139–68 Carfax.

Masuda, Y. (1980) *The Information Society*, Bethesda, MD: World Future Society.

McKersie, R.B. and Walton, R.E. (1991) 'Organisational Change', in *The Corporation of the 1990s: Information Technology and Organisational Transformation*, Scott-Morton, M.S. (ed.) USA: Oxford University Press.

McRae, H. (1995) in an article entitled, 'The Giants must learn how to roar', *Independent on Sunday*, 12 March.

Meiklejohn, I. (1990) 'Whole Role for Hybrid', *Management Today*, pp. 113–16, March.

Miles, R.E. and Snow, C.C. (1986) 'Organisations: New Concepts for New Forms', *California Management Review*, XXVIII.

Mintzberg, H. (1979) *The Structuring of Organisations*, Prentice Hall: Englewood Cliffs, N.J.: Prentice Hall.

Moncrieff. J., Pidgeon, H. and Smallwood, J. (1997) 'Strategy as a Dynamic Process – A System Perspective' a paper for SEMS 2nd International Conference, published in *Dynamics of Strategy*, University of Surrey, pp. 268–81 April.

Moss-Kanter, R. (1983) *The Change Masters*, New York: Union.

Mumford, E. (1996) 'Risky ideas in a risky society', *Journal of Information Technology*, (11): 321–31.

Murray, F. and Willmott, H. (1997) 'Putting IT in its Place: Towards Flexible Integration in the Network Age', in B.P. Bloomfield, R. Coombs, D. Knights, and D. Littler (eds) *Information Technology and Organisations: Strategies, Networks, and Integration*, 8: 160–80.

Naisbitt, J. and Arbudene, P. (1982) *Megatrends*; Naisbitt, J. and Arbudene, P. (1986) *Re-inventing the Corporation*, London: Futura Publications.

Neumann, S. (1994) *Strategic Information Systems: Competition Through Information Technologies*, New York: Maxwell Macmillan International.

Newell, S. *The Healthy Organisation: Fairnesss, Ethics and Effective Management*, London: Routledge.

Nohria, N. (1992) 'Is a network perspective a useful way of studying organisations?', in N. Nokria and R.G. Eccles (eds) *Networks and Organisations*, 1–22, Boston, Mass.: Harvard Business School Press.

Nolan, Norton and Co, PR material, 1993.

Nolan, R. (1984) 'Managing the advanced stages of computer technology: key research issues' in *The Information Systems Research Challenge*, F. W. McFarlan, (ed.) Boston: Havard Business School Press, pp. 195–214.

REFERENCES

Nolan, R. (1979) 'Managing the crises in data processing', *Harvard Business Review,* 57 (2) March–April.

Nolan, R., Pollock, A.J. and Ware, J.P. (1989) 'Toward the Design of the Networked Organisation' in *Stage by Stage* 9 (1): 1–12 Nolan, Norton and Co., Lexington, MA.

O'Brien, D. and Wainwright, J. (1993) 'Winning as a team of teams – transforming the mindset of the organisation at National Provincial Building Society' in *Business Change and Re-engineering* 1 (3): 19–25, John Wiley and Sons Ltd and Cornwallis Emmanuel Ltd, Winchester

O'Brien, D. (1993) 'Process and the People Challenge', ICL Financial Services Conference, published by ICL.

Origo Services (1993) 'Electronic trading a mutually agreed view of the future' An industry vision document July.

OST (1995) 'Progress Through Partnership: IT and Electronics', Technology Foresight, HMSO.

OST (1994) Downing, H. (ed.) 'The Demographics Roadmap: IT and Electronics', *Technology Foresight Programme,* OST, August.

Ostrof, F. and Smith, D. (1992) 'The horizontal organisation', *The McKinsey Quarterly* (1) 149–68.

Palmer, C. and Ottley, S. (1990) 'From Potential to Reality: Hybrids – critical force in the application of IT in the 1990s', BCS Report, London.

Pascale, R. (1990) 'Managing on the Edge: How successful companies use conflict to stay ahead', London: Penguin Books.

Pascale, R. T. and Athos, A. G. (1981) *The Art of Japanese Management,* Harmondsworth: Penguin.

Pearson, J. and Skinner, C. (1993) 'Business Process Re-engineering in the UK Financial Services Industry', published by the University of Bristol.

Pedler, M., Burgoyne, J. and Boydell, T. (1991) *The Learning Company – A strategy for Sustainable Development,* McGraw-Hill.

Peters, T. (1994) from Series on Excellence in the *Independent on Sunday.*

Porat, M. (1977) 'The Information Economy: Definition and Measurement', US Dept of Commerce, Washington DC.

Price Waterhouse (1993) IT Reviews 1992/93, London.

Price Waterhouse (1994) 'IT Review 1993/94', London.

Quinn, J. B., Anderson, P., Finkelstein, S. (1996) 'Managing Professional Intellect: Making the most of the best', *Harvard Business Review,* March–April.

Quinn, J. B. (1992) *Intelligent Enterprise,* New York, NY: The Free Press.

Quinn, J. B. (1980) *Strategies for Change: Logical Incrementalism,* Homewood, IL: Irwin.

Quinn, J. B. (1989) 'Managing Strategic Change ' in D. Asch, and C. Bowman, (eds) *Readings in Strategic Management,* London: Macmillan.

Rajan, A. (1988) 'Information Technology and Managers', IMS Report.

Rajan, A. (1989) *New Technology and Employment in Insurance, Banking and Building Societies,* Aldershot: Gower.

Rajan, A., Rajan, L. and Van Eupen, P. (1990) *Capital People: Skills, Strategies for Survival in the Nineties,* London: Industrial Society Press.

Roach, S. (1991) 'The Services Under Siege – The Restructuring Imperative', *Harvard Business Review,* Sept–Oct.

REFERENCES

Rockart, J.F. and Short J.E. (1989) 'Information Technology in the 1990s: Managing organisational interdependence', *Sloan Management Review* Winter: 7–17.

Rockart, J.F. and Short J.E. (1991) 'The Networked Organisation and the Management of Interdependence' in *The Corporation of the 1990s, Information Technology and Organisational Transformation*, M.S. Scott-Morton (ed.) Oxford: Oxford University Press, pp. 189–219.

Sampler, J.L. (1996) 'Exploring the relationship between information technology and organisational structure' in M.J. Earl, (ed.) *Information Management: The Organisational Dimension*, (1) 5–22, Oxford: Oxford University Press.

Scarbrough, H. (ed.) (1996) *The Management of Expertise*, London: Macmillan Press Ltd.

Scarbrough, H. (ed.) (1992) 'The IT Challenge: IT and Strategy in Financial Services', Business Information Technology Series, London: Prentice Hall.

Scott-Morton, M.S. (ed.) (1991) *The Corporation of the 1990s, Information Technology and Organisational Transformation*, USA: Oxford University Press.

Senge, P. (1991) *The Fifth Discipline: The art and Practice of the Learning Organisation*, New York: Doubleday/Currency.

Silvestro, R., Fitzgerald, L., Johnston, R. and Voss, C. (1992) 'Towards a classification of service processes', *International Journal of Service Industry Management*, 3 (3): 62–75, MCB University Press.

Sinfield, K. and Coghlan, J. (1993) presentation for the 'IT for Business Excellence Awards' organised by *The Sunday Times* and Andersen Consulting.

Somogyi, E.K. and Galliers R.D. (1987) 'From data processing to strategic information systems – a historical perspective,' London: Abacus Press.

Spikes Cavell and Co (1995) 'The UK's Top 100 IT Users', in Corporate IT Strategy, May.

Steiner, T.D. and Teixeira, D.B. (1990) 'Technology in Banking: Creating value and destroying profits', Homewood Ill.: Business One. Ref. quoted in Scarbrough as stated.

Sveiby, E. and Lloyd, T. (1988) *Managing Knowhow*, London: Bloomsbury.

Synott, W.R. (1987) *The Information Weapon: Winning Customers and Markets with Technology*, Chichester: John Wiley and Sons.

Takac, P.F. (1994) 'Outsourcing a key to controlling escalating IT costs?' *International Journal of Technology Management* 9 (2): 139–155.

The TQM Magazine 7 (1) (1995).

Thompson, M. (1992) 'Performance Related Pay: The Employee Experience', Institute of Manpower Studies, University of Sussex.

Toffler, A. (1970) *Future Shock*, New York: Random House.

Treacy, M.E. (1986) 'Towards a cumulative tradition of research on IT as a strategic business factor', Sloan Working Paper, Centre of Information Systems Research, Sloan School of Management, MIT, (15): 1771–786 March.

University of Nottingham Insurance Centre (UNIC) (1995) 'Insurance Company Performance, 1993: A Statistical Summary of the Top 200 UK Insurers', published by University of Nottingham.

VanLengen, C.A. and Morgan, J.N. (1993) 'Chargeback and the maturity of IS use.' *Information and Management* (25) North Holland.

Venkatraman, N. (1991) 'IT-induced Business Reconfiguration', (5): 122–58, in *The*

Corporation of the 1990s, Scott-Morton, M.S. (ed.) Oxford: Oxford University Press.

Walter, P.F and Walter, A.B. 'The significance of the next generation: technical keynote presentation', in Gruenberger, F. (ed.), *Fourth Generation Computers: User Requirements and Transition*, Englewood Cliffs, N.J.: Prentice Hall pp. 11–29.

Ward, J., Griffiths, P., and Whitmore, P. (1990) *Strategic Planning for Information Systems*, Chichester: John Wiley and Sons.

Watkins, J.W. (1988) *Harnessing Information Technology: What are the UK insurers doing?*, Bristol Business School.

Watkins, J.W. (1989) 'IT and the UK Insurance Market' in *Managing Information Technology in Insurance: A Guide to Key Issues*, A., Sturdy, (ed.) Harlow: Longman.

Watkins, J.W. (1992) 'Information Systems in the Financial Services Sector', *MIP Journal* p. 10.

Watkins, J.W. (1993) 'The Future of Professionals in the Retail Financial Services Sector' in *Managing Service Companies in the 1990s*, C., Armistead (ed.) London: Kogan Page.

Watkins, J.W. (1994) 'Managing the Transition: A Comprehensive Study of the Changing Use of IT in the Retail Financial Services Sector', published by the University of Bristol.

Watkins, J.W. (1995) from interviews carried out by the author in the banking sector.

Watkins, J.W. (1994) 'Business Process Redesign in the UK Retail Financial Services Sector', *The Journal of Corporate Transformation*, Spring pp. 38–48.

Watkins, J.W. (1996) 'The Future of the European Professional', Proceedings of the Eucen Conference, pp. 17–34, Italy: University of Catania.

Watkins, J. and Bryce, V. (1993) 'HORATIO 1: A Survey of Human Resources Ratios in the Financial Services Sector', published jointly by KPMG Management Consulting and the University of Bristol.

Watkins, J.W. and Drury, L. (1992) 'From Evolution to Revolution: The Pressures on Professional Life in the 1990s', University of Bristol, December.

Watkins, J.W. and Drury, L. (1994) 'Positioning for the Unknown: Career Development for Professionals in the 1990s', University of Bristol, Spring.

Watkins, J.W. and Drury, L. (1994) 'The Pressures on Professional Life in the 1990s', *International Journal of the Legal Profession*, 1 (3): 369–85, Carfax December.

Watkins, J.W. and Harding, K. (1990) 'Focusing on Business Success: A Comprehensive Study of the Changing Use of IT in the Insurance Industry', published by Bristol University in conjunction with IBM, September.

Watkins, J.W. and Wickrama-Sekera, U. (1991) 'Focusing on Business Success: A Comprehensive Study of the Changing Use of IT in the Building Society Sector', published by Bristol University in conjunction with Mornington Building Society, September.

Webber, A.M. (1993) 'What's so New about the New Economy?', *Harvard Business Review*, 71 (1): 25.

Wiseman, C. (1985) *Strategy and Computers*, Irwin: Dow-Jones.

Whitmore, P. (1985) in Ward, J., Griffiths, P., and Whitmore, P. (eds) (1990) 'Strategic Planning for Information Systems', Chichester: John Wiley & Sons.

Whittington, R. (1993) *What is strategy and does it matter?*, London: Routledge pp. 23.

REFERENCES

Wyllie, J. and Sprigge, B. (1990) in *Computing, Communications and Media: Trend Monitor*, Northants: Aslib/TMI.

Yates, J. and Benjamin, R.I. (1991) 'The Past and Present as a Window on the Future' in M.S., Scott-Morton, (ed.) *The Corporation of the 1990s*, Oxford: Oxford University Press, Oxford.

Zuboff, S. (1989) *In The Age of the Smart Machine: The Future of Work and Power*, Heinemann.

'Technology improves sales performance', a synopsis of a report by Datamonitor on IT in the UK Life Insurance Sector, Insurance Marketing Review, 4 (28) February 1995.

INDEX

251

DATE DUE

APR 1 9 2000